I Wish You Well

The Lives and Loves of a Night Owl

BY THE SAME AUTHOR

Grisly Trails and Ghostly Tales
Nightmare on your Street: More Grisly Trails and Ghostly Tales

The Lives and Loves of a Night Owl

The Autobiography

Alan Robson MBE

To Rosie
Thank you for holding my heart

'Night goes down and finds me alone
In a space and time of my own,
Lost in dreams in a world full of shadows!'

From *Night Owl* by Gerry Rafferty

First published in Great Britain in 1994 by
Virgin Books
an imprint of Virgin Publishing Ltd
332 Ladbroke Grove
London W10 5AH

A catalogue record for this book is available from the British Library.

ISBN 1 85227 409 3

Typeset by TW Typesetting, Plymouth, Devon
Printed and bound in Great Britain by
Mackays of Chatham plc, Chatham, Kent

Contents

Illustrations

1 Geordie Roots and Branches

THE CHARGE OF THE LIGHT BRIGADE, Custer's foray into the Little Big Horn, Chamberlain believing Hitler's lies, all rank as a few of the greatest mistakes of all time. Around February 1955 my parents were in the process of making another. It was then that a particularly persistent sperm managed to cause the 'Nightmare on Wor Street'. At a time when my dad was working every hour that God sent to try and support my mother and their twelve-year-old daughter Brenda, the last thing they needed was another mouth to feed. By then it was too late; that once more 'for old times sake' created me, the latest addition to arrive screaming into the Robson clan. In centuries before, the Robsons had been Border reivers and rogues along with the Milburns, Charltons and Armstrongs, but more recently they had taken to rather more civilised lifestyles.

In days gone by my ancestors ranged from 'foy' boatmen, rowing the cables from the tall ships to the quayside at North Shields in the 1800s, to coal merchants along Scotswood Road. None of my family was particularly well known but many seem to be cast in roles that did leave a mark in the history books, which is certainly more than can be said for me.

My great great grandparents were from the Crowe family in Cambo village, where he became head groomsman to Sir John Swinburne, she the housemaid below stairs. He was responsible for breeding a prize-winning bull that was named the finest in Britain, and to this day a photograph of the champion hangs on the wall in the tack room of Capheaton Hall.

My great grandmother, their daughter, also worked at the Hall as a sewing maid for Lady Swinburne. She married a young man she met at a horse show and together they had four children. The eldest died in infancy, and the Grandad had contracted pneumonia and died at the age of only 28. On leaving service she moved to Stargate where she became a skilled dressmaker. She was well known in the village because due to scarlet fever which she had suffered as a child she became profoundly deaf and used a long ear trumpet that everyone had to shout down.

My dad's father established a successful business as a coal man in Benwell. It was also this man who brought a white whale, caught in the icy North Sea, to Newcastle's Hancock Museum on one of his horse-drawn coal carts. It is now preserved in a case on one of the staircase walls. Old Tommy was a bit of a ladies' man, being married twice, quite scandalous in its day, and having many affairs. I realise there are a lot of Robsons in the North-East, but I don't think he was responsible for all of them. There was talk of other children being born 'on the wrong side of the blanket' but none he would put his name to. He did, however, officially have five sons and a daughter. My memory of him was that he was a chunky, hard-faced man, keener on belligerence than affection. This may well have been exacerbated by the fact that his second wife Mary was a tiny shrew of a woman with horn-rimmed glasses. They lived in a tatty flat on Armstrong Road in Benwell, while my mam and dad occupied the flat downstairs. I remember the old black range that sat right in the centre of their living room, surrounded by old scratchety wooden furniture that certainly would never have made the *Antiques Roadshow*. Although they owned their own business, including stables, they were far from wealthy. My grandfather's clothes were always old and oft repaired, unless he was out 'tomming' – chasing the ladies – when he would be immaculate. In his later years, when he was suffering from Alzheimer's disease, he would wander, tramp like, to his old haunts in North Shields. It was a mystery to everyone how he could get from Newcastle to the docks in such a state of utter confusion.

My memories of them are fixed on their old house, where I was in my infancy: the cold oil-clothed floors, polished wood floor tiles and a square of carpet just big enough to fill the centre of the room. Downstairs I would hear my grandparents rowing, his bass voice booming over her annoying high-pitched whine. He always won!

Ultimately it would boil down to him getting his own way, and she vanishing into the kitchen, hoping that the way to her man's heart really was through his stomach. Judging by his affairs, it seemed obvious she was aiming a little high.

She was the archetypal Geordie woman, with headsquare, old coat and little sheepskin booties. A nosey, busybody of a woman who, if you vanished for a second, would be looking in your drawers, cupboards and wardrobes. In her own house she seemed to be forever cooking thousands of things at once. The range always had on it a pan of broth, scones, bread, a freshly slaughtered chicken broiling and an old black metal kettle hissing. This mixture would bubble and boil creating a mixture of smells that were instantly recognisable. It was in that old black range that my grandmother once inadvertently closed the oven door without realising her cat was inside sleeping and cooked it to death. The woman was more concerned about the congealed mess she had to clean up than the animal's suffering.

My father also suffered from this lack of concern for animals when he was a youngster. He was given charge of the stables and was told to muck out and look after the horses that drew the coal carts. In the stables he kept a most peculiar pet, a huge pig that became his very best friend. Perhaps because he wasn't given anything that could loosely be described as love by his parents, he transferred his affections to a tiny piglet he named Bessie. No matter how much work he was given, the end of the day would see him playing with his raucous, fun-loving pig. It followed him around like a dog, shared any meals with him, and when it was dark and the day's tasks cleared away he would curl up with Bessie in the hay and fall into a deep and contented sleep. Nowadays rich people have discovered just how loving Vietnamese pot-bellied pigs can be; well, just call my dad a man ahead of his time. That pig was his best friend for years; he watched it grow from a newborn eight-inch-long piglet into a huge lady pig that used to let him have rides on her back around the yard. Then one day, returning from school, he started his chores and called out for Bessie. There was no reply. Normally she would come trundling across the yard, squealing her joy at seeing him, her tiny curled tail swishing as she went. Even if she couldn't get to him, he would hear her voice telling him where to run to. That dark October day she was silent, and there was a long trail of crimson stretched across the yard. He raced into the house and tugged at his mother's sleeve as she peeled potatoes over the rough-hewn marble sink.

'Where's Bessie, and what's that red in the yard?'

His mother chose to avoid the issue, believing, as many parents do, that bribery works.

'Look, your dad will be back from his rounds and you've got to go to the shops!' she replied.

Despite his concern, he knew better than to back answer her. So off he went, first to the greengrocer to get some potatoes, then into the butchers for pork sandwiches for the family tea. As he stood there waiting to be served, he took in that tell-tale smell of the shop, sawdust on the floor, various carcasses hung up, blood dripping from their noses. There was the owner in his stained shirt and blue-and-white striped apron. He was a fat, red-faced man with a drinker's nose covered with tiny bursting veins.

'Helly Tommy,' said the butcher. 'What's it to be today?'

At this my dad fumbled with his note, and asked for five pork sandwiches and some chops.

The butcher walked to the side of the counter picking up his heavy metal cleaver and asked, 'Well, would you like them off Bessie then?'

At first this didn't sink in. What did he mean? Bessie was his, she wasn't like the pigs he'd seen in the shop. She was his pet, he loved her, she was his only true friend! Without wanting to, he spun around and there hanging from a hook was Bessie, cut in two and dripping in gore, forming tiny scarlet sawdust balls on the shop floor. The butcher proceeded to carve pieces from the animal as my father stood there dumbstruck, unable to move, unwilling to talk. The chops were wrapped and sandwiches were placed into a brown paper bag from beneath the counter. Then it was back home where his father would expect him to eat Bessie.

'If you don't eat that I'm going to have them,' shouted his dad at the dinner table. 'Divvn't waste good food, young man!'

My father walked into the stables and broke his heart. From that day onwards he kept his feelings very much to himself, as if to guard himself from being hurt again.

My family was never renowned for sentimentality, so when my father was a lad it was taken for granted that he would go down the pit. My dad was frightened of very little, but going underground terrified him, he was torn between his claustrophobic fear of the colliery, and his very real fear of his father who would think nothing of kicking him all over the yard. So when the day came to start work, my dad being aged about fourteen, he was given his bait, a few sandwiches and an apple, and in his short trousers and ragged herringbone jacket headed towards the pit. As each step took him nearer he began to sweat, and as soon as he was within sight of the gates he turned and ran. Tears poured down his face as he just raced through the back lanes until he found a yard far enough away so they couldn't drag him back. It was far away from his father's coal round or all hell would have been let loose. It is a child's logic that says if you go back home around the time your shift was due to surface, then your folks would never suspect that you weren't there. In his heart he knew that the foreman would call to find out why little Tommy had not shown up, but for the moment he would be safe. After a day in hiding he slowly plodded up to the house to be grabbed by his mother who was crying. There behind him was the stern face of the wild-eyed coal man. He couldn't quite comprehend how they had tumbled him so soon? Finally the full story emerged. A shift full of new lads had gone underground and within their first hour at the pit-face the roof had collapsed killing twelve of them and severely injuring over forty. The entire community had gathered around the pit head. Had he gone down, he most likely would have died that day. His mother saw this as a sign from fate, and instead of life as a pitman he became an apprentice bricklayer instead.

During the Second World War he served with the Border Regiment, later transferring to the 'Loyals' – the loyal Lancashire Regiment. He seldom spoke of his various adventures, but as a child I always viewed him as a hero. I always pawed over the few crumpled photographs of him with his army pals. Yet his Achilles' heel seemed to be his parents. They gave him so much frustration, always trying to control him. Living so close at hand meant they considered him always 'on call'. They would have him mending this, fixing that, running to buy something or just generally whining to him.

Even as a tot I could feel the tension between my father and his father, both too alike to ever get on. My early toddling years were spent listening to my parents plotting to get out from the clutches of his parents.

My father was also a Thomas, Thomas Francis Walker Robson (the Walkers being distant relatives too), and he shared the family trait of never truly showing emotion. I am sure he loved as deeply as anyone, yet never spoke the words. As an adult I understand and love him; as a child I felt he was lost to me. The only place I could go when in need of affection was my mother, all her five foot one inches full of cuddles. As a child she was my refuge, my port in any storm and more importantly the only one who could save me from my dad. My sister was twelve going on thirteen when I was born, and to her I was a human doll, something to be paraded around the streets in a pram with her mates. One of my earliest memories was hating being played with by her two friends. Yes, it is fun to be fussed with as a child, but being fondled by strangers is only fun when you can fondle back. To have my naked genitalia, barely a baby carrot, on display to the street wasn't my idea of having a good time.

My mother's name was originally Audrey Ivy Green. Her parents came from Lemington, and it seemed inevitable at the time that her parents would be linked to the North's traditional industry, coal. My other grandfather, Stan Green, worked at Stargate pit and later at Walbottle until a string of horrendous accidents and a serious lung disease ended his career.

When young Stanley was only seventeen he enlisted to fight in the First World War which had just begun in 1914. He was too young to be called up, but he lied about his age and off he went. He made sure he was in with the horses, as his parents had owned many and were cabbies. His own father had been the coachman who had driven the carriage carrying the King and Queen across the brand new High Level Bridge. Stan's regiment was the 9th and 10th Northumberland Hussars and they were involved in some of the bloodiest campaigns of the war. Despite being barely five feet five inches he was as hard as nails, renowned by many as one of the 'hard lads' of his day. My father always told a story of how one day they went for a pint into a really rough pub in Pink Lane, Newcastle, in the 1950s. A huge man started a fight, but by the end of the fracas the tough little pitman had knocked him out and strewn several of his friends across the furniture. No one messed with him. He almost fed on aggression, using it against anyone who dared face him. He seemed to know everyone, and was a good loyal friend, but if anyone crossed him he made sure they paid in full. After he retired due to ill health the world seemed to collapse around him. His friends were at work all day and he rarely saw them. He was no longer party to everything that was happening in the village. The lack of a job to do all but ruined him, and he turned to the bottle becoming an alcoholic. This, added to his fighting skills, made him a real handful to many publicans throughout the North, and caused even more problems at home.

Stan's wife, Cissie, was a big round woman, about five feet tall and roughly that round. She suffered many beatings at his hands. When we visited her she would tell us how she always knew if he was going to hit her. She was so used to this man she could tell if he was happily drunk or if she was in for a hiding; more often than not it was the latter. He never raised his hand to his children, my mother Audrey, her sister Maureen or her brother Bill. They were merely spectators of the savagery. When he eventually died I wasn't sure whether it was a blessing or a curse; at least my lovely nana was free of him. It was after his death that she became a walking pharmacy, taking dozens of pills and potions every day. She was my loyalist defender, the only human on the planet that could keep my father under her thumb. My mother could reason with him, yet my Nana Green was completely in control.

My Uncle Bill was in the Royal Navy during the war and was involved in the sinking of the *Bismarck*. He was on HMS *Coventry* in pursuit of the German war machine's newest acquisition. It was in May 1941 that he watched helplessly as his best friend was lost when Germany's fastest battleship sunk HMS *Hood* and only a handful of the 1,421 crew survived. Uncle Bill's injuries were so severe as a result of being torpedoed and spending too long in the water, that he was told that he would never be able to father a child. So he decided that, despite being a great lover of the female form, he would never be able to offer a woman a proper family life and nobly chose never to marry. He would've made a great dad, but he stayed true to his beliefs, remaining with my nana until she died.

My mother Audrey was always a traditional mum, believing that a woman's place is in the home. Her only job was during the war making bombs at Vickers-Armstrongs. She met my dad at a meeting of a cycling club and from single cycles they were soon on a tandem.

My father, Thomas Francis Walker Robson, seemed to get called Tony for some strange reason. I called him a lot worse than that when I was growing up. He returned from the war with several decorations and the knowledge that he had a 'war baby' at home, for Brenda had been born while he was away. He was a time-served bricklayer, later becoming a jobbing builder. However, when the building trade slumped he got a job with the Northern Gas Board where he worked doing emergency repairs. He's a good, solid man, always the first to help others, and I have never forgotten the solid example he set me.

This is the backdrop to my early years: a mixture of strange examples, set by a bizarre array of people with more hang-ups than you'd find at a psychiatrists' conference.

2 Enfant Terrible

I HAVE VERY FEW MEMORIES of my very early years, except the happiest day that I spent in that old flat on Armstrong Road. I was sitting playing with some wooden blocks my dad had made for me out of old scraps of timber, when there was a rapping on the door. It was my dad who had forgotten his key. My mother was wearing a white pinny over a print dress and ran to answer it. I had never seen my father happier. He had managed to secure a down payment on a terraced house in Hugh Gardens, barely 150 yards away. He was ecstatic, his face beaming more than I had ever seen. He was so charged with joy, he actually picked me up and kissed me, and he never did that! My mother was dancing around screaming and hugging until there was a tell-tale banging from downstairs and a husky roar of 'Keep that bloody noise down up there!'

That would be the last order my grandfather would ever give in that flat. Within a wink of an eye the four of us were up the street at 203 Hugh Gardens. A simple two-bedroomed terraced house, that we turned into a three bedroomed. We didn't knock down walls. The front room became Brenda's room, and I was upstairs opposite my parents. I was too young to know the difference, but they seemed really happy, and I benefited from that.

It's from this point that my memories begin to flood, so many skeletons hammering on the closet door, ghosts waiting to be exorcised. Up to the age of four I was a right wimp, clinging so closely to my mother's petticoats that I might as well have been her third leg. The very first trauma I suffered was a month before my fifth birthday when out of the blue my mother told me I was going to school the following day. Now I was the kind of bairn who would cry if my mother refused to take me into the toilet with her; how was I going to cope with being away from her for an entire day? That had never ever happened before and I certainly didn't want it to start now. I had wondered why she had been stockpiling jumpers and grey shorts, and as to why she had made a drawstring bag for my black, well-worn, sandshoes. I remember crying myself to sleep, my dad pushing me into my bedroom and shouting, 'If I hear a peep out of you tonight I'll tan your backside'.

Even as a four-year-old I knew that to be tanned by his shovel-like hands was not to be recommended, so I kept my sobbing to a whimper under the covers. When my mother walked past the foot of the stairs, I'd cry louder to attract her attention, being swift to stifle my tears if his heavy steps plodded by. It was all to no avail. The very next day I was woken at 7.30 a.m. and watched the disciplined way that my mother prepared meticulously for my school début. I really couldn't understand how she could survive without me. Every day I'd accompany her to the shops, stop chatting to neighbours, help her tidy up; now she'd have to cope all on her own. I probably made more mess than I ever cleared, but this is what we did. In the street I had very few friends, only one my age and he was a pain in the backside.

The only person I trusted was my mother; she would never do anything to hurt me. But that day my face was red and sore from crying, my mouth twisted downwards, and I had two candles beneath my nostrils. This picture was framed by a carrot top, my hair recently basin-cut and short enough for any teacher to approve of. I was put into a brand new shirt, a rarity indeed, and a pair of pressed grey shorts. Over the top I was given a grey jumper that she had knitted for me; it didn't fit me as a four-year-old, but she insisted that I would grow into it. I did, by the time I was about nine. As my mother had betrayed me, I was certain that she didn't love me any more, so I switched off my love for her. 'That'll teach her!' I thought to myself as I sat on the black plastic settee in the living room. The room was tiny, the window looking out on to an old dark grey yard, still with its air-raid shelter from fifteen years earlier.

'Come on, Alan. It's time to go,' came her shout from the hall as she was putting on a woolly hat and her grey coat. I ignored her; I was going nowhere! She kept fussing with her make-up, and zipped on her little furry boots.

'Alan, come on!' she shouted. Still I refused to go. Surely after spending all my life with her she owed me something?

Finally, she appeared at the door giving me an authoritative glance, which I turned away from. Then her wool mittened hand grabbed my arm and proceeded to drag me. I grabbed hold of the settee, determined to win this tug of war. I didn't, and soon found myself walking down Hugh Gardens to Armstrong Road, then along towards Atkinson Road School. From all directions, all the five-year-olds were joining the older children on their very first pilgrimage.

'But Mam, I'm only four!' I pleaded.

'Yes, but you're five at the beginning of next month!' came her stern reply.

'But Mam, I'll be the youngest one in my class!' came another winge.

In fact, I *was* the youngest one in the school. She knew this, but didn't want to give me more reasons to be unhappy. As we neared the school gates I saw that she was crying too. Not my kind of self-centred tears, but 'I love you' tears. I didn't perceive them to be that at the time, but I'm sure they were.

When we got to the school, a dark red brick building, all the mams and dads were being guided into the main hall to receive a talk from the headmaster, a balding chap called Mr Gill. He seemed very nice and one by one I noticed parents 'slipping away'. As soon as their children were talking to friends they were sneaking out. This wasn't going to work with me. I knew that I was going to keep a tight hold of my mother's hand, and if she let go, even for a second, I would scream the school down. She tried twice and I did.

Finally, I was singled out as the black sheep and as the rest of the new intake went to their respective classes my mother and I were guided to the headmaster's office. They talked for a while, speaking to one another as if I wasn't there. I was and I paid attention. They were going to take me to my new class, and while I was playing in the Wendy House, she would slip out.

When we got to the classroom, I was confronted with more children than I'd ever seen before. There were no such things in

Benwell as kindergarten schools, and as I'd never really played out much, this was a serious shock. My only contact with other children had been through my sister and her friends and that hadn't been fun. I had no interest in the cheap cardboard Wendy House, I knew that was part of their ruse, but that sand tray looked interesting. I may have been to the beach before but couldn't remember it. That was sand, and in it was a toy plough, several big plastic moulds where you tipped sand in and it made a crab shape. That was clever!

'Do you want a go, Alan?' asked the nice lady, who I later discovered was my very first teacher.

I shook my head, but my eyes watched as another spotty boy made a sandcastle out of a bucket and stuck a feather in the top. Wow! it looked just like a castle! I hadn't seen a castle except in books, but there was a little one in the sand tray. The next five minutes are a blank, I just remember stuffing sand into another mould and creating a star shape. I felt really proud, then spun around to show my mother just what a genius she had as a son, but she was gone. It could only have been in a split second, but she had been spirited away.

I panicked. I was alone. The teacher wasn't there either, as she'd left to show my mam the way out. Within seconds a gang of little tots had grabbed 'the crying boy' by the ankles and had pushed him into the sand tray. I felt the sand go into my mouth and eyes; I tried to swallow but it clung to my throat. Then the teacher rescued me and cleaned me up. I wasn't crying any more; I was just angry and frightened. At dinner time my mother arrived to take me home for a tin of watered-down tomato soup. I was thrilled; this school was all over with really quickly. I was away from my attackers and back with my mam. Granted she had let me down, but at least she'd come back for me. Then as soon as I'd eaten my bread and soup she was getting me dressed again. 'Are we going to the shops now?' I enquired enthusiastically, as I still hadn't had my weekly comic yet.

'No, you've got to go back to school!' she answered.

My world folded like a deckchair. Back to face my worst enemies. I'd never had enemies; I didn't know how to deal with them. But I'd have to learn!

3 The Snotty Street Monster

WITHIN MONTHS I had transformed from that scared and lost little lamb into the biggest baddest bully in Atkinson Road Infants. We would run around the streets playing games like Japs and English, knocky nine doors and street football down the back lanes. Literally every spare moment was taken up with something. There were very few organised events for the under-tens so you had no option but to think for yourself. When my dad was out I would sneak a gang of pals into my bedroom to listen to my battered old second-hand record player with the speaker built into the lid. The quality was awful, but between us we only had about eight records, so knew all the words of both sides off by heart. Occasionally, we borrowed some of the old 78s from my mam's radiogram for a laugh. We'd all sit on the floor with a big bottle of Villa Dandelion & Burdock and loads of biscuits. So many crumbs would end up in the bottle that the last few mouthfuls were more like bread pudding than a drink.

A lot of the posher kids at school, the ones with creases in their shorts and shop-bought jumpers, used to go to scouts at the church that stood at the bottom of Hugh Gardens. So after a lot of ear-bending my mother persuaded me to go. I wasn't old enough to be a scout. First I had to be a cub. So without being able to afford a uniform, I turned up woggleless for my induction. They all paraded like soldiers and recited this pledge of sorts. Then I went in and this pompous man in his fifties told everyone that as I didn't have a uniform they would have to raise the money to get me one. Even at that age I was utterly humiliated. I didn't want to be a charity case. Maybe a lot of my clothes were homemade or bought from jumble sales, but I still had pride. Being new, I had little option but to let it go. I had been there less than an hour when we were told to split into groups. This creepy character called Roger was in charge of my group. His jumper was smothered in badges and he was obviously rich because the badges had been sewn on by a sewing machine. He had the full kit and lived on Ladykirk Road, at that time one of the posher streets. Throughout our discussion group Roger kept digging at me. Finally, after dozens of caustic remarks, I was on my way to the toilet when I heard him say, 'So we'll have to get the little tramp a uniform!' Without thinking, I just ran back and punched him in the side of the head as hard as I could and he fell on to the hall's cork floor crying his eyes out. Although he was two years older than me and a leading scout he obviously hadn't quite mastered 'Be Prepared'. At that, about six other scouts dived towards me and played football with my head! I ended up being thrown out and sent home for fighting. Apparently you couldn't get a badge for that. Let there be no doubt at all that I had come off worst. My ribs were badly bruised and my nose was covered with a smearing of blood and snot. On getting home in that condition there was only one possible consequence. I'd get another hiding from my dad. Unperturbed, I was soon back out in the lanes playing football. I was soon lost in the excitement of the game; playing in goal, I was the mad waif diving around the concrete path to stop the others from scoring. There were more scars on my bare knees than spots on my mate's brow, and he had acne!

All of us used to look forward to Thursday nights when a local hall opened up to the young people offering a wide variety of activities. A young curate ran the thing at a hall just opposite Benwell Library. 'Wor gang' was more than a bit sceptical because we were young, wild and free; aged seven to ten, we didn't want to get tied down. We tried it anyway and discovered that a lot of our pals from school were going, so stayed. This became a regular part of the week. The young curate seemed totally committed to giving us all a good time. He would have been about 25 with a modern 'Beatlecut' and his chubby round face was an endless stream of smiles. He would wear black sandshoes under his black trousers and his collar under a very colourful short-sleeved woolly. We'd play 'pirates', table tennis, darts or that game where if someone hits you with a ball you're out. Then by about eight o'clock a lot of mams and dads would appear to collect their children, leaving 'the rough lot' to walk back along to Hugh Gardens or Suttons Dwellings. This is when a new habit started forming. When all the other organisers had gone, about five of us were left with this nice curate. So each week he started laying on little treats, a few cakes, a packet of sweets each and some pop. It was the fact that he made it 'our' secret that made it quite exciting. We would all sit with the light off, because no one was allowed in the hall after eight. So for up to half an hour we'd secretly snack and get cuddled and tickled by this friendly man of the cloth. His favourite was a young lad called Leslie, the youngest of our group who lived in Clara Street. He always got the warmest cuddles and once even got walked home by the vicar, who knew his parents. We thought the world of him, he was there to listen to our problems helping far beyond his calling. It was a freezing December that our bond was broken. Due to the deep flurries of snow only two of our crowd managed to get to the hall this Thursday evening. After the rest disappeared, out went the lights and the two of us and the curate sat illuminated only by the lamppost outside in the street, giving the room its ruddy glow. We had tons of rubbish to eat and the curate told us that he didn't have any pop, enquiring if we would like apple juice instead. I must admit we would accept anything. Our tiny amounts of pocket money would barely cover a comic and a couple of chews, so this kind of extravagance was something to be wallowed in. The apple juice was very sharp and I began feeling a little giddy, but still attempted to eat my friends' share of the sweets. I remember the curate talking away to me while all around was fast disappearing into a blur. I remember him cuddling me and saying that I felt cold. Those were the days when everyone wore short trousers irrespective of the weather. I recall his chubby warm hands rubbing my thighs, and each time the fingers seemed to rub further up my legs and beneath the material of my shorts. I had seen him do this to my friends and thought nothing of it. He was obviously just a very loving man and he was giving us affection. Child abuse was never discussed in the early sixties and we had no idea that it went on. We were with a man of the church, a man to be respected and looked up to. The vicar of the parish was an older, rather posher, man who visited our homes and was totally trustworthy and willing to help anyone. To a child that collar meant he was safe to be with, didn't it?

By this time I knew that he was touching my underpants and leaving his hand there, all the while jabbering on about pop music, football and school. Although I was aware of what was happening, I felt sleepy and tired. Finally I threw up in the darkness. The curate swore as the warm bilious concoction spilled itself over his legs and he grabbed toilet paper from the nearby loo to swab himself clean. My friend Tony was at least as giddy as I was and ended up in a fit of the giggles.

So we were escorted home through the snow, neither of us capable of putting one foot in front of the other. I was stopping to be sick every five minutes and Tony roared with laughter and kept throwing himself head-first into the deeper drifts, reappearing covered in flakes and howling. All the while the curate was trying desperately to deal with the situation. Some years later, I realised that we had been spiked with cider. Was it all innocent or had we been used and abused by someone we trusted as our friend? At times I like to give him the benefit of the doubt, but the truth is I will never know for sure.

We only went back on another couple of occasions. We always kept our distance from the curate and never stayed behind again.

It's really strange how on straining to remember the things that happened in those days you end up with a mixture of sweet and sour. I was still a bit of a bully at school, where I had the nickname 'Pop' for a variety of reasons including that no matter what problem anyone had they would always look to me. Anyone who called me 'carrot' or 'ginger nuts' got a knuckle sandwich. Then out of nowhere another pastime appeared as if by magic. For years we had treated girls very badly. They were boring, they didn't play football, they had dolls, what a soppy cissy lot they were! Then a few boys in the junior school started having things called girlfriends. I couldn't think of a single reason why until my friends started getting them too, and I couldn't be missed out. So I started talking to them and discovered they were very nice indeed. They really were very different from boys, and I wanted to know more about these alien creatures. It was then that I met my very first 'love'. Her name was Susan Swan and she was lovely. So whenever I bought a 'lucky bag' and the gift was a luminous green plastic ring with a blue plastic stone set into it, I would leave it in her desk as a token of my undying affection. I was obsessed by this girl, but she would have nothing to do with me. The more she ignored me the more I wanted her to be my girlfriend. At the age of about seven I crept into the bottom of the family food cupboard, just beside the gas meter, and drew a huge heart with 'I Love Susan Swan' in the middle of it. My dad ended up giving me a good hiding for that when he found it almost five years later! This was the beginning of my catalogue of disasters with the fair sex. So I'd go to school the next day and take it out on the younger boys by giving them a good bullying.

Then I tried with Carole Pearson, a small angular-faced girl from Suttons Dwellings. She asked me to go and see her. I was thrilled and raced around there wearing my best T-shirt. It was even clean! She asked me if I'd shin up a huge drainpipe to retrieve her tennis ball which was wedged between the pipe and the wall. This I did gladly, zooming up like a chimpanzee about twenty feet up the side of the flats. I threw the ball down and shinned down to receive my prize. But she had gone! Next day I was like a bear with a sore head. I thumped people for even looking at me!

Next I asked out a girl called Vivien and to my total surprise she said 'Yes'. So once more the best T-shirt came out and, as she'd asked, I went to her house and rang the doorbell. I gave it two rings and then heard the upstairs window open. On glancing up I saw Vivien looking quite cute, her curly hair hanging down in ringlets. 'Don't move, I'll come straight down!' she shouted. So I was feeling thoroughly pleased with myself. I stood there smiling waiting for the door to open and within a split second I was completely covered with rotten vegetables. There up at the window was Vivien and four of her pals. They'd emptied a bucket full of slops all over me. There were potato peelings across my shoulders, tomato seeds in my hair and I was soaked by the awful decaying soup created by the gunk that had started fermenting. I had a few tears on the way home, and a lot more tears when my dad saw the mess I was in. At school the following day I was even beating my friends up and if the teacher had said a word I'd have cuffed him too.

The part of Benwell that I lived in always had its fair share of villains, but they never robbed their own. Anyone who did was rooted out and given a kicking down the back streets. There was a kind of honour about it. The community was tight, everyone knew everyone and that was their protection. They were mostly good people, perhaps with not as much money as some, but they lived life to the full, and would share their last crumb. That was except for one woman in Clara Street! She was a human Rottweiler, with huge glasses that were as wide as she was and black hair in a bun that seemed glued to her head under a brown net. She always seemed to wear the same pinny, perhaps for the same reason other poisonous creatures have specific markings to frighten off anything that may want to mess with it. No matter what we did in that back lane it was wrong. If we put books on roller skates and screeched down, we were making too much noise. If we played football, we were banging the ball off her wall. If we walked down to the shop, we were told, 'Go play outside your own back door!' She was fierce and we did not dare wind her up, because she was the type that would come and see your dad, and there was no way any of us wanted that to happen.

In those daft young days I really loved my mam, insisting that she give me some 'loving' time every day, a half-hour when we just cuddled and talked. If any of the lads had found out, my life wouldn't have been worth living. My dad was always the one I was frightened of – the callouses on his hands were bigger than any muscle I had. He kept his builder's belt in the bottom of the cupboard, and if ever I stepped out of line he insisted that I get the belt – the under-ten equivalent of asking a man sitting on the electric chair to plug it in. Believe me, my bottom felt equally hot afterwards. In a way, he was my hero too. Everyone in the street loved my dad and I rather enjoyed basking in his reflected glory. He would look after the older folks in the street, fixing their burst pipes, re-tiling their roofs, building garden walls, putting new electric sockets in, and only charging what it cost him for materials. He'd do other jobs for cash too, to try and supplement the lousy wages that he was paid on the sites. He was literally never home, always working, always helping someone, always out of my reach. I never told that man that I loved him until I was 35 years old.

My hero worship peaked when I was playing football in the

lanes, and a Scottish and Newcastle Breweries' van drove past. I had just climbed over a backyard wall to get my plastic football back. This meant, as any back street footballer will tell you, that it was a throw-in. So I held the ball above my head and waited for the van to pass. As it did so, I pretended that I was going to throw the ball. The van screeched to a halt and out stepped a huge Tasmanian-Devil-shaped man, roaring and growling, who slammed me backwards against the wall and punched me in the face. Simultaneously, a lump was appearing on the back and front of my skull. He was the son of a neighbour renowned for being a bit of a thug. Well, this incident took place in front of not only my mates, but also, from the top of the street, my dad walking home from work carrying his heavy builder's bag. He handed it to my young pal Tony, who collapsed under its weight, and ran down to sort it out. The bruiser who was clouting me was about sixteen stone and an animal, yet my dad hit him only once and he was on the ground. The vice-like grip of Robson senior lifted him up and smacked his head off the side of his van wedging him back in his seat.

'If you ever lift your hand to my lad, I'll rip your bloody head off. Do you hear me?' The brewery man nodded, fumbling to put the key in the ignition, my dad slammed his door catching his elbow as it closed, and the van tore out of the lane, the swelling over the driver's eye accelerating almost as fast as the vehicle. My gang cheered and clapped, except for Tony who was trying to get out from under my dad's builder's bag. I felt so proud. He picked me off the ground and I expected sympathy, but I expected wrong.

'What the hell did you do to get him that annoyed, you stupid little bugger?' At that I was bodily carried home for the interrogation and punishment. It was a savage but just court. I spent so much time in my room I remember to this day that there were 2,558 squares on the wallpaper! The example he set was so clear: everything was black and white. There were no grey areas. A person was either good or bad, and this swiftly rubbed off on me. Throughout his life this naivety would cost him, as it has subsequently cost me. He was ripped off and betrayed by so-called friends and family alike who took advantage of his kindliness. Promising mutual respect in return, but ultimately just taking and taking from him. He was true to himself and true to my mother.

Mind you, he did spend an awful lot of time with that woman from the wet-fish shop, and we were never short of cod!

One of my adventures was when this lady, Ivy, the owner of Benwell's wet-fish shop, called over. I remember her as a sleek silver-haired woman with very short hair, very manly in stature and always wearing trousers and big cardigans. Apparently she thought that she had a rat in her backyard and needed my dad to get it out for her. So he grabbed a torch and a masonry hammer and headed out for the hunt, dragging me with him, perhaps as bait. Her backyard was roofed in and had a light, but the forty-watt bulb made next to no difference at all as we listened in the darkness for the tell-tale scuttling behind the smelly fish pallets that were stacked up high. Slowly but surely my dad managed to establish where it was, directly under a pallet right next to where I was standing. So infinite was my faith in this man I genuinely wasn't frightened of anything. He was with me, so I was safe.

'Alan, just you jump on top of that pallet and you'll trap him!'

So I leaped down on it with all my five stone or so, and a high-pitched squeal was heard. It was so desperate that it really chilled my blood and I leaped off as quickly as I'd leaped on. My dad tore into action, jumping on to the pallet and stamping it flat with his steel-toe-capped boots. It was over – the rat was dead! So Ivy opened the back door and the inner yard was finally illuminated, to show the pallet barely an inch off the ground. I recall thinking all this fuss over a tiny little rat; it must be really small to get under there. At that moment my dad picked the beast up by his tail. The body was at least a foot long! He casually lifted Ivy's dustbin lid and tossed the rat inside, walking back across to our house completely unconcerned. I shook for almost an hour.

Within three months I would see him corner another rat in our yard. He got it trapped in a corner while trying to squash its head with a shovel. Knowing just how big the beggars were, I watched from the comfort of the living-room window. My dad standing up straight was about five foot nine inches and very broad and strong, yet this rat leapt at his head, flying over his shoulder. It climbed on to the dividing wall between the houses and vanished. That curtailed any games I'd planned for that yard for some months to follow.

The rat story was told to all my friends and added to my status because not many others had ever been big game hunting. I had a cousin who lived near the school, and she seemed fascinated by the adventure, and we became quite pally. Cousin or not, at that age all I knew for sure was she was a girl, and she was the very first girl who I persuaded to 'show me hers' but only if I showed her mine. You must remember that there was nothing sexual whatsoever about this. It was pure innocent curiosity, although I'm sure our parents wouldn't have agreed. So one day in her front hall, between the closed front door and the closed internal door, I pulled down my shorts and my little white market-stall Y-fronts. She stared fascinated by my minute wee willy winkle. Finally she burst out laughing. Sadly that wouldn't be the only time in my life that happened. Then it was her turn, so down came her little knickers and up she hoisted her skirt. I looked, then I looked again. There was nothing there at all! I felt so cheated. Once again, I'd let a girl take advantage of me. I'd kept my side of the bargain as always, only to leave completely deflated. On getting to school the following Monday I heard that a girl called Margaret, who lived by the brickfield, where Benwell's Health Centre now stands, was charging lads threepence to watch her go to the toilet. I wasn't going to fall for that one. I was now a man of the world. I knew there was nothing to see.

Directly across the front path there was a pretty woman who I only knew as Carole's mam. Carole was a right snotty little brat that I was sometimes asked to look after. This I did with threats and the occasional twisted arm. I hated her. She was about two years younger than me and treated me with utter contempt. She attended a different school, so wasn't aware of my reputation as being one of the school's 'hard lads'. So therefore she wasn't scared to give me lip. I was too young to be gallant, so would cuff her to keep her in place. Adelaide Terrace in Benwell had one large brothel nearby and several places where prostitutes could be found just waiting for a pick up. I would regularly see these girls meeting men. All I noted at that age was the number of boyfriends these girls had. The brothel was in an ordinary two-up, two-down, house, behind one of the shops. Every night was party night there. I was once playing football up against a wall in the back lane, just by myself, when I spotted Carole's mam walking home from work. It was about 6.30 p.m. and it was very dark except for under the streetlamp where I was playing. I thought for a grown-up this woman was very smart indeed, bright ginger hair, short skirt, high boots, all the latest Carnaby Street fashions. Then a car drew up alongside her, following her slowly, all the while the male driver talking to her. He grabbed her arm and tried to persuade her to get into his car as she struggled and screamed. Finally the car roared away as she fell backwards on to the pavement, her legs akimbo. She was screaming 'Bastard' at the car, so without considering the implications, I grabbed a half-brick and hurled it, smashing the rear windscreen. As the car pulled out on to the Terrace and away people appeared from all sides to help Carole's mam back to her feet. Although she had in effect saved herself from the unwanted attentions of a kerb crawler, she gave me the credit. This won me a free two-ounce paper packet of peeled prawns from the fish shop and a bar of Caramac chocolate. No super hero could ever have been better rewarded.

Indirectly, this made me reconsider my role as school bully, particularly as many of the other pupils were now growing faster than me and seeking revenge. Apart from that, I was also learning that most of these little kids had older brothers who didn't take kindly to bullies. So I changed direction. Perhaps I was more suited to being a good guy than a bad guy. It was around this time that my love for the super hero type of comic transferred to television. At long last my dad bought a second-hand black-and-white television from one of the cheap shops along Westgate Road. We didn't have a proper aerial and had to wave the cable around until a picture appeared. The best place was around the clock and then around the hanging mirror. Now I could watch Adam West as Batman. I was totally knocked out by it. My seamstress mother and sister were instructed to make me a Batman costume for my birthday. It was created: a light blue T-shirt with a yellow felt circle with a lop-sided bat on it, blue swimming trunks, black felt glued to a pair of black sandshoes for the bat boots, a black remnant of material as a cape and a black balaclava with felt added for my mask. It looked ridiculous but I loved it. Now I could use my fighting skills to protect Hugh Gardens from any master criminals who dared to show their faces. If they weren't about, I'd smack any kid who took the mickey out of me. The neighbours would watch me as I walked along walls, climbed up lampposts and charged down the street in search of any mission that needed accomplishing. My mother has a photograph of me in my outfit and I want it sealed in a lead coffin so that not even Superman's X-ray vision can catch a glimpse of it. I used genuinely to believe that people couldn't tell who it was when I had this costume on. Since I didn't wear tights, my milk-pale legs and swimming trunks were there to be seen even in winter. I must have looked a complete prat. Whenever our friendly policeman walked down the street I'd don my disguise and walk alongside him, so everyone would feel reassured that the area was safe in our hands. Big Bobby and Little Batboy were out on patrol. To this policeman's credit, he would always talk to me as an equal, saying things like 'Well, Batboy, thanks to you crime is down in these parts!' I'd stick my chest out with pride and reply, 'Well, don't forget to tell Commissioner Gordon that all he has to do if he needs my help is flash the Batsign on the clouds and I'll come running!' Isn't this proof beyond words that my life as an intellectual was never terribly likely? Everyone in the street knew that I was the gormless pillock in the navy-blue knickers, but most were kind enough to protect my supposed anonymity. If anyone did accidentally call me Alan, I would give them a quiet talk, explaining how my life would be in peril if the underworld discovered my true identity. They swore to keep the secret and the street was safe again.

What it did do was fuel my interest in films. Along on Condecum Road there was an ABC cinema. Soon I was a badge-wearing member of the Saturday morning ABC club. Each Saturday kids could get in if they brought jam-jars instead of money or old Villa pop bottles, because the theatre could get a threepence refund off each one. The cinema would be jam-packed too, most of us never ever putting actual money over the counter. We would watch adventures of The Lone Ranger, Flash Gordon and various other heroes, yell at the screen, share sweets and give our folks a well-earned break. My love of movies consolidated my obsession with right and wrong. Each of these heroes, be they Errol Flynn or John Wayne, honoured women, protected them, loved them. Each one did 'the right thing' even if it led to them undergoing tremendous suffering. I looked around at the real world and saw that men no longer treated women like that, not that I could see anyway. But the world of the movies was the one I wanted to live in. On leaving the theatre I was filled with this passion to be that hero, to do the right thing, to be looked at adoringly by a woman who saw you that way. It may sound like a bucket of bilge but I believed it!

So once again I decided to try and win the affection of a woman, this time trying rather nearer to home. Further down our street lived two girls, Susan Hindson and Angela Macfarlane. Every lad at school had a girlfriend except me, and I couldn't think why. The only thing that kept me from getting upset about it was knowing that Batman didn't have a girlfriend either. I rationalised that maybe 'us crimefighters' have to live alone. Even so, I was trying really hard. Once in a competition with another Hugh Gardener, Terry Davidson, I ate a banana skin and the peel of an entire orange to prove how much I wanted to go out with Susan. I won, because Terry refused the banana skin. So she invited me into her alley where I was promptly sick down her wall. My endless unrequited pursuit of this woman ended after years of flirting when all the lads got hold of me, stripped all my clothes off me and dumped me in her garden. The twenty or so of them wouldn't let me out and rang the doorbell. Thank the Lord nobody was home, but the neighbours saw what had happened and got my clothes back for me. I couldn't beat them all up, otherwise they would have known I was Batboy!

I started trying to get other girls to date me. A lovely lass with dark curls called Carol Bone got on well with me, so I asked her out only to discover she was seeing a boy in the older year. He was the very first person to break my nose, but sadly not the last. This deterred me from aiming so close to home, but realistically it was the only place I met girls.

Once the bruising had gone down and the bones had been repaired, returning my nose to roughly the centre of my head, I decided to try again. There was a really rough girl from down Joan Street. She'd never had a boyfriend. I decided to ask her out. Her reply was instant – a crack on the nose that gave me a mask like the Lone Ranger and came close to sending me back to hospital again.

Hospitals, in fact, were becoming a way of life, as my mother had been seriously ill, spending almost three years in and out of Hexham Hospital. Most nights my dad would borrow a friend's car and take me straight from school to see her. There I'd be allowed in for a two-second cuddle, then I'd have to wait for the rest of the hour out in the corridor. I took with me a huge wallpaper pattern book, my scrapbook. I'd spend hours cutting out and sticking in pictures of my favourite movie stars. It started being mostly the heroic men, but ended in mostly gorgeous actresses with as few clothes on as possible. The nurses were great, but I was being starved of love. My dad thought love was him taking me, barking all the way, and barking all the way back. I can see now that he was frightened. He has always been totally wrapped up in love for my mother and he was scared he was going to lose her. He had never been apart from her since their marriage, except during the Second World War.

One night while my mother was still in hospital, there was an awful accident at school. Myself and three friends were swinging on the heavy metal gate of the school when it came off its hinges and hit a passer-by, splitting his head open like a coconut. The man was trapped under the gate, with us all lying on him. We jumped quickly off, and the others tried to shift the gate whilst I had the presence of mind to race into the school and phone for an ambulance. By the time we'd all spoken to the police and were allowed home I was over 30 minutes late, and my dad was at the top of Hugh Gardens sitting in the borrowed Zephyr Zodiac, revving his frustration on the accelerator pedal. As I opened the door he grabbed me, belting my backside hard. I tried to sob an explanation to him all the way along the Military Road. It made no difference. Everything in his world was still black or white. I had said that I would be there at that time and I hadn't been. It didn't matter to him that a man was critically ill in hospital. My word was sacrosanct.

Once the calming and loving influence of my mam was returned to the family home I started my chasing of the elusive girlfriend. I sought them here, I sought them there, I couldn't find the buggers anywhere! In my desperation I turned where no self-respecting boy would dare to look, into the world of country dancing, that twee silly world of 'The big ship sailed down the alley alley O!' Benwell had plenty of alleys but we'd never seen a ship in any of them. Then there was 'In and out the dusty bluebells'. In our part of Benwell there was no grass let alone bluebells. Mind, if there were, they would certainly be dusty. Practically every house had a coal fire and we hadn't heard of smokeless fuel. Here was a group of young girls that my charm had never worked on. I was instantly paired with Kathleen, the school smelly. I had a great deal of sympathy with her; it was not her fault that she had devastatingly bad body odour. She was always clean and tidy and grew up into a fine woman, but as a bairn she was a stinker. None of the other lads would touch her. Even while dancing they fended off her touch, as if she had leprosy rather than BO. She was my partner for about a month and taught me all the steps and how to hold my breath for up to three minutes at a time. I was now fully equipped to be either the twinkle toes of the country dancing class or a pearl fisherman. As I couldn't swim, the choice was obvious. So I chatted to everyone and made myself known and it was there that I met my very first girlfriend, Carole Snowden. She was almost a foot taller than most of the girls in the class and was a good five inches taller than me. She agreed to see me, but not when my gang was about – 'I don't like you when you're with them, but when you're with me you're dead canny.' That's as high a compliment as a girl of that age could deliver. It won her a quarter-pound of Weekend chocolates and a kiss that was as passionate as the kind you give your granny. I used to walk her home to her house on Ethel Street and we'd hold hands if nobody was watching. Come on. I did have a reputation to uphold. I was the only country-dancing Batboy in Benwell. I couldn't let the image slip. If you showed signs of weakness, you paid a heavy price. I loved country dancing with Carole because when she swung me round my feet would come off the ground. To say I used to walk on air was an accurate description. That was as romantic as it got in those days. She'd come and watch me play football, cheering whenever I got near the ball, even if I let a goal in. She was tremendous for my self-confidence, particularly with women. She made me forget my previous ineptitude and lulled me into a false sense of security for all of the disasters that would lie ahead.

4 The Prodigal Black Sheep

IT WAS A TYPICAL WEDNESDAY NIGHT. Young Robson was kicking his football around in the back lane, when one of the lads blasted it wide and it ran right down the hill on to Armstrong Road. I raced after it, stopping it as it trailed down yet another steeper hill alongside Suttons Dwellings.

Once down there, I glanced about and saw a bus pulling up at the stop near Maria Street. A group of giggling girls in their late teens stepped out of the door at the back, walked around to the front of the bus and started to cross the road just as a green mini speeded to overtake the bus. I screamed 'Stop!' only to see one girl completely driven over and another hurled at least 30 feet into the air. Others were clipped and lay on the road. Such a tiny car, such complete carnage. Women on the bus fainted seeing a head crushed flat on to the road. One of the girls ran to her friend, who was lying in a tangle like a rag doll. Her neck had been broken and she was dead. I was barely ten and remember trying to drag her away. Another girl was screaming at the driver, a young man, who was crying 'I'm sorry, I'm so sorry' over and over again. I looked at the blood. It was everywhere – splashed along the side of the bus, in huge pools on the grey tarmac and even dripping from the faces of friends who stared at the result of one split second of thoughtlessness. That picture is still vivid in my mind. I remember thinking how useless I was. I couldn't help in any way. All I achieved was getting in the way, and making a young girl's grief even worse.

They say that tragedy comes in threes. Well, only two days later there was a huge fire in a house next to the brickfield, where a pal,

Stephen Wheatman, and I watched as a dog, a little sheltie, was burned to death up against a window. Hundreds of people watched, yet no one dared go close enough to rescue it. I was screaming at everybody to break the window, but they just pushed me back. I found a rock and when it connected the force of the fire exploded the glass and bystanders were cut by the flying shards. It was too late for the dog – it lay cooking on the window sill. Seeing things like this does have a marked effect on a young mind. It demonstrated just how important every single second of our life is. How one wrong decision can ruin your life.

Then came Saturday. Usually, when I leapt out of the front door of number 203 Hugh Gardens I would wave to the old lady who lived in the upstairs flat. She couldn't get out much so sat at the window shouting 'Hello' to everyone who passed. I had noticed for the past two or three days she hadn't been there and I'd even mentioned it to my mam. It was explained away that she sometimes stayed at her daughters or maybe she was poorly. That Saturday morning as I left the house, a couple were hammering on her front door, but getting no reply. The couple were her daughter and son-in-law, and they were anxious because she had been expecting their visit.

The local policeman, Batboy's friend, appeared on the scene and spotted the open upstairs window. He called me over: 'Alan, over here, son.' I walked across. 'Do you think you could shin up that drainpipe, climb through the window and open the front door?'

I nodded. For a second I thought I should decline, run inside, get my Batboy costume on, and then reappear just in time to save the day. But seeing the road accident had rocketed me into reality. Fantasy had its place, and it wasn't here.

The drainpipe was too small to support the huge policeman's weight, but he did stand directly beneath me, to catch me in his arms should I fall. I didn't, reaching the ledge easily, and poked my leg inside. I was wearing my very first pair of long trousers and I was being careful not to scuff the knees. I eased my body through the half-open window, tentatively feeling down until my foot touched something solid enough to carry my weight. My nostrils were filled with a sweet, sickly, distinct smell, a smell that I'd never known before. I looked around the room and there she was, lying on the floor between the unmade bed and a cluttered dressing-table. Her face was more green than white, with dried froth around her mouth, and her eyes stared at me. I screamed, a kind of girlish scream, and raced down the stairs but couldn't get the door open. It was a classic case of more haste, less speed. All that was preventing me was the sneck, yet I was now in full panic. Once I solved this puzzle the door opened and I sucked in as much fresh air as my nose and lungs could handle. Such a gasp made me dizzy and my legs turned to jelly. The policeman then took full control and another neighbour gave me a hot cup of tea. That was the cure adopted for every disaster ranging from toothache to a thermonuclear war. My friend Mr Bobby, who was actually the same shape as Mr Blobby, explained that the smell came from a complete release of bodily fluid and internal gases. That didn't make me feel any better at all. A statement was taken and then the ambulance arrived to carry her away. I had a few nightmares after that and had to find a way to end them. I had said hello to that lady every day for almost five years, yet that wasn't her that I found on the floor. It was merely the husk, the vehicle that her body travelled around in. She'd gone, abandoning the vehicle so it didn't slow her down. She'd traded it in for a faster, more modern model, and was now free to begin a new adventure. Heavy philosophy for a youngster, but had I let it eat away at me, my mind would have imploded. It would have transferred itself to my parents. Every day I would have to rush home to make sure they were all right. I had to create a device that convinced me, so I could push myself back on to the tracks again.

It was around this time that I was the victim of an accident by a local dentist. An error in judgement that would completely change my life for almost ten years. Like many, I was petrified of the dentist, having such a sweet tooth that fillings and extractions were certainly commonplace in my early years. I vividly remember the rubber smell of the mask placed across my face as he started pumping gas into me. The dreams were always violent, vicious tales of me being trapped, often actually in a cage, and people outside trying to hurt me. All the while the dentist heaved on his pliers to remove the errant peg. I remember waking up in the waiting room with a huge hole in my gum where a tooth had been. I remember poking my tongue into the gap, feeling a little squirt of blood gush into my mouth. There next to me would be my mother, holding a white metal basin half-full of bloody squidge that I'd been dribbling in my sleep. Then a scarf would be put across my mouth and I'd wobble home.

I'd suffered this about fifteen to twenty times with baby teeth and my grown-up ones. Then the dentist got the smart idea to get an X-ray taken. For Benwell at that time an X-ray was unheard of and just something else that a little boy could be frightened of. At long last I was persuaded to attend the old Dental Hospital just down the road from Newcastle's Civic Centre. There the pictures were taken – for once a dental experience that didn't whiten my knuckles and loosen my bowels. However, through the door three weeks later came a little card asking my mother to take me back to the dentist. It seems that this innocent and painless photograph had uncovered a monster lurking beneath the surface of my head. There in a skull picture of my mouth was a huge tooth growing the wrong way. It was lying on its side embedded inside my gum directly above where my two front teeth were meant to be.

'It has to come out,' said the dentist. 'In fact, if you look there are three teeth there and two have to be cut from the gum. One is his new front tooth, one is a tooth his mouth hasn't room for and the other . . . well, I don't know where that's come from!'

If he didn't know, I'm sure that I didn't. My baby teeth had lasted longer than expected and I was longing for my second big front tooth to appear. I had suffered several cruel remarks about the tell-tale gap. My mother said it was there because I must have been kissing all the girls. I wish! So the appointment was made at the Dental Hospital and I had about four weeks to worry. In the meanwhile one of the new teeth appeared in my front gap, the dentist was informed and he said it was obviously the one that there was no room for so it had to be removed to make way for the proper front tooth. So once again I was gassed and the perfectly healthy tooth was pulled. No sooner had I got over this nightmare than it was time to trail back into Newcastle city centre for the big operation. My mam was crying and kept saying that she would rather go through the operation than me. I happily would have let her. However, the reality was that if anyone had wanted to take out her teeth, she just had to spit them into a handkerchief. So there I was in a strange room with a young nurse who had obviously fallen under my spell. I hadn't even asked her out yet she was holding my hand and stroking it gently. Then in walked this small, bespectacled, pompous man.

'Ah, Master Robson. I see we'll be getting this nasty tooth out for you?'

I nodded, knowing it wasn't nasty. It hadn't done me any harm. It didn't even hurt!

'I've spoken to your mother. She says that she doesn't mind if some students watch the process. After all, this is a training hospital you know!' I had no say. As it was, he hadn't asked my mother, she was pacing the corridor frantic for the well-being of 'her bairn'. Mind you, she wasn't half as frantic as I was. Then in poured a river of faces, about twenty dental students all gaping at this wriggling ten-year-old.

'We're not going to knock out the patient,' said the surgeon. 'The entire operation will be done merely with a numbing injection.' I almost soiled the chair; I'd never had any work done without gas; I'd even insisted on it as a child for the fillings. So a needle that looked almost as large as a fire extinguisher was poked into my gum, again and again and again. My upper lip felt like a rubber hoover ring and I couldn't talk. I scrunched my eyes up and dared not open them.

'First, I'm going to make the first incision!' A running commentary, that was all I needed. I could close my eyes, but I couldn't close my ears. I felt something in my mouth, not so much the cut but I felt something warm running into my mouth. That was blood, he'd cut me, the old sod had cut me. The back street toughie came out in me and my mind was using every swear word at him. How could he humiliate me by having all of these people watching my suffering? Were they all sick in the head or something? Tears rolled down my cheeks, I was trapped and there was no escape. The ordeal took almost an hour to complete and I can still feel the pulling of the fourteen stitches inserted in my upper gum. Then the students disappeared, giving the old dentist a polite round of applause as he dinked this huge tooth with sinews and nerves dangling from it into a glass dish. I didn't want to applaud him. I wanted to catch him in the groin with my brogues. He had directed the entire operation towards the students instead of considering me. He was no professional.

After a while the nurse guided me to my mam, who was waiting with a droopy expression, red eyes and my scarf. With my scarf wrapped around my mouth, still full of blood, we headed out to get the bus home. With each and every blast of wind, it was as if someone was sticking knives into my face. I cried every day for almost a month. Even when the stitches were removed I suffered a great deal of discomfort. It was then that my own dentist examined me, and the follow-up X-ray, declaring that he'd accidentally taken out the wrong front tooth. I would always have a sizeable gap. By this time the other tooth was starting to slide into the space. There was the new Robson mouth – one little teeny weeny tooth and one that looked like a paddle in comparison.

This actually did change my life. Suddenly, the little self-confidence I had was totally gone. Each time I smiled someone made a remark. 'Goofy' was a common one. As the season of goodwill approached, I wish I had a penny for every time friends and family said, 'I bet all you want for Christmas is your two front teeth!' I felt so ashamed – even the ugliest kids in my school at least had two teeth up front. I'd just turned eleven for Heaven's sake. I started learning to smile without showing my teeth, laughing with the lips firmly together. The embarrassment continued even in school where the teachers joined in the ritual humiliation. When reading aloud in class I noticed that the gap created problems – you either spat through it by accident or it would whistle. Each time it did, half-a-dozen mimics would pile in: 'Thay thea-thide again Alan!' I would just sit down and shut up. Instead of chastising the teasers, I would be in the wrong for not finishing the piece. The only real pals I had were the remnants of the gang from Hugh Gardens. Girls wouldn't even consider going out with 'Goofy'.

Benwell's Adelaide Terrace was up for a major revitalisation. The branch of Woolworths was closing, and half of the buildings were going to be pulled down so that a glitzy new shopping centre could rise from the ruins. Most of Benwell actually preferred things the way they were with little quaint shops, owned by people everyone knew. It was quite a buzzing place, with much of the activity centred around the Milk Bar, a sort of 'Happy Days' style establishment with a big juke box blasting out all the hits of the day. It sold nothing stronger than coffee, but it was always full of teenagers having a dance, or just ganging up with their pals, mixing with pensioners who were in for a cuppa or a slice of simnel cake. The Milk Bar earned its living mainly from the younger crowd, buying sweets, pop or ice-creams in fancy dishes. It was next to the post office, just along from Nora's wool shop. Wool was the essential commodity in an area where hardly anyone had the price of a pullover and each one had to be knitted by hand. But despite the uproar against the scheme, the entire block was demolished.

The shells of the old buildings made a perfect playground for the Hugh Gardens posse. We were in there hunting for anything to play with, and young Robson as always was doing the most dangerous and stupid things imaginable. It was there that whilst walking along one of the roof joists I slipped, landing with one leg either side of the rotting timber. It snapped and I fell down about fifteen feet on to the rubble floor. A passer-by in a car whisked me up to Newcastle General Hospital. I looked down at my grey school trousers and saw that the crotch was covered with blood. I felt sick and woozy as they laid me down on a huge trolley, pushed me into a cubicle and pulled the curtain closed behind me. After this, a middle-aged lady doctor removed my trousers and pants and there were my forming genitals, looking more like sweet-and-sour pork. They were impregnated by huge wooden spelks, each one an agony to remove. She smeared the swollen testes with a cream, and sent me to another room for a tetanus injection. Then I was placed back in the bloody trousers and sent home. The blood, what appeared to be gallons of it, was from a tiny cut on the sac too slight to need stitching.

From that moment on, I concentrated on my football, playing for the youth club team in Mill Lane, the local pub juniors team and the school eleven. Even at that time we couldn't always afford a proper football, not even a plastic one. It is in such times that necessity becomes the mother of invention. We'd often heard some of the old fellows talking about how they used to play with a 'clootie ball', a ball made out of cloth, filled with rags. Wasn't that a brilliant idea? So I raced into the house and to my surprise I found in the bottom of my mam's sewing cupboard an old round cushion. I tugged at the lining and it was full of tiny pieces of foam rubber. There next to it was a paper bag full of even more spongy pieces. So I jammed as many as I could into this cloth lining, trying to form as circular a shape as I could and then proceeded to fold the edge and then sewed it up. The lads had a ball at last and out we went. Before the game we all tried to dribble this 'clootie ba' ' down the street, while we gathered the entire squad. It was then that I kicked the distorted sphere as hard as I could, and it landed in a lady's tiny garden. To my absolute horror the ball had burst and there completely covering a grassy patch no bigger than two-yards square lay close to a thousand pieces of multi-coloured sponge. We were all down on our hands and knees picking them up from four-inch deep grass for almost three hours.

I still believed if I gave it maximum commitment that I'd be capable of earning a job in soccer. My school work was reasonable, but football was my passion. I was always in the top class at school but I was always the one with the worst marks, the lad who seemed perpetually likely to sink into the next class down. I was certainly one of the roughest there, always surrounded by immaculately dressed kids. Myself, George Walker and David Dowson were the three in hand-me-downs and second-hand stuff. George would go on to stuff the snobs by getting ten O levels and David, another schoolyard fighter, became a butcher in Benwell. He's one of the few lads I still bump into, and he's a good man. I'm proud that he's done so well. Nobody ever really thought that any good could come out of the West End kids. If you lived in Blakelaw or Fenham it was OK, but Benwell, Norwich Street flats or Scotswood Road even then had a stigma. So each of us pushed hard to prove everybody wrong, particularly in the area of sport. I was the school goalkeeper at football, the wicketkeeper in cricket and captain of the volley ball team. I ran in the 100m, 200m, 440m and the relay events, and competed in the long jump and high jump. I couldn't get enough of it. Not only would I play in all of these games, most nights I'd be training, practising, giving it 100 per cent. It would be my way of making it. No obvious career was opening itself up to me and I was desperate for any direction. Then I did well in a cup game, playing for my school John Marlay against Rutherford School on Newcastle's West Road. I had played a cracker, diving at people's feet, saving a penalty and in the dying seconds turning a thunderbolt of a shot over the bar. A scout for Newcastle United must have seen the game for completely out of the blue I was offered a trial for the youth team. There wasn't a bigger honour for any Newcastle lad than to get a chance to play for the Magpies. I was there for all of the home games and to think I'd be out there playing on that very pitch was a dream come true. The dream became a nightmare, for my side lost 8–2. I played all right, but was obviously held to blame for the goals, as they ended up signing up half of my team's defence. That was the end of my serious efforts to become a pro, another dream totally dashed.

Even in our house I always enjoyed taking risks, and to this day I am certain that my own father would have killed me had he known exactly where I was late one night. My dad was always careful with money. It was too hard to come by for him to be any other way. Rather than buy a new television he'd always just get an old second-hand reconditioned one. This meant that inevitably it was backwards and forwards to the repair shop. Finally, my dad complained so bitterly that they gave him a newer black-and-white model for downstairs. Forever frugal, my dad brought the original set upstairs and put it in the corner of their bedroom. So after about ten o'clock when I was already in bed, they would sneak up and watch the late films. To a young lad who was movie-mad this was much too great a temptation, so I used to wait until the film had started, then after tying the belt of my pyjamas as tightly as possible, I'd commando crawl across the landing from my bedroom, staying flat so they'd not see me slip beneath their bed, where I'd watch the rest of the film before creeping back.

One night there was a film on TV starring my mam's favourite, Claudette Colbert. It was called *It Happened One Night* and never was there a more appropriately named film. My mother had gone on about this film for ages, so there was no way that I was missing out. The pair of them often would say to me how bad a film was, as an excuse to get me to bed, then the following morning they would go on non-stop about how brilliant it had been. I wasn't going to be caught again. So rather like a soldier sneaking beneath the wire into no man's land, I slid my way across the polished wood-tiled landing, on to the worn carpet and under the bed. Once established, I was enjoying the knockabout comedy when the bed started moving. The springs actually bounced on to my back, knocking me flat to the ground. Then I started to hear noises, grunting, panting and to my absolute horror I realised they were making love. Now I knew they had before – I was the result – but

I didn't want to believe it. I had often asked about sex, but my mam refused to say anything and my dad was never in long enough to explain. Yet there they were lost in their love for each other. No matter how magnificent the experience, it is for two people not three. I thought about moving. I thought also of the consequences if I got caught, so stayed put. My mind swirled as I tried to concentrate on the film. The other noises made me wonder if sex was painful. At one point my mam sounded in so much agony I wanted to shout 'Hey, leave her alone', but didn't have the guts. Finally, summoning every ounce of courage, I crawled from under the bed and out of the room, pulling their glass bedroom door to after me. I got into bed in a real sweat. Although I had enjoyed dozens of films and football matches that way, I never dared again.

My sister Brenda occasionally took me out to the shops and to the pictures. The only problem was it would always be to things that she rather wanted to see. I quite liked being with our Brenda because she always paid and I'd get an ice-cream, which were normally out of my range. Then came Julie Andrews in *The Sound of Music* and the beginning of a huge chasm that would slice our family in two. She dragged me along to the Queens Cinema, where the Queens Arcade now is in Newcastle, and I must admit that, as a twelve-year-old, I thought it was very good. What I didn't realise was that it would completely capture Brenda's imagination. I ended up being dragged back to see it 21 times, while Brenda returned well into the hundreds. Her religious beliefs had been in a state of flux for some time – she'd visited many churches to see if any of them held the answer for her. The rest of the family were loosely Church of England. In other words, they never went to church at all. Brenda decided upon Catholicism, eventually took orders and became a nun. My mother was appalled. She cried for months. She knew that sooner or later we would both leave home, but never expected this. Finally, after deep family talks Brenda entered the Convent of Marie Reparatrice, from there disappearing to another private order in Ireland. This almost killed my mother who was already weak from her various internal problems. Brenda believed it was her calling and nothing could dissuade her. Yet truth has a way of always being stranger than fiction. All those times Brenda had watched Julie Andrews' joining the convent, discovering that she wasn't 'an asset to the Abbey', then going out to marry a wealthy German and look after his children. That is precisely what Brenda did. After six or seven years, she came out, joined an international penpal agency, met a wealthy German called Eifler not Von Trapp, married him and became the mother of two beautiful daughters. She now lives on a huge patch of land in Stetternich, near Jülich in Germany.

That left me in a house that remained sad for many years. My dad just kept on going, but when we were all together my mother would inevitably mention Brenda and start to cry. Through all those years my mother was very sullen and hard to motivate. Only the times when their friends were around seemed to perk her up. I had always felt that I was my mam's favourite and this was a huge personal blow to me. Suddenly, it was obvious that she thought non-stop about her lost daughter. I was there right beside her, yet nothing I could do ever helped. Not only had Brenda gone, in a way I had lost my mam too. Yes, she still loved me. I have never doubted that, but this family crisis showed me a kind of batting order. Brenda was, and really always had been closer to mam. It was from that day I started calling my mother Audrey and still do. My love for her has never waned, but I never felt 'special' again!

To say that Benwell was a safe place isn't totally true. There were various gangs that hung out, and if they caught you, you'd take a beating. I used to run three newspaper rounds at Jack Ward's, the newsagents, on Clara Street, one in the morning and two at night. This was the only way I could supplement my pocket money. Some of the money went to my mam for insurance policies, and the rest was mine. It was my cinema cash and helped buy books and comics that I loved. My rounds were always the most tiring – blocks of flats, streets that stretched from Elswick Road right down to Scotswood Road. Along a narrow, darkened alleyway I would be attacked at least one night a week by the Pipe Track Lane Aggro Boys. They were a gang of skinheads who knew that I was starting to wear my hair long. They would kick me around on the ground, and on one occasion hit me with a metal bar causing me to have nine stitches in my brow. I also suffered serious cuts and bruising and had four teeth kicked out of my head. Still I refused to give in. Every day I'd go back down, facing them, and if I found one of them alone I'd chin him, knowing that the following day I'd get caught and be made to pay for it. One day I was so frightened by all this that my dad, who was now working for the Northern Gas Board, lay waiting in a van to try and catch the bigger lads that regularly preyed on me. I was about thirteen, while the bigger thugs were in their late teens. The two worst were Lislo Wol and Celtic Mick, both a pair of bruisers, regularly coming up to Benwell with their gang, who were far more fierce than ours.

It was a strange thing but eventually I managed to earn their respect, and they started leaving me alone. In the end, they'd actually say hello. So to show how much I appreciated it, I wrote on my canvas paper bag PTLAB, the initials of the Pipe Track Lane Aggro Boys. That very day I was at the bottom of my street delivering papers when Slatyford Aggro Boys got off the bus and turned me over after reading it. I've always been lucky like that.

It was down Pipe Track Lane that I met the very next object of my desire. After some detective work I discovered her name was Sarah-Jane and I asked her out. To my surprise she said 'Yes I've fancied you for ages!' I practically flew back to the paper shop. I was so elated that despite my gappy teeth this pretty girl had agreed to be my girlfriend. So I instantly emptied my piggy bank (yes, a real ceramic one) and planned my very first proper date. By this time I'd moved downstairs into what used to be our Brenda's room on the ground floor, to get out from under the close scrutiny of my parents. There I had a bottle of Villa Sasperella, a plate of crisps, some chocolate raisins and my record player with the speaker in the lid. I dug out the best records I had and put on the sloppiest one. Then in she walked, short cotton skirt, little ankle socks, broad round sandals and a white cardigan. To me she was Ursula Andress walking out of the sea in *Dr No*. She sat down next to the old gas fire my dad had installed in there warming herself, stuffing crisps into her mouth and getting comfortable. I excused myself and raced into the kitchen to find my mam and to get two plastic beakers for our pop.

'Mam,' said I. 'I have got the most beautiful girl in the world next door.'

My mother was totally uninterested. 'Yes, dear, that's nice,' she said and kept on peeling vegetables for my dad's tea.

My bladder was showing signs of nervousness, so I visited the outside toilet and quickly washed my hands. I tried to calm myself.

I had to be cool. That's what the girls liked. Then grabbing the two beakers, I took a deep breath and walked back to my room.

Sarah-Jane had gone. So had my record player and the records. I never saw her or them again.

I felt so humiliated, but I didn't want my mam to know. I pretended that Sarah-Jane was there for about an hour and a half, talking to myself in male and female voices. I ate the remaining crumbs of crisps and chewed on the sweets whilst feeling sick to my stomach.

As I approached my middle teens I became even more desperate to find a girlfriend and maybe even try this sex thing. So I saw this young girl working just on a Saturday in a florist's on Adelaide Terrace. Her name was Hazel and she lived miles away near Palatine Products at Delaval Road. Even so, I was undeterred. With the princely sum of a pound I'd saved from my pocket money, and doing my best to hide my gappy grin, I waltzed into the florist and ordered a bouquet of flowers. It was only a small bunch, but the young ginger-haired girl picked one out and handed me a card. I paid my money, took the bunch of carnations and placed the card inside. Then I turned to her and handed her the flowers: 'They're for you!' At that, I raced out of the shop, my courage running out with me. On the card I had written: 'I'd love to go out with you. I'll meet you outside Palatine Products tonight at 6 p.m.' I stood there for two hours watching the house where she lived. She appeared at the window at regular intervals but never came out.

I tried something similar with another girl called Lynn Davies who had been in the infants with me. A dark-eyed girl, she had been a friend, so I thought that fact alone would give me an edge. This time my attempt was made on Christmas Eve, when I just turned up at her door with a big present. She accepted it courteously, then slammed the door in my face. I slipped a note through her door saying that I'd meet her at the top of her street. It was bitterly cold, the snow was ice, and like the nuggets of the day, we never wore heavy coats. It wasn't cool to show the cold so I was turning rapidly blue. I waited for another freezing couple of hours but she never showed up. She did introduce me to one of her friends though, a Cyndi Lauper lookalike with long white-tighted legs called Susan.

'Mind Alan,' warned Lynn, 'don't make her laugh or she'll wet herself!'

I giggled as I took Susan's arm. I felt terrific. It was how it was meant to be. So this very first time we were together we promenaded around Adelaide Terrace, and I was persuaded to buy everyone a hot pasty. We knew how to live in those days. The only problem was that there was a huge queue in the baker's shop on the corner of the Terrace and Ethel Street. So we all waited outside, Susan leaning on the glass of the shop. I cracked a joke and she started laughing, from laughter to giggles, then to snorts like a hyena. Lynn was right, for she promptly wet herself. However knowledgeable I am about the problems of the bladder now, then I was so embarrassed that I just walked away. The great love affair died. Anything to do with wee-wee was taboo!

Every night at the top of Hugh Gardens, right next to the baked potato shop, stood the prettiest prostitute in Benwell. She really was a picture, with her mousy hair piled high on her head and wearing a short micro-mini dress covered by a yellow and black plastic raincoat and high knee-length white boots. They were called kinky boots at the time, but I'm sure she knew more about that than I did. Using all the monies that I had collected as a paper boy, I decided to hire her services. I had a total of £1 3*s* 11*d*. So I walked across to this angel-faced woman in her late twenties, me a spotty-faced, gap-toothed kid barely fourteen, and asked her how much.

'Just piss off,' came her reply.

I was quite taken aback. Did she realise that I was a wealthy young man and, more to the point, I was dead good at nipping and tickling?

'No, Miss. I want you to be my girlfriend.' Eyes like big blue dinner plates shined up at her in the chilly night air. Our breaths formed clouds before us.

Her eyes started to smile. 'Come back in a few years son!' she said. She leaned over and kissed me on the cheek. A big red butterfly remained for the world to see.

'How much was that?' I enquired.

The street lady chuckled. 'That was for nothing.'

'I've had plenty of that!' I replied. 'Here, look. I've got money!'

My hands fell open showing a crumpled ten-bob note and various hot sticky coins.

With her long ring-bedecked fingers she closed my hands around the money. Her red nail varnish was so shiny it reflected the glare of the street lamp. 'Listen kid, save it for a proper girl-friend!'

She looked so beautiful, smiling at me sincerely and kindly, when a car pulled up. She leaned into the window, said a few words, and then slid her long legs inside and was gone. My passion was turned towards the baked potato shop where I used almost a third of a year's savings on a baked potato with prawns. I said to myself, 'This is a damn sight better than nipping somebody!' The sad truth was that no one was holding or touching me and I so wanted that, I needed that!

Although I had never had an erection let alone any other form of sexual urge, the entire year at school claimed to be at it like knives and I needed to join in. There was nothing else for it. I'd have to go for the lass above the butcher's. She was about sixteen and had sex with everybody and anybody, and the stories about her were rife. After the pubs closed, they would literally queue to have her. She'd sleep with men for money or gifts, with children for comics or sweets, and was the nearest thing to a nymphomaniac that existed in my world. One of my older mates, Micky, told me that he had sex with her for two cigarettes. So I took the remnants of my nest egg, a packet of my dad's Embassy Tipped and a bottle of wine from the cupboard. I knew that I would be caught and have to pay a heavy penalty for taking them, but I felt as if I was the only lad in the school who hadn't 'done it', so tonight it had to be! She was just getting in from school when I stopped her. 'Excuse me, but I want you and I have these for you!' I said.

She looked at me as if I was a dog turd on her shoe. She pulled the cellophane off the packet and pulled out a ciggy. She threw the rest of the pack in her school bag, grabbed the wine and pocketed the money.

'So what do you want, then?' she barked.

'Everything. I want sex and things!' came my weak half-whispered reply.

She reached down and tweaked at my groin. 'You've got nowt

to have sex with!' She turned towards her door, pushing it open. 'Now fuck off, you toothless git!' She slammed the door in my face. The bottom of the barrel had been scraped and I was still alone, lost and unloved.

5 Remember the Days of the Old Schoolyard

My schooldays were certainly not the best years of my life. It was a time of fighting, swearing, hiding and struggling to keep up with the others in my class. In the schoolroom I was one of the weakest students in the top set, while outside I was 'Pop', the lad everyone came to, to get their problems solved. It was odd having teachers chastise me, paying me so little genuine concern, whilst the other lads held me in high esteem. When we weren't hanging out on street corners I used to take a foray to Newcastle's Hancock Museum to look at the stuffed animals and the mummy. My mother was quite chuffed when I'd say I was going there, or to Newcastle's Central Library, believing her little waster from the backstreets was seeking culture. The truth was that as I was too young for pubs and clubs they were the only places outside of school where you could meet girls. School parties from all over the North poured into them, and rather like a fox would try and corner a lamb, I'd try and separate a girl from the flock. Over the years at the Hancock Museum or the Laing Art Gallery or the Joicey Museum, I chatted up hundreds of girls and ended up courting none of them. One of the older girls had told her sister that I had no 'machismo'. I was frantic – what was it? I thought it must be some gadget that older boys used to buy to impress the girls. I even went into the electronics shop Aitken Brothers in town and asked for one. I wondered why they'd laughed. As usual I was the class clown, a mask that laughed and made others do likewise, but all the while feeling very much alone.

I was regularly strapped, my bottom suffered canings and my newspaper round was almost lost due to the amount of times I was put on detention. Then totally against my character, I began volunteering to stay behind after school every Monday night for extra work. We had a new student teacher called Miss Tagg and she was really nice, not so much attractive as just female. We did have some female teachers but this girl was young and enjoyed a laugh. As I was regularly striking out with every girl I met I got a huge crush on this lady. Each week she ran extra classes to teach us about mythology. I was already an expert, for the excuses I gave for not doing homework fell loosely into the same category. Still, I really was studying and to my surprise found the subject thoroughly fascinating and still do. My love for Miss Tagg was a fragile rose that would eventually lie crushed and broken on the last day of term. On that day a bespectacled wimp in a small car picked her up and gave her the kind of snog you never saw on TV in the sixties. Especially when you didn't own a telly!

Throughout my school life at an all-boys secondary school, I was taught to swim by experts, teachers, instructors, friends and family all without success. I swam like a brick. During our swimming periods everyone else had a whale of a time, while I plodged in the shallows with a polystyrene float. To help get around this, I acted the fool to cover my humiliation. One day my body began to change without my consent and led me to almost take my life. There was I, with the scratchiest pair of navy blue swimming trunks, my spindly body like a piece of diseased bacon rind but probably more white. I was on the top board running around, pretending I was going to dive off. I would jump off backwards, catching hold of the board and climb back up. Everyone knew I couldn't swim but used to laugh at my antics. Then one day as our lesson neared its end, in walked a class full of girls from the school next door. Their teacher was a beautiful redheaded lady in her early twenties in the most sensational bikini I had ever seen. Having only been to the beach a couple of times, I had never seen anything like this. There I was, standing on the top board in full view, my eyes fixed on this woman, like every other lad in the water. This included the three lads still in their school uniforms who had verrucas and weren't allowed in the water. My eyes were rather like saucers as I looked this woman up and down. To my eternal shame I started to feel my swimmy trunks expanding. I had never had an erection before and there it was, pushing at the elastic that ran across the top, battling to escape. I could've fainted, yet the more I thought about it, the harder it became and the less likely to disappear. Finally, I felt as if everybody was looking at it. They weren't, but it's rather like the spot on your cheek, nobody knows it's there, but you're certain everyone's staring at it. So I did the only thing I could do – I jumped in!

I went straight to the bottom, killing my very first manly feeling in the process. Friends were saying, 'Eeh, Alan's jumped in the deep end, off the top board and he can't swim,' and the others were laughing until they realised that I wasn't coming up. Several of them dragged me to the surface and pushed me into the arms of a teacher who pumped my stomach and sent me home.

Our English teacher, a small balding chap called Mr Doney, was a lovely man and the only one that I could really relate to. His idiosyncrasy was to wave his legs around under the desk while he taught you. He lit the blue touch-paper of my imagination about language, words, books and literature. Everyone around me spoke broad Geordie – no one from outside our patch could understand a word. Yet in the middle of all this dialect, here was a man who could paint pictures with sentences, who could take you out of the classroom with stories and who made me exercise my imagination with just a pen and a blank sheet of paper. He said, 'Language is power. It is the way to control your life and the lives of others!' He was right. I had reached a stage where I didn't believe that I could possibly be interested in school work and he saved me. I'll never be able to thank him enough.

At the age of only fifteen I wrote a book called *Terra Moon* and my love for words has never left me!

When O level examinations came along, I achieved only five. It would take me almost six more years of day release, night classes and correspondence courses to get the education I needed to help me on my way. I ended up with one A level and a Diploma in Literary Appreciation, my proudest educational achievement.

6 My Parents Were Always Right and I Felt I Was Always Left

I ADMIT TO BEING BORN the black sheep of the Robson family, forever off on my own ploughing a lone furrow in the field of life. When I look over my shoulder, I have racked my brain to find out why. I always wanted to be a part of whatever was happening, yet I never seemed to fit in. I look at symptoms like feeling that my sister was always preferred to me; I'm sure my parents genuinely did love us equally, yet I always felt at the bottom of the bill. Once my sister had left the family to join the convent, I had felt that it was my chance to become number one. Quite the reverse happened. I found myself almost pushed out altogether, as if somehow her leaving had to be taken out on someone, and I was the only one there. I remember this time as the angry years, when for the only time during my childhood there was any friction in the great love my parents have always been lucky to share. A love that would lead to over fifty years of marriage, and an example that I would never be able to follow. I was so desperate too, so determined to 'do the right thing' and 'make them proud'. Perhaps there was even a bit of 'I'll show the buggers'.

I only remember the highs and lows, not the fairly happy average childhood days in between. The highs were the times when I did get fussed over, the lows when I was ignored or almost forgotten about.

I remember being dragged down south to Abingdon in Berkshire to spend time with a fun-loving, firebrand of a woman, my Auntie Elsie. I didn't know anybody down there, but was assured that they were family so it was all right. My dad had borrowed his pal's car and I was so frightened, never having had a holiday, that every ten miles was wee-wee time. On getting there, some eight hours after setting off, I met the strangers who were my blood. Elsie was great, and I took an instant, loving attitude towards her. My dad's sister had the fine northern trait of being just friendly enough to put you at ease. Her husband Will kept me rather more at a distance, but perhaps this holiday was going to be all right after all.

Within twenty-five minutes of arriving, they had all decided to go to the pub. So what was I to do? After a bit of running about, Elsie returned to say that her daughter would take me for the night. So my comics were gathered together, a bag of bribery flavoured sweets and my pyjamas and I headed to my next stop. These folk weren't my kind of people, they spoke a different language, as if they had a pickled onion in each cheek. The only kind of talk I was used to was from along Scotswood Road or Armstrong Road in Newcastle. There I was with a youngish man and woman and two girls, all viewing me as if I was ET and I'd just landed.

I remember screaming and crying. My mam was concerned, my dad wanted away for a fun night out and Elsie was keen to show them the town. The more I used my lungs to demonstrate my anxiety at being taken on holiday then dumped, the more this couple used phrases like, 'Oh, he'll calm down when you've gone', 'Don't worry, we'll put the television on, that'll quieten him down!' and the classic 'Get yourself away. Don't let him spoil your night!'

I'd never been away from my parents before, I'd never met these people, yet here I was trapped. I tried to get out of their back door but it had an upper bolt and even a sprightly six-year-old couldn't reach it. I started screaming even louder as my parents walked to the car so they could remember the torment I was feeling while they downed their beer and drambuie. I had never ever felt that terrified before. They had made a choice, the choice to leave me behind. I had often heard the jokes they would crack to friends about how I was the 'mistake' and I never forgot those comments. Each time I remembered, I felt hurt by it. To this day, it gives me a heavy heart. Now they had left me! From the very second that I heard the car pull away the mother tried to placate me, without success. Then the two girls made me even more hyper, by shouting 'Cry baby' and other welcoming phrases. Finally, at the eleventh hour, the man came forward and tried to reason, whilst having a heavy undertone of threat in his voice. I had been in Abingdon for less than an hour and I was being told to go to a strange bed, in a strange house full of strange people that I didn't like. My first holiday and I hated it. It set me against holidays from that day on.

My school activities became another sore point with me, because apart from two school concerts that my mam attended, neither of my folks ever came to see me do anything. I played in every sport, I was in the choir for six years, in football we won the County Shield, in cricket we reached a high standard and at volley ball we won every league going. I asked, even begged my mam and dad to come and see me, but it never fitted in with what they were doing. I now appreciate the amount of work my father did at that time, but over all of those years they could've come to see me. I wanted to make them proud; I wanted to show them that I was finally capable of doing something. But they seemed always more concerned about Brenda, the runaway nun. I wanted to run away as well, but I was too frightened.

As well as the lows came the highs, the times that my dad's closest friend, Joe Jobling, would take me along nature trails, showing me my first owl, my first hawk and helping me catch my first fish. Although whilst under orders I caught quite a few things, I never really liked it. The fish always looked in pain. It was bad enough that they'd just eaten a maggot, let alone get hooked in the mouth.

Once, when fishing off the pier at Seahouses, using an old kipper as my only bait, a seagull swooped down, taking the bait before it hit the water. The hook was in its beak and I had to reel in this white, flapping bundle of angry feathers. Had my dad not been there with his fisherman's pliers, that huge albatross of a herring gull would've dragged me to the Farne Islands.

Surprisingly, these were the happier times, despite me having an unnerving way of ending up in trouble. I used to watch my dad, always capable, always calm in a crisis, always solid as a rock. I so wanted to be like him, though I would never tell him so. He seemed to love me from a distance, only ever having something to say if I'd stepped out of line. One day whilst fishing at Ford Castle I saw him standing on a tiny grassy knoll about a yard out in the river. He looked like Izaak Walton's complete angler. So with my cheaply bought junkshop rod, I leaped on to another little island in the stream – and felt my second-hand jumble-sale wellies begin to sink. My dad always insisted on silence whilst fishing, so I was reluctant to shout. Down I went, under the surface of the water as it began pouring into the top of my boots and drowning my socks. The water was bitter cold and I was still going down. Finally, I shouted to my dad for help. He just laughed and let me sink a bit further before he flopped over to me and pulled me free. He tried to find my wellies now lost in the quicksand, but he never did. They had cost pennies at the church fayre, but I paid the penalty for losing them over the next three days. I remember most of these day trips as happy, sunny times, where I saw my first adder, picked up my first toad, milked my first cow, saw my first lamb born and learned that the entire world wasn't made of concrete and brick. As we never owned a car I was indebted to the Joblings for giving us the chance to seek out this amazing thing called 'the country' so near and yet so far.

My dad for most of his life has seemed to be almost impervious to pain, and I was always expected to follow his lead. My mother was often unwell, so the conclusion I came to was obvious. Women are weedy and need looking after, men work every hour that God sends and are never poorly. Once a dog savaged my dad's face and he walked in with his lip hanging off, blood dripping down his face and soaking into his white shirt collar. My mother almost fainted, but my dad casually wandered the two miles up to the General Hospital for a few stitches. When he returned, he was more concerned about my mam. This is a hard act to follow when you're a little kid. I did try once when I needed stitches in my brow after getting hit in the face with a rock. On getting home I tried to tough it out despite having a face like a Mekon in the Dan Dare comics. My mam sat me on the marble bench in that Benwell kitchen and tried to wash off the trickle of blood that had started seeping through the over slack embroidery. As soon as she did, I passed out with the pain, fell off the bench on to the concrete floor and was rushed back to hospital again.

My mother is so full of love for everybody. When she was in this kind of fettle I adored her, and couldn't get enough. Yet within me there was something – I don't really understand what it was – that made me keep everything more at arm's length. Perhaps it was that degree of insecurity that turned innocent events into abject paranoia. Those nights coming back from such wonderfully happy days, in the darkness singing 'Keep Right On Till The End Of The Road', a family and friends united, I felt that I belonged, that I was an important part and so secure. But something always happened. Sometimes it would be a pub. In those days no one under the age of eighteen would be allowed in. From the idyllic warmth of such a closeness, I would be excluded. In a pitch-black pub car park I would be asked to 'go to sleep' in the back of the car or I'd be handed a packet of crisps and a bottle of pop, as if it made up for the fear and loneliness that I felt. It was as if I didn't really belong and had merely been kidding myself.

Although they never saw me as a black sheep, I knew that I was. The times I spoke of things like this they never really listened. 'He's only a child. What does he know?' Finally, in my early teens, I persuaded them to leave me at home during the holidays, rather than be a burden to them. At first, I suggested this knowing that they would never leave me, because they loved me too much. To my surprise and horror, they accepted it rather too readily. Once again this fuelled my insecurity and a distance began to grow between us that would never ever really change. I love them, I honour them, it is because of them that I am who I am. But I have known since being very small that I would never have the type of unique closeness with my parents that my sister enjoys. I blame myself in the main, for misreading signals, for turning away from those who love me, for being jealous and for being a mistake. A bastard sperm with a will of its own. It still drives me to try and make them proud. No matter if I married Princess Diana and was crowned King, I still feel that I would be left grounded. Once, I was named the country's top rock DJ in a national magazine, I couldn't wait to phone my mam. At last, proof that I had really achieved something never done before by any north-eastern radio presenter. I remember the call vividly: 'Mam, you'll never believe it, I've just been voted Britain's top rock presenter!', my chest panting in excitement and pride. 'That's nice, son,' came her stock reply. 'But did I tell you our Brenda is coming over next week? She's bringing the bairns. I'm really looking forward to seeing them!'

I love my sister and brother-in-law, and surprisingly I feel maybe more loving to their two beautiful daughters, my nieces Michaela Audrey and Fiona. My jealousy allows me to love Brenda from a distance. For deep in my subconscious I blame her for stealing so much love from my mother and father. I know it is stupid, that it is irrational, but I feel it in every ounce of my being.

When my parents accepted my proposal that they leave me at home alone while they travelled to Scotland, Germany, Spain or Italy, I got my first nervous taste of self-sufficiency. After the initial worry, I lapped it up. With my portion of holiday money I'd nip into the Tatler Cinema on Northumberland Street to watch the cartoons, go to the Odeon on my own, or cruise Newcastle's Handyside Arcade, the hippy haven of its day. At the weekends I'd bring all my mates in to watch TV, listen to Jethro Tull, Black Sabbath, Free and my favourites of the day, Deep Purple. We'd all walk around with hair down to our waists, either carrying a guitar to look cool or a copy of our favourite album to prove we were 'funky dudes'. We were often called hippies, yet even at that time I didn't know anybody who worked harder than I did. While I was still at school I used to work with a pal called Dick Freeman, an amateur film maker, making outfits, writing scripts, doing Goon show sketches on to a battered old tape recorder and making our own films on his cine-camera. He may still have the vampire movie we made at 6 a.m. on a Sunday morning in Jesmond Dene. He played the Dracula role, I the gap-toothed hero who ended up staking him in the heart. We wore our costumes on the bus both in and out, only putting on our make up when we got there, otherwise we'd have looked far too cissy. After the film was finished I went down to the Dene, even then far from clean, and washed off my make-up. Whatever was in that water transformed me in real life into a lumpy, scabby zit monster within four hours.

Now, after school, I was working on scripts, writing school shows and preparing a sort of amateur dramatics company to go around old folks homes. Because I couldn't write music I'd pinch famous tunes and put my own words to them. At Bolam House Old Folks Home, near Westgate Road, I recall performing my own musical, *Cleopatra*, aided and abetted by a group of mates who really couldn't be bothered. I sweated through the hour-long show, while the old dears snoozed and tried to follow the mindboggling plot. To the tune of 'California Here I Come' I wowed them as Mark Anthony with showstopping lyrics like: 'Cleopatra here I come, Caesar's dead but don't be glum. I'll woo ya, sing to ya night and day, I'll hug ya, not bug ya, Hear me, Cleo, as I say that I would gladly walk a mile, just for that Egyptian smile. Open up that River Nile. Cleopatra here I come!' Surprisingly, I never got the chance to do Shakespeare on stage.

My mode of dress was bizarre at best, ridiculous at worst, and my dad's reaction was predictable. Here was his son wearing tapestry jackets that my mam made out of furnishing fabric, loon pants, embroidered T-shirts, hair bands, love beads, a black cape and around my neck a huge cross and my bell of spiritual awareness. He was appalled and whenever I walked in if he was with his pals he'd openly call me a puff in front of them. 'Here he is the puff – what a huckle!' and they'd all have a good laugh about it. The fact that I was so lousy at getting myself a girlfriend didn't help. He'd only ever seen me with a group of fellow 'hairy Dans'.

At that time I was friendly with an older girl called Gill. We never dated, but we did knock around in the same gang. During one of those daft tickling sessions I'd taken my opportunity to reach inside her blouse and felt her breast. My very first touch of female flesh. It wasn't anything like a sexual sensation, but it was unique and unforgettable. She hit my face so hard my nose went right around my head before it started to bleed. We did stay friends, but from that day on she wore assault-proof tops in my presence.

In my desperation to, as always, live up to my father's expectations, Gill agreed to let me borrow her and pretend to be my girlfriend for one night only. So the next time I heard that my dad's pals would be around, particularly a sarcastic, beaver-faced bloke from Slatyford called Tommy, I invited her around. Gill had short dark hair, a small, slightly shop-soiled bust and the longest legs you've ever seen. She wore the tiniest mini skirt in the world, giving you a tantalising glimpse of her pants if you watched her long enough. Men always did. So I walked through the living room to get a drink to the usual taunts, then opened the door and in walked Gill. She deserved an Oscar for her performance. She stood there like a model, allowing the eyes to pop out of their heads. She walked across to me, and with her being taller she stooped down to give me a peck on the cheek, making it look as sexy as she could. Even if this didn't work on them, I was sure it was working on me. I was so desperate, I could get aroused by a strong wind, dropping a bus ticket on my lap or the noises made by next door's mongrel. She came back from the toilet, hung herself around me like a slave girl and we walked out to my room. My dad never called me those names again.

At the age of about 13, life was more savage than ever. I had long hair and lived in an area full of skinheads that prowled in gangs to seek you out. The entire ethic of long hair was the peace and love thing, but I spent an awful lot of time punching people, leaving me with two more broken noses and countless other scars. I remember being called on regularly by pals to go and wreak revenge on the various gangs that raided our turf. We never ever bothered anybody who didn't bother us, but if we were attacked we matched force with force. Once, a gang of crazies from Rye Hill actually grabbed Sparky Bright's girlfriend and he came hammering on my door absolutely demented. They had her pinned against the wall of Elswick Cemetery and were going to shave her hair off. So I grabbed a lump of wood and the two of us ran back to sort them out. By the time I got there, half her hair was trimmed, she was screaming and passers-by crossed the road so as not to get involved. Ian 'Sparky' Bright was my best friend. He was the only man who could play a tune whilst breaking wind. He pointed me to where these five or six yobs were and I piled in like Conan the Barbarian, smacking them away from the girl who ran to Ian as they skedaddled. Like most times that I help a friend, I'm left in the middle of six troublemakers in Doc Martens. They played keepie-up with my head while Sparky took his girl to his house to claim his reward. I ended up with a slash from a Stanley knife that very nearly took my nose off and needed fourteen stitches. Because I'd started the fight, my folks were told that I'd fallen off a wall. They didn't know that I used to be Batboy and would never do that.

My worst run-in with skinheads came when I was trying to win over one of my unrequited loves, Helen Joyce, who lived in Scotswood. On my way back from a visit I missed the last bus, leaving me no choice but to walk home along Armstrong Road. It was a dark night in September. I would be about fourteen and had very long hair, and knew that I had to pass the Bobby Shafto, a pub that had a reputation as being the gathering place for every waster in Scotswood. As I neared the place, I spotted twenty or thirty people hanging around outside. Their ages ranged from 12 to 25. Some were carrying wooden staves and one had a huge whiskery German shepherd dog. So rather than invite a confrontation, I decided to sneak up a side street, then continue my trek home along Elswick Road, which was a far safer route. The only problem was that it was the day of riding boots. Everyone wore either them or Doc Martens. To make the boots a bit more tough, we'd cover the soles with segs. Trying to sneak anywhere with sixty-odd segs in your boots isn't a wise proposition. Walking quietly at 11.30 p.m. at night still sounds like the entire German Army marching into Poland. Within minutes I was spotted and the entire gang gave chase as I raced up the hill to try and get away. I reached the top of the street, finding myself where Fergusons Lane meets Whickham View, as one of the bastards set the German shepherd on me. I still tried to run away but it caught me easily. It snarled and bit open my jeans and without thinking I just swung a boot at it. To my surprise, I'd hit it hard on the shoulder, sending it on to the road where it righted itself and turned to attack me again. At that moment a number 33 bus was heading back to Slatyford depot and drove straight over the animal. I can still remember the noise it made as its life was squeezed out of it. The bus driver screeched to a halt, but on seeing the screaming throng of thugs descending on him, he merely accelerated and drove off. Blood ran black in the darkness into the gutter as the dog's insides resembled a painter's palette. I looked at the dog's owner and was close enough to see the tears in his eyes. Hurling rocks and stones, his friends ran to catch me. I knew then that if they had caught me I would have died. The same group had appeared some weeks earlier on a Tyne-Tees Television show that had tried to reveal the skinhead culture. There was nothing cultured about them. They would batter anyone, man or woman, who came into their patch. As the years went on, they continued preying on their own people. They were the hard-core hooligans of their day. It is amazing the gush of energy you get when you're running for your life. I sprinted like Linford Christie until I reached Delaval Road, then I walked awhile to catch my breath. On glancing behind me I could see no sign of them – I didn't know that they had cut along a side-street running parallel to where I was. Just as I reached the corner there were five of them within twenty feet of me. So with no time to build up I was off again, like a frightened rabbit being chased by hyenas. They stayed with me, sometimes gaining, sometimes dropping back all the way to Benwell.

Then I realised that I couldn't go home. If I did, they'd identify the house and the windows would be smashed, and they'd wait until they got me. So instead I raced into the maze that was Suttons Dwellings. I knew every landing, every garage, every hidey hole. I dived over the wall down Hugh Gardens back lane. There I hid lying flat on top of a garage until they were out of sight and earshot. Then I crawled over the wall and sneaked into the house. As my front door closed, I heard feet running, swear words being cursed and threats of what they would do to me. The upper part of the Robson front door was glass, so I couldn't put the light on. It would signal my presence and lead to trouble. My dad was on night shift and I couldn't put my mam at risk. I sat on the floor panting, almost sick from exertion, my heart racing, sure that the yobs would hear it playing the bongos in my chest. At that moment, my mam shouted down: 'Is that you, Alan?'

I dared not answer.

She called again, 'Is that you, Alan?', as I walked on my knees along the passage and up the stairs to let her know I was in safe. Glancing nervously out of her upstairs window, I could clearly see them standing at the top of Hugh Gardens. That was another night when I was too frightened to sleep.

7 The Melting Pot

I FEEL VERY NEANDERTHAL remembering the countless confrontations with other gangs, where we'd find ourselves rolling around in the dirty back lanes, trying to strike a telling blow. Clothes were dirtied, knuckles skinned, bodies bruised, all to achieve absolutely nothing. Yet, if you were victorious, you walked away feeling as if you were King Arthur having defeated the Black Knight. In fact, all that had happened was you'd spoiled their day, as they had ruined yours on dozens of other occasions.

In the early months of 1969, as a gormless 14-year-old, I was invited to go on 'a rumble' with some lads from school. I didn't know these kids very well, but they knew that I'd been involved in fights before and that I'd get stuck in. I was used to gangs protecting their turf, so presumed that this was a foray against another team who had attacked them. In those days we always gave very colourful excuses for our brutalities, so I put this one down to 'honour'. They had told me that a group of Asian lads had been causing trouble, and one of them had punched one of the girls from Clara Street. So what could any lad do? We had no option but to seek out these rapscallions and wreak our childish vengeance. On reaching an area of Newcastle known as the Big Lamp we piled off the bus, all nine of us, and walked back towards where these lads were known to live. We peered around the corner and saw around eight Asian girls carrying on with skipping ropes, balls and such, and there leaning on a wall was a young lad reading a comic.

'That's him,' said one of the gang. The lad was almost 200 yards away.

I chipped in, 'How can you tell from this far away?'

As they began slowly walking down the road, I realised that they didn't care if they'd got the right lad. They started swearing about the black this, and the black that, and I realised that they just wanted to thump somebody of a different colour. As we neared the girls I recognised one of them – her father ran a paper shop close to Whickham View. I shouted a friendly 'Hello' to her, as the rest of the mob looked at me disparagingly.

'Don't talk to the bastards,' spat the unelected leader of this surly mob, a spotty monster with a mop of curly hair called 'Cocker' (his surname was Coxon). All the while I was getting a bad feeling about this, yet before I could rationalise what was going on four of the gang had grabbed the young Asian lad, dragging him away into a side alley. Nadia shouted, 'Alan that's my brother, let him go!'

I really didn't know what to do. My parents had never ever given any truck to racism. Despite the usual playground mickey-taking, I couldn't comprehend what it was. It may have been naive, but if someone was black, brown or yellow that was irrelevant to me. What mattered was if they were decent people. Yet here I was inadvertently 'Paki-bashing'.

When I got around the corner about six of the kids were aiming punches at the little fellow. I stepped in front of the others saying 'Look, let me have a word with him!' The gang backed off him. 'All right son, why did you hit a girl called Ellen yesterday afternoon?'

The youngster looked totally puzzled. 'I didn't hit anybody yesterday. I was down the coast with my dad.'

Out of the mob another fist slapped across his brow. They weren't going to listen to reason or to me. Once again the young lad screamed in terror as the beating continued. Behind me Nadia was running to him, and as she reached the tangle of bodies Cocker swung out a backhander and slapped her to the ground. The one rule about fighting was that you *never* hit a lady, so I instinctively pulled Cocker back, punching him hard on the side of the chin. Within seconds he had me wedged up against the wall and had butted me in the face.

I lay on the ground dazed. I couldn't even squeeze myself into a ball to protect myself. I was so giddy I was hardly aware of the feet that kicked at my head, stamped on my back and hoofed hard into my stomach. Finally it was over, and I was lying face down in a scruffy wet gutter, inches from putrid dog dirt, with blood streaming down the side of my face. I looked across at the Asian lad who was crying. His black and white striped shirt was torn away at the shoulder but he looked OK. He was being cuddled by Nadia who had a swollen cheek. She was talking to him and trying to lift him to his feet.

At this point, three Asian men ran around the corner, saw me and pulled me from the ground. This hadn't been a good day, now Cocker's gang would be another mob to watch out for. Still, at least I didn't have any broken bones. As I was helped to stand there wasn't a part of my body that wasn't singing in pain. I was just on the verge of thanking them when a fist rammed itself into my left eye. I rocked backwards cracking my head off the red brick wall. The lights went out.

I awoke in the back yard of a terraced house. A foul smell had roused me, emanating from a tiny tube of smelling salts. I had a lump the size of a goose egg on the back of my head and fortunately the lump on my eye acted as a reasonable counterbalance. An Indian lady was rubbing something greasy on to my eye. To this day I don't know what it was but it felt good, warm and soothing. She was talking to me, but not in any language I recognised, so I just tried to smile. The inside of my mouth was full of gouges where my lips had been kicked against my teeth, and every movement made the wounds open, squeezing blood into my mouth.

We were at the top of about eight stone steps, and there below me stood the man who had hit me. I got that sinking feeling that he was coming to give me some more, but instead he handed me a can of Pepsi he'd bought at the corner shop. It removed the vile taste of blood from my throat and cut through the difficult silence. He had thought that I was one of the gang who had attacked the Asian lad, but Nadia had explained what had happened.

My legs were cut and my jeans stuck to the wounds as they began to scab, so I thanked the lady and decided to get home. The older Asian man and Nadia put me on to a bus and off I went. When I got home I dived into a bath, once more blaming my injuries on football.

'Eeh, our Alan,' said my mother, as she did every time. 'I don't know why you play that game, you're always getting hurt!'

I thought a lot about that day, trying to work out why they would want to hit someone for no reason. At school I began suffering some racist abuse – 'Wog lover' or 'you White Paki' and once in a school assembly Coxon shouted, 'Robson's a fucking nignog.' My mates paid no attention to it, and I suppose it took some weight off many of the Asians who had previously taken all the stick themselves. These thick-headed kids, all from the bottom class in my year, dished out as much hatred as they could, yet towards the Indian lad who played football for the school team, they were as meek as a kitten. It is the same hypocrisy that spews out bigotry in one breath and in another cheers a black athlete who wins a gold medal for Britain.

My hard time continued when Nadia introduced me to a Pakistani girl called Kathleen from Fergusons Lane, Newcastle. We used to knock around the streets together. I suppose we went out, but never really officially. When we were on the verge of courting properly, her parents pulled the plug. I talked to them about it but their minds were set like concrete. Although they quite liked me as a person, they didn't want their daughter in a mixed-race relationship. To me I could make no sense of it – wasn't this racism too? I was suffering threats and violence at school because I wasn't prejudiced, now I was being turned away from a girl for that very reason too. I wasn't trying to be black, or choosing to stay white, I was just being me. This did make me realise that there are people so poorly educated that they believe they are somehow superior to anybody who isn't the same shade as they are. Anyone who actually does feel that way is absolute proof that the reverse is true. For the rest of my time at school I was often drawn into fisticuffs over my beliefs – there seemed to be no escape from fighting. My mother just couldn't believe the amount of football that I was playing, and yet I was always getting hurt. 'Eeh, our Alan, why don't you take up cricket before you get killed?'

I was beginning to get a real taste at fifteen of wanting to perform. I still loved football but realised that I really wouldn't ever be *that* good, so scoured for something else I could do. I was now part of a little troupe of amateur singers, dancers and actors but we couldn't find anywhere to rehearse, for the school stopped us after one of our number was caught canoodling with a girl from the neighbouring school in the props cupboard. Then one of the lads told us about a group of people called the Torchbearers who had a big hall on Westgate Hill, on the edge of Newcastle City Centre. They had meetings every Sunday at about six, so we all decided to go and see if they'd let us rehearse.

To our absolute horror, we discovered it was a church, a temple in fact for the Salvation Army. Still we persevered and although we had downed a bottle of cider between us, we were still sober enough to give it a go. The message was very straightforward, but one of the ceremonies really shocked me. Towards the end of the 'meeting', the officer up on the stage preaching would give a real fire-and-brimstone speech about how the Devil would take us down to hell if we didn't repent. He shouted how if we were sinners we had to run down to what he called the 'Mercy Seat'. It was merely a bit of carpet on the stage where you had to kneel to be forgiven. I watched as old ladies ran down crying their eyes out, screaming about how they'd upset their daughters, sworn at the postman, forgot to come the week before, etc. Half the congregation were homeless folk, many just coming in for a warm. I watched people destroying themselves, complete wrecks having been made to feel so guilty for the kind of things most folk end up doing every day. Then I noticed that each one was being ministered to by really attractive girls in uniforms. You may just recall how desperate I was for a girlfriend, I may have mentioned that a few million times. Well within a split second, to the absolute disgust of my mates, I was off. Repenting for everything, for starting the Second World War, shooting John F. Kennedy, England getting knocked out of the World Cup, anything I could think of. After all that, the woman who ministered to me was almost 80!

To be honest, they did help us out. They let us rehearse at the City Temple for a while, and without joining the 'Sally' we did go to a good few social nights. They had tons of really good looking girls there, and I knew the chorus of Kumbayah. In my time I saw goodness among them and hypocrisy. I saw men and women who had given up everything for their beliefs, and other high-ranking officers with huge houses and three cars in the family. After the service some of the uniformed lads used to borrow our coats to hide their uniforms so they could sneak into The Black Bull, the pub that used to be opposite the Temple just down from the Pavilion Cinema in those days. We were told all of the things that Salvationists weren't allowed to do, mostly universally ignored when away from the Temple. I knew one lad called John who was an alcoholic and who also popped all kinds of drugs. Some girls were sex mad and one young lad in his twenties was thrown out for getting a married woman pregnant while he was engaged to another Salvationist girl. My view of religion was very strange indeed. I had seen what my sister's convictions had done to my parents, had a Church of England curate touching where he shouldn't and now all this.

By the middle of my fifteenth year I had done a fair bit of stage work, singing and acting, and had joined a local rock band called Highway as lead vocalist – anyone who could afford to buy a microphone instantly became this. We mainly sang old Free and Wishbone Ash songs very badly. The guys didn't really have the push to make it happen.

One night we were all at what is now Newcastle United Supporters Club to watch a pro-band and get a bit of experience. Purely by chance, I'd met a pretty curly-haired girl who'd agreed to accompany us. I grabbed her believing that she was my very first girlfriend. I had only kissed her twice, just pecks too, but I had high hopes for a proper slavvery one later on. Half-way through the night I spotted her going out of the auditorium with my cousin Brian who is about two years older than me and a bit bigger too. The band were doing an instrumental number, 'Albatross', the old Fleetwood Mac tune, when I raced out of the door to find Brian snogging with *my* girlfriend. They were sitting at the top of the steep stairs leading down to the main door. I stood there for a few moments before they even saw me. Brian was about to blurt out some kind of irrelevant explanation, when I swung my boot into his face. A brutish act that I didn't even think about, it was in the heat of anger and bitterness, and sent him spinning down the stairs. The fight was over after one blow. Then two men picked me up and threw me out, giving me a good kicking in the process. My ribs were bruised, my band sacked me, my girlfriend was gone and I'd badly hurt my dad's brother's son.

This was trouble with a capital T. Over the next twenty-four hours I was treated like a leper by everyone, friends and family alike until I finally decided to swallow my pride, visit my cousin and apologise. My dad had almost exploded with rage, as had my Uncle Jack, Brian's dad.

I knocked at their door on St John's Road in Benwell. Brian opened the door. Without a word of a lie, if I hadn't known it was him I would not have recognised him. He resembled John Hurt as 'Elephant Man' John Merrick – his head swollen, black sunken eyes, his lip split, his nose swollen and scrapes across his hands. I did feel bad about doing this to him, and sincerely apologised, expecting him to fire back any number of phrases, each one ending in the word 'off'. To my surprise he said, 'I don't blame you for doing that. I would have, if I'd caught you with my girlfriend!' Our friendship healed faster than his wounds, although things would never really be as they had been.

Back at the City Temple I found myself being eyed up by a girl called Julie who lived in Scotswood. It was inevitable that I would ask her out, as no girl had given me the time of day, let alone a come-hither glance. I found out what school she went to and before long I was walking her home. My mates took the mickey out of her because her family didn't have a lot. Because of this she always wore the same brown coat, and she did have an aroma all her own. Not quite Givenchy, more congealed turnip. Still, I persevered and got my introduction to serious kissing. I had no experience of how girls liked to be kissed, but I had seen my mates kiss their lasses, and I'd watched *Gone with the Wind*. I can remember walking her along to her bus stop, or walking her miles home when we didn't have the fare. Wherever I'd leave her we'd kiss non-stop until the bus arrived, once getting separated by an elderly lady wielding her umbrella yelling, 'There's a time and a place for that kind of thing!' We used to kiss so hard that our lips would actually hurt – me believing that you had to press really hard. I was useless, but did try. It was with Julie that I touched my first female body parts. The strange thing was that I never ever really fancied her, but at least I had a girlfriend, even if I was getting skitted about who it was. You must remember that the conversation in an all-boys school was mainly about girls or football. Lads had a number of degrees of success:

1 Hoying the lips on (kissing)
2 Tonsils (kissing with your tongue)
3 Getting your top (touching her breasts)
4 Getting your bottom (touching her down below)
5 The lot (sex).

Not very gallant I admit, but every lad knew the code. I never *ever* spoke about what I did or didn't do in the company of ladies, no gentleman would. I was raised on Errol Flynn's Robin Hood as a role model. Even at that age I valued the privacy of such things, and have difficulty even writing about them all these years on. For that reason I won't give the ladies' surnames out of respect.

During a kiss and cuddle I found myself reaching for and successfully touching Julie . . . down there. I was nearly sick! I don't know what I expected, but what I felt certainly wasn't that. Her breasts had felt small and smooth, sleek and streamlined. I still didn't fancy her, but mother nature had done a good job. Down there was damp and sticky, and I reacted like someone who had inadvertently put his hand in baby sick. My reaction was undisguised and on registering it she pulled away. She finished with me within the week. Once more my lack of experience with women had left me on my own. My naivety had cost me my first proper female friend.

During the day I was at school, then doing paper rounds, then off with Ray Horsley to work as an electrician's apprentice or singing with local bands. My most successful was an outfit called Ashton Priory, and we worked in a lot of clubs throughout the North-East, none of them aware that I was actually too young to get into any of them. I had long hair and a moustache, and no one ever let on. The tough club audiences are swift to let you know if you're no good, and I wasn't really. So to cover my ineptitude I'd tell jokes and stories in between songs. Eventually my act started with a song, ended with a song and was non-stop patter. It was then I became a stand-up comedian. My act was fairly successful and some clubs advertised me as 'the world's youngest comedian'. I used lots of ideas and routines that I had written years before. After almost two years with roughly the same act it had to change. To take time out to write meant I wasn't working, so I looked around for something to keep me in the public eye. Around this time I met and befriended Rob Green and his girlfriend Caroline. He was a six-foot six-inch vacuum-cleaner repairer and shared my love for loud music. One day, looking through a catalogue my mam had, I saw a twin disco turntable and some flashing lights. The seed of an idea began to grow. I persuaded my mam to let me spend some of the £7 4*s* 11*d* I received a week getting that cheap disco set from her Kays catalogue. On the printed page it looked about three yards long and the flashing lights looked as if they were strong enough to illuminate Newcastle Airport if necessary. On actually getting them home I discovered the twin turntables were only seven inches wide and the lights were as small as a shoe box. I already had a sizeable collection of records but that didn't go any way towards saving me from the disasters that I had just walked headlong into. Before the equipment was even received I'd arranged gigs at some of the clubs that I'd worked as a singer and a comedian, and I'd got myself a local agent too. The first show was upstairs in a Gateshead pub called the Azure Blue. All of my friends were invited, it was totally full and a tremendous night was had by all. The only problem was to celebrate my success I was bought so many drinks that I collapsed in the van on the way home.

It was the second show we did that really taught us how small we really were. We were playing at Hallgarth Hall in Winlaton, which was a huge club, and even with the deck and our two tiny speakers set up we looked pathetic on that huge stage.Our tiny light unit didn't light a yard in front of it, let alone a dance floor that could easily accommodate about 300 people and another 300 still seated. So within hours of the show starting, we nailed lumps of wood to one another, bought two dozen light sockets and bulbs, and stood them around the edge of the stage. These I worked all night using two micro switches under the soles of my feet. To get the sound to match the lights I had to almost tap dance every single song. We didn't have close to the volume such a massive hall required so we stood our speakers next to their microphones and used their powerful amplification to do a decent job. Every single penny from that moment went towards equipment, records, lights, projectors, dry-ice machines and pyrotechnics. I was beginning to learn how to work audiences, grab a crowd and actually entertain properly. Practically every show we did received rave reviews but once again it's the oddities that yield the warmest memories.

There was the time we provided a wedding reception disco for a devoutly religious couple at a temple in Byker. After my second disc – ironically 'It Don't Come Easy' – the riot began. Men and women were rolling all over the gear, knocking down the speaker stacks. The show was over before it began, costing us over £132 and this 'devoutly religious' couple refused to pay us our astronomical fee of £3.

I also remember the Milvain Club, off Newcastle's West Road. Whilst I was answering a call of nature, the record 'Who Loves You' by the Four Seasons stuck, angering the rough crowd so much that they tipped the deck over causing £80 worth of damage. The fee we didn't get there was £4.

At South Bank in Middlesbrough, a monster of a man with a gut the size of the National Debt ordered me to play Led Zeppelin's 'Dazed & Confused' for him, saying he'd wreck all our gear if we refused. Erring on the side of caution, I played it – much to the disgust of the rest of the audience. The crowd all wanted Motown and they all sat down except for him. Half-way through, he promptly puked all over me than fell on the turntables. Once again that was a night we returned home unpaid and well out of pocket. Don't ever tell me that showbiz isn't glamorous.

Yet as well as all the 'bummers' that every performer suffers, there are the others where everything goes right and you're left exhilarated. The adrenalin courses through your veins like molten lava. Maybe the cheers and applause feed that longing that I've got to be wanted, needed and loved. Yet around every corner I would find someone who would take from me, betray me and leave me questioning whether there was anyone that I could trust. Having read Fred Astaire's autobiography I never realised that I would need to 'Pick myself up, dust myself off and start all over again!' as often as I have.

8 Rebel Without a Pause

WITH ALL OF THE confidence of a baby bird on the edge of a nest I kept trying to prove that I could cast off puberty. Subconsciously my parents didn't just rule the household, they ruled me too. Their example of what family life should be shone like a beacon, and although it was totally against my grain, I felt duty bound to follow. I'd work at school during the day and never ever have a single evening free between training and performing.

This was the real beginning of what life would inevitably become. My dad had always worked every hour God sent, to try and look after us as well as he could. What lay ahead for me was a rollercoaster of graft, and when one job ended another began.

Educationally I was thrashing about in the dark. I had no idea what I was going to do. Practical as ever, my father said, every ten minutes for almost five years, 'Get a trade behind you son.' For years as a callow youth he'd had me trailing around the streets as an unpaid navvy while he did building jobs. I'd mixed sand and cement, chipped old cement off bricks to recycle them, set up plumb-lines and humped his tools. To him it was almost art, to me it was callouses on your hands, muck on your fingers and black fingernails that eventually fell off. When all the lads were off to play football, I'd be eyeing them enviously while knee-deep in some trench.

Watching him work taught me many lessons, as he'd build walls around gardens, extensions to houses or the full gambit of building jobs. He'd take time to do it properly, checking and rechecking until it was perfect. All over Benwell, to this very day, there are walls he built, when others have long since decayed, fallen or been vandalised. He did it right! I hated the work for myself, but he could graft, non-stop, for upwards of twenty hours a day at times, only ever stopping when the job was done. To me that was how life was, perhaps the rich could afford to sit idly by, but to keep a roof over our head we had to give 100 per cent. So at fifteen I had five newspaper rounds at Eric Ward's paper shop, including the legendary round, up the block of flats that was known as 'shite alley' by the lads, as the heavy paper bag had to be carried up 50 flights of stairs. At the same time, a couple of nights a week Ray Horsley and I would do electrical jobs throughout the North, and add to that the training and followed by various gigs as a singer/comedian in the clubs. At that time kids from my background seemed to have three options open to them – the dole, the army or the Ministry. The Department of Health and Social Security offices in Newcastle accommodate over 14,000 staff in a single complex and can swallow up hundreds of local would-be clerks. I had so desperately wanted to be a footballer, now I so desperately wanted to be a singer and I certainly could've been were it not for one thing – my voice!

To try and scrape cash together I'd go to 'Go As You Please' nights, a kind of amateur night, where the nightly prizes ranged from £5 (a fortune) to a leg of lamb wrapped up in cellophane. It was at a huge club in Aycliffe that, accidentally on purpose, the entire band Highway just happened to be in the audience for one of these contests. I hated doing them, but we had to find some way to get a gig. We would always wait until the very end, after the audience had laughed at the local drunk singing 'Be Bop A Lula' or the suntanned pensioner belting out '*Y Viva España*' without using proper notes. That night three different people had all tried singing 'Is This The Way To Amarillo' and the crowd were certainly getting restless. So this was when we got plugged in, took off our jackets to reveal snazzy shirts and took them by storm. Sounding good under those circumstances wasn't hard – you smiled a lot, played in tune and belted out some rock'n'roll, ideally Elvis. People even got up and danced. The club had about 1300 people in there, all singing and hurling themselves about. So the concert chairman, who was almost sober, slid our drummer £3 for us to play for another hour. We did, won the competition hands down and packed our gear into the back of a battered estate car, then popped into the office for our prize. What could it be? Surely a club that huge would pay maybe £10 for a full night's free entertainment. So we waited, and all of the omens were good. All the staff were smiling, the audience were all congratulating us and we were overdosing on adrenalin. As a fifteen-year-old, I was trembling at the thought of picking up cash like this. The most money I had ever had in my life was £2. There were six of us in the band and my mathematical abilities hadn't made me tumble to the fact that I'd only be due just over £1, and after the petrol was paid it would be less than that. The red-nosed man in the scruffy jacket opened the safe in the corner of the tatty office, carefully obscuring the combination from our view. Then before he turned around it was slammed shut. He had something in his hand – was it a £5, a £10 or, Heaven preserve us, a £20 note? It was in fact only a key, the key that opened his metal cupboard. Once open, we saw our prize . . . a basket of fruit! Three apples, three oranges, two pears, two bananas, a pineapple and almost a carrier bag full of straw padding. In the car on the way home it was eaten before we reached Durham. The oranges we'd thrown out of the car window at some skinheads who'd taunted us as we were leaving the club.

At this time, I tried to have at least one night out with 'the lads' in search of 'the lasses'. I would go to a hard rock cellar at the back of The Royal Turks on Grey Street in Newcastle. It was called The Chain Locker and had a cave décor that made the music so loud it hurt. It was wonderful and soon became the cult rockers' haunt. A pub called The Man in the Moon (opposite Newcastle's Central Library) was another hot spot for seeking women, but if you just wanted a good drink it was The Lowther. This led to a very nasty run-in with the demon drink. At school everyone was judged on how many they could sink in a night's boozing. It had to be 'lunatic soup' – Newcastle Brown Ale – and we all tried hard to build up the amount we could take. It cost me every penny to afford it, but at my peak (in retrospect my trough) I could drink twelve bottles of Brown in a night. The trip home involved urinating down back streets, being sick and falling unconscious into people's gardens. The number of times that I got on the wrong bus and ended up even further from home I couldn't begin to count. Once, on a bus to Walker (the opposite direction to where I wanted to be), I was sick in the hood of the anorak of the man sitting in front. Because it was the last bus and he was half-cut he never realised. I only hope it wasn't raining when he went outside.

I feel quite ashamed about all this now, not so much because I did so many stupid things, more because of the heartache it caused my mother. Her own father had been an alcoholic and from a very early age she was bombarding me with advice on drink. Basically I wasn't to touch it. At New Year I was allowed a thimble-full of ginger wine if I was lucky. I kept the secret very well for months, until one night I had been told to get home for no later than ten o'clock. It was nearer eleven and I was mortal drunk. On getting to the house I heard the sound of guests – my dad had invited the Joblings around and they were having a few laughs. So I had to get in, get to the loo and get to bed, and that way I'd avoid any serious telling off.

Being drunk I was staggering, but all I had to do was take a deep breath, say 'Hi', nip through to the toilet in as straight a line as I could manage, then do the same thing back. So I opened the living-room door, took a deep breath and set off. 'Hello everybody,' they all replied. I didn't see the long coffee table that they'd placed in the middle of the floor. It was full of salmon and beef-spread sandwiches and bowls of pickled onions. I went straight over the top, pulling everything on to the floor on top of me. My well-rehearsed sober lines disappeared into slurred apologies as I was smacked and carried to my bedroom and punished. I didn't feel a thing!

My drinking had reached a stupid level and I found myself missing training, missing nights working with Ray and being kept in by my dad. I would feel the need to pinch a drink from his booze cupboard, and to my eternal shame I'd take the odd pound out of his pocket to buy cans or a bottle of cider, needing to have that 'kick'. It wasn't even that I liked the taste of any of it. I'd just been conditioned that that was what you did. That was the excuse you used to meet your mates, chat up girls, go to dances.

Because of the brew, although I'd attended dozens of concerts I had so few memories of any of the bands, for by the time they got on stage I was already stoned. I had also dabbled with cannabis, mandrax and speed, all readily available and often handed around like smarties. Bands like Free, Led Zeppelin, Deep Purple, Black Sabbath all came and went and the only common thread at the end of any show was that my ears were popping and I was drunk. Once after seeing Roy Wood's Wizzard, I remember being kicked in the stomach by a bouncer because I was lying on the carpet face down. He ordered me to get up and I couldn't move – my long ginger hair was stuck to a huge wodge of bubblegum. Rather than gently pull me free, the doorman put his hand in his pocket, pulled out a penknife and sliced the hair off my head, picked me up and threw me out on to the street. I was still lying there on the pavement almost an hour later when my mates got out and helped me home.

I was a mess and my dreams and ambitions were drowning in a sea of booze but I couldn't help myself. Some nights I'd wake up sweating feeling the need for a drink, yet even if I sneaked into my dad's cupboard under the stairs and swallowed some down it made things worse rather than better. My favourite drink was always the next one. I couldn't live with it and yet I couldn't live without it. It seemed a total waste of time for me to worry about the future, because had I carried on full tilt as I was doing, I would not have had any future! My mother didn't want to believe that I had any kind of problem, choosing to ignore those nights that I'd be falling around. My dad was never there, always working, so I succeeded in hiding most of the signs. There is nothing more stubborn than a drunk trying to convince you that he isn't.

Those times my dad was in, we would lock horns. It was almost as if I were challenging to be head of the herd. That position actually was totally safe, but the drink made me kid myself. One night when I'd arranged to meet 'the lads' at The Chain Locker, my dad put his foot down. My mam hadn't been well, not since her operations, and my dad quite reasonably told me to stay home and keep an eye on her, as he was off to do a nightshift. There was no way I was going to do that, the lads were waiting for me. Still he insisted, as I ignored his protestations and put my coat on, collecting my cash from a drawer in the old sideboard. My dad raced across the living room, grabbing at my collar with his enormous fist, pushing me off my feet up the wall. He was yelling and swearing at me for being selfish and inconsiderate, I was swearing and grabbing at him, and we both were ready to punch the other – the only time I have ever been that close. We were no more than a hair's breadth from fighting each other, when my mam suddenly fainted in front of the fireplace. We both dropped one another and darted over to see if she was all right. My dad vanished into the kitchen for a facecloth to dampen her brow as I cradled her head in my hands. As soon as he had gone, her eyes opened. 'Look, I'm all right. Just get away now while you can!' she whispered. It had been her ploy to end the conflict. I scuttled away into the night, while she papered over the cracks of our straining family relationships.

9 From Here to Maturity

Most Saturdays would see me on the terraces of St James's Park with Ray Horsley. Through rain or hail or snow we'd be there. At one game I was thrown out after a slight contretemps with a man twice my size. At that time the way men relieved themselves was fairly simple. They would unzip their flies, widdle where they stood, covering their John Thomases with their programmes. The wee ran down the steps to the very front where the little kids stood. Well, it was a freezing cold day and Newcastle were playing Nottingham Forest when I felt something running down the back of my leg. The huge man behind me was wetting all over my trousers, the coldness of the air made my legs icy and steam was rising. At this moment Ray had actually made his way to the primitive toilets they had in the popular end in those days, leaving me on my own. Most of the people around me were disgusted at this Neanderthal, but his mates laughed. So I swung around and punched him hard under his chin. To my horror, his right eye shot out of its socket and smashed on the concrete floor. I had no idea he had a glass eye! Within seconds, his friends were punching and kicking me, as the entire bank of supporters pushed me down to the front. There amidst the battle, a pair of blue arms lifted me out and carted me out of the ground. Ray watched the rest of the game, meeting me afterwards by his light-blue Anglia car parked up along Corporation Street next to the brewery.

I was still fifteen and I'd left school, although I wouldn't be 16 until after the summer holidays. I suddenly found myself with more time on my hands than I had ever had before. Ray wanted to take me on as his full-time apprentice but his gaffer wouldn't let him, so I had to seek work elsewhere. I had signed on but wasn't entitled to any money until after the holidays, so I improvised. Every day I'd find the local bin men and offer to do all of their work for that day for £3. The half-dozen lads would team up, give me the money and they could nip to the pub, home with the wife or off to the pictures. By the end of the holidays I had shoulders like a shot putter and I had made enough money for some cracking nights out.

My dad had told me that he had contacts on building sites and could try and get me in where he worked at the Northern Gas Board. I loved him, I respected him and was very proud of everything he stood for, yet at that time I'm not really sure that we liked each other very much. So off I went on my own in search of work.

After a few months on the dole I joined Terry Brewis Electricals as an apprentice electrician. Right from the very first day I realised that I wasn't going to fit in. I was rough and ready from Benwell, his other lads were all 'Yes sir, no sir, three bags full sir'. Still, I grafted harder than anybody, although I wasn't exactly cut out to be an electrician. I had so many electric shocks that to this day my nipples glow in the dark. Everyone thought I was a heavy smoker because the tips of my fingers were all brown and burned.

Once, one of the lads switched the electric on just as I was wiring a junction box and it had me trapped welded to the wire. He kept me like that for what seemed to be hours – it was his idea of a joke. I shook non-stop for days.

Still, I kept my nose clean, I didn't cause any trouble and just tried to learn as much as I could. Months later, I was on a site with the big chief Terry Brewis, and doing all the dirty jobs, as I was the youngest one there. Brewis was an arrogant man and it became apparent that he had taken an avid dislike to me. We were doing the electrics on a cul-de-sac of eight remodernised houses in Heaton, Newcastle. I had been told to wade in human waste to attach cables to a main that ran next to the smashed sewage pipes, I'd had to balance on roofs covered with ice and I'd been made to clean up after everyone else. The other apprentices didn't have to do any of this, so I knew that he was trying to force me out. He could never complain about my work, since I started before anyone else and always worked longer. I ate my bait while I was working and didn't take tea breaks. This annoyed the hell out of everyone, as it made them look bad. At the time I didn't realise this. I was merely trying to show that I was worth keeping on, yet the reverse was more likely. Every twenty minutes, as soon as I was doing some intricate piece of wiring, I'd be ordered to 'get the bacon sandwiches' or 'pop down to the bakery for a hot pie' or 'nip to the off-licence for some cans'. Anything but do the job I was being very badly paid for. Once, while I was busy upstairs, someone urinated into my tupperware bait box, soaking into my sandwiches.

Another day, I was sent all the way to South Shields to collect a long weight that they needed the following day. I presumed that they needed something heavy that was a certain shape to protect some of the more crucial cabling. So on getting to the firm's warehouse I asked the storeman for the long weight and he disappeared down the warehouse. Over an hour later he returned with five of his mates.

He said, 'What do you want again?'

I replied, 'A long weight.' They all collapsed laughing. 'Don't you think you've had a long enough wait by now?' the warehouseman chuckled. So off I went feeling totally stupid all the way back to the site.

I was the butt of everyone's jokes but I made sure they wouldn't rattle me. My dad had told many stories of how tough it was to get along on the buildings, so I just stuck to my tasks and put up with the chiding.

It was a hot day in early spring when we moved on to the final house on the site. Already Brewis was making 'finishing noises', saying he might not have enough work for me after the job was done. So the apprenticeship would be ruined. It was almost impossible to pick up an apprenticeship already six months in. After all the bullshit that I had taken from these people, the mocking, the shocks, the humiliation and still I was going to be dumped. The anger was growing daily as the work progressed almost as fast.

One morning, Brewis told me to climb under the floor pulling cables with me, and then to poke them through various holes in the skirting boards where sockets would be attached. Like a Jack Russell terrier, I scuttled down between two floorboards, clutching tightly to the cable, and proceeded to carry out his instructions.

Then, just as I was pushing the final wire through, I heard hammering – to my horror they were nailing me under the floor! It was barely eleven in the morning and I was trapped. I cried out, I begged them to let me out but all I received back was a flurry of insults. 'Fuck off, you little ginger cunt!' They really were fine examples of their species. I had been frightened by spiders ever since one climbed across my mouth when I was a baby. I'd also swallowed a mouth-full of cobwebs in an old attic, so to be in the pitch blackness covered in gossamer was the equivalent of being trapped in my worst nightmare.

In the blackness I could hear things scuttling about and I'd back into a corner away from the sound. It is at times like this that you remember that people have said things like 'Rats can sense your fear'. Down there, the rats could easily have smelled it too. They kept me in that state of terror, ignoring my pleas, until almost five o'clock. Black mud-stained tears trickled down my filthy face, my hands were trembling out of control and my stomach seemed invaded by swarms of butterflies, as I staggered out of the hole. The entire crew were rolling on the floor at the state of me and there in the middle of them was Brewis grinning like the Cheshire Cat.

Despite being very shaky I ran at him, and in my fury I lashed out hitting him hard in the mouth with my fist. I felt my knuckle rip open on the sharpness of his teeth. There was an awful snapping noise and his front tooth was now in half. Two of the men pulled me off and as they held me Brewis, who was over six feet tall and built like Stallone, swung his fist into my face smashing my nose to pieces. I collapsed in a dead faint, only waking in the waiting room of accident and emergency at Newcastle General Hospital. They had left me with an orderly who propped me up and was waiting for the doctor to tend my wounds. I felt very ill indeed and before anyone could see to me I had to be given a total washing down. Once again, that poor hammered nose had to be put back together.

I returned home with two eyes like a panda. My mother was upset by my appearance, but my dad handled it in a very matter of fact way. It reminded me of the way he'd been when I'd been attacked by a dog as a tot. I had no fear of the many big dogs around the streets. You'd slap their snouts if they pestered you and they'd run off. Yet during a back lane kick around a tiny Yorkshire terrier had sunk its teeth in the muscle behind my shin and ripped it away. I'd limped into the house and begged help from my dad who insisted on showing all his friends my open wound before helping me to hospital. The cut was so deep you could actually see the bone and I was in shock, yet still we had to walk the two miles to the hospital. It was almost as if whatever injury I received it wasn't as bad as one he once had, so it wasn't any big deal. Still, this time I expected it, so it came as no real surprise.

The following day was a Saturday and since they never put me down for the weekend overtime I had until Monday to get pulled round for work. I wasn't even sure if I dared return, not in light of what had gone on. But I did have to get my outstanding pay and, if I left, my P45. If I quit I would get no dole, so I decided to face Brewis. By this time he had a temporary cap on his front tooth and was not pleased to see me. It was then he told me that I'd been sacked for walking off the site and that I shouldn't expect a reference. All that work had been wasted and now I was more unemployable than ever.

Life on the dole is a nightmare to anyone, and I took to it badly. I had so many dreams, yet one by one they were being flattened. I applied for job after job, yet each time the reference would shoot me down. One potential employer showed me what Brewis had put: 'Robson is a lazy, belligerent troublemaker who cost me a fortune in wasted hours. He'd regularly take time off, leave for home early and sought any excuse to vanish to the shops.' It was the reverse of the truth but it was universally believed, and once they heard I was from Benwell it seemed to underline their fears.

My old school had a bad reputation that occasionally surfaced in the press and employers had long memories. On the last day of my last term at John Marlay, our headmaster warned us to try and give our school a good reputation, because it would help us find work. He was ignored and on the way home the wasters set one school bus on fire and poured paint out of the windows of another over people and cars. The worst incident made the front page when a brick was thrown through a bus window putting someone into intensive care. I may have been fairly wild, but I wasn't stupid enough to get involved in that kind of thing! Instead, all decent lads paid the penalty for attending the same school. So it was the dole.

The pittance I received barely paid for stamps for the batches of application forms I filled in. I rarely got any replies. Those I did receive were shot down by my only reference to date.

Then after months of wasting my time, I started working as a singer again. The voice was still fairly poor, so I ended up telling jokes in between the songs. Eventually I was starting with a song, ending with a song and doing stand-up comedy. I was reasonably successful, but desperately needed a day job to fund the unrealistic dreams of a career in entertainment. The three Benwell choices of dole, army or DHSS seemed the only ones. I'd tried the dole twice by this time, and it wasn't fun. I didn't fancy the army because I had hair right down my back . So I was left no other option but the Longbenton DHSS.

The careers office sent me to take an entrants' examination to join as a clerical officer, but due to my downing of four bottles of Brown Dutch courage I made a complete mess. To my surprise they offered me a place in the pensions section as a clerical assistant. So after an interview I was guided into what looked like an aircraft hanger full of long desks and hundreds of people. My long ginger hair made me look like John the Baptist after a heavy night, but I was in my only suit – a wide-lapelled lavender number with big flared trousers. I wore a lighter lavender shirt with a dark lavender tie and maroon platform boots. What a fashion victim!

I was introduced to a rather portly lady with make-up so thickly applied to her face it was cracking in places. She was an executive officer in charge of pensions I think, and she treated me with complete disdain. She passed me over to a girl in her middle twenties who seemed very pleasant and said, 'Right Alan, today all I'd like you to do is sit here and check these cards. If there is a tick in this box, stamp the section below. If not, put the cards in this file!'

It was very simple and I sat there doing this for almost an hour. Then I tugged the girl's sleeve and said, 'I've done all of them, now what can I do?'

She gave me a look as if I was stupid. 'Well, that's all you do. Get some more from the next section and keep busy!'

Although I was grateful to have a job, the monotony was intense. 'Surely there's more to this job than that?' I barked.

'No, it needs to be done!' came the young lady's answer.

'Now whoa, just hang on,' said young Robson. 'Let me get this straight. All you do all day, all month, all year is put stamps on boxes?'

She nodded as I stood up, walked to the end of the long desk and placed my stamper into the hands of the crinkle-faced executive and stormed out.

Now what could I tell my mam about that? I waited until after five and returned home. Excitedly I told her how they loved me and how they would be writing to me to tell me when a full-time job arose. She was thrilled and I got some peace. The truth was that I was back on the dole again. In my desperation I wrote to the Civil Service Commission telling them how appalled I had been to be sent to a job where I couldn't use my brain. I really let fly and ended saying, 'I wanted to be part of the Civil Service and feel terribly let down. I have initiative and am prepared to work very hard. It is a shame to waste those qualities in a dead-end job.'

Two months later, out of the blue, I received a letter from the Commission offering me another job with the Ministry of Agriculture, Fisheries and Food. Within days I was installed as the clerk for ADAS, the Agricultural Development and Advisory Service, working as a clerk to two scientific departments, Entomology, which dealt with insect pests, and Plant Pathology (plant diseases).

It was here that I would start restoring my rather infamous reputation. The people were tremendous and I was made welcome right from the very beginning. My love of nature was soon put to good use, as were my artistic abilities, as they used me to work on displays to use in talks. Apart from that, I'd daily be in laboratories or out on field trials of fertilisers and weedkillers.

There were so many wild adventures as clerk and latterly assistant scientific officer, yet the ones best remembered were the disasters.

It was one of those glorious sunny days where nothing could possibly go wrong. It was chilly but bright and three of us were travelling up to Alnwick to check on a crop of oil-seed rape that had suffered pest infestation. On the way a hawk had swooped past the cab of the vehicle snatching up a tiny vole that had made its presence too obvious on that lazy Tuesday afternoon. We were set to clear a patch of the field using a very dangerous chemical weedkiller called paraquat. Because of the risks we all had to wear masks, gloves and white plastic overalls that even covered our heads. So we looked like something out of a fifties science-fiction film rather than the men from the ministry, but we did the job. I wore a tank of the liquid on my back and walked down crop lines spraying to the left and to the right. The other chaps had used up their tanks and had secured them in the boot of the Land Rover. Yet there was I with half a tank of the stuff left. They had left me with the keys having walked along the road to the local pub for their dinner. So rather than look as if I'd only done half the job, I carried the tank to a ditch at the edge of the field and just dumped it. The next time I returned to that field, about three weeks later, the big bushy hedge that acted as a fence for the field was completely dead. Due to the underground camber the poison had run the entire length of the field. Being a bit of a George Washington I told the truth to my boss, who gave me a reprimand and an official warning.

It was one of my tasks to open the post for my two departments and one morning a huge brown envelope arrived amongst the regular batch of letters. I love opening parcels so I ripped off the edging and pushed my hand inside. There was a squelch and I knew that what I had in my hand was absolutely disgusting. I could smell excreta and knowing my hand was in it I didn't want to pull it out and confirm my worst suspicions. When I actually did, I found that not only was I up to my elbow in dung, but the gunge was covered in thousands of beetles who promptly crawled off, running across the desk and into the inkwells, into drawers and cupboards. Apparently, a farmer had found thousands of strange beetles in his farmyard so had bundled up some dung crawling with them and sent them in to the ministry to identify. We were still finding bugs almost a year later.

10 The Verge of the Real World

EVERYONE THINKS THAT they're grown up at sixteen. I certainly did, yet I had so many shocks and horrors waiting to tell me what life was really all about.

Fortunately, the rebel seemed to have found the perfect job. I was still desperately trying to be an individual and I could wear whatever clothes I wanted at the Ministry of Agriculture, because they gave you a big white coat to wear over the top. I really loved laboratory work despite having no science qualifications. The bosses of the two departments, a Mr French and a Mr Ford seemed to like me, and I gave them my best.

On a bitterly cold May morning, I remember putting on an old Parka coat, with the rats' fur around the hood, and meeting a particularly airy Land Rover on our way to the Scottish borders. Apparently some farmer had a problem with his strawberry crop and needed the 'Men from the Ministry' to check it out. I sat in the back and cold air seemed to be rushing in from a thousand small gaps in the vehicle's sub-frame. At last we reached a field out in the wilds of north Northumberland. There were no buildings for miles, no toilets, no chip shops and I had no bait. It had taken us almost three hours to pick everyone up and get there, so we set straight to work. There protected by a heavy green net was the strawberry crop. My job was to remove the netting, while the scientific officers dug out collection jars to take a representative sample of the crop. I blundered in, just ripping the thing back, sending rabbits scampering out into the meadow that edged the crop. The sun was beginning to shine and our exertions soon warmed us up.

The team leader was a thick-set man called Derek, who smoked a pipe and always had to be in charge. He was a real salt-of-the-earth bloke. As the removal of the mesh was almost complete, Derek grabbed the last piece of webbing, so he could later say that he had helped. The rest of us knew what he was doing and grinned to ourselves, because we had done all the tricky bits. With a wry smile on his lips he tugged at the last remaining swathe of net, pulling it free. At that very second, something hit him full in the face knocking him backwards on to the damp grass. He was dazed for a second and opened his eyes as we rushed the 30 or 40 yards from the opposite end to see what was happening. When we reached him he was shaking his head and just opening his eyes. There on his chest was a pheasant doing exactly the same. They made eye contact simultaneously and both reacted the same: Derek screamed, the pheasant screamed and they both flew off in different directions. After a few seconds the big man's calm returned and all he had as a memento was the least hint of a black eye and a puddle of drying pheasant droppings on his dungarees.

Our next task was to divide the field into squares, then make sure we had sample strawberries from each part, all neatly labelled and stored in the back of the Land Rover. It was back breaking work, as we had to do the entire job in one single day. At lunch-time the rest of the crew shared their sandwiches, we 'appropriated' some of the farmer's apples that were underripe and flagged down the local milkman who sold us a couple of pints. The day had blossomed into a gloriously sunny afternoon, and as we sat on the grass at the edge of the field exchanging stories, I had a brief glimpse of contentment. All my life I would seek to taste more of it, yet it is so very elusive. Big Derek called us back to the rows of strawberries and after five hours non-stop we had collected enough. All the time we had been picking, we'd been attacked by hundreds of tiny hopping bugs that as soon as you touched the plant they were on would leap up into your face. The ones I didn't breathe in would be swallowed and coughed back up. It was awful for me, but I couldn't imagine how bad it must have been for them. It was nearing five-thirty now, and still nice and light, when the boss said, 'OK, lads, if you want some strawberries to take home you can have as many as you want!' Derek was already crouched filling his small tupperware bait box. I was from Benwell, strawberries were the equivalent of caviare, a food for only the very rich and I grabbed two huge plastic sacks and began collecting as many as I could. This is where I learned the value of working for yourself. In five hours I had worked very hard and had certainly pulled and collected my weight in strawbs. I had less than an hour to collect strawberries for myself and worked like a hurricane, finishing with two huge sackfuls.

After dropping off the containers at the laboratory I was given a lift home with my prize. I had about twenty pounds weight of fruit, so delivered bagfuls to all of our neighbours, all my friends, leaving one of the full sacks with a teacher who worked at a local school for handicapped children. I used to help out most weekends during the day and knew that they would be thrilled with such a treat. My mother filled her old-fashioned clip-lock fridge and searched her larder for some Carnation milk. We ate to bursting point, all three of us sitting back feeling very pleased with ourselves.

The following day I was at the lab bright and early and was given hundreds of glass slides to examine, each one taken from a strawberry that we'd collected the day before. I was mortified to discover they were crawling on the outside with minuscule red spider mites and on the inside tiny transparent sucking worms were feeding on the soft fruit. On average, each strawberry had up to ten worms and six spiders. The previous night I had massacred hundreds of them, feeding these creatures to everybody I knew. When I got home that night I found my mother had made strawberry tarts, a strawberry flan, strawberry mousse, strawberry cakes but I had gone off the idea completely. I have never felt the same way about them since.

In the evenings after work I was connected with three different groups, one a knockabout outfit run by a close pal Colin Smiles, another that used to cruise the go-as-you-please competitions and Ashton Priory. It was with the latter that I made my first breakthrough, writing my own material but having to sing all the old favourites to placate the turbulent audiences in the tricky northern clubs. I remember times when we'd be singing and the entire audience would be throwing tables at each other. I recall being in a big club in Newton Aycliffe and while singing the Leo Sayers hit 'The Show Must Go On' five thugs with baseball bats began wrecking the place. They walked to the edge of the stage and hammered down on the front spotlights shattering them and plunging us into darkness. We backed away as they got on to the stage and started pounding the club's mixing desk just as I was singing 'I wish somebody would tear down the walls of this theatre and let me out!' I meant it.

There were so many adventures on the road, vans filled with ageing equipment, cars full of friends, wives and girlfriends and great shows. Granted, I couldn't sing to save my life, but I could carry a tune and was learning how to cope with audiences of all kinds.

Whilst at Agriculture I was named as the youngest ever trade union representative of the CPSA and was asked to go to a conference in Margate. That was a real eye-opener in so very many ways. I had heard that conferences were places where everybody leaps into bed with everyone else, and such was the case. I, sadly, was roomed with another delegate with an appalling personal odour problem and haemorrhoids. One night after the conference, I inadvertently found him lying face down on my bed placing ointment up his rear end. The entire experience lost its shine from that point on. I was mentioned in the national press for the very first time. *The Daily Telegraph* described me as 'an angry young man' for speaking out against monies being wasted on senior civil servants' perks!

The conference took place at the same time as the Sunderland *v* Leeds United cup final in 1973. I was staying in a bed and breakfast hotel with about forty delegates from Yorkshire all supporting Leeds. I loved all the north-eastern sides and cheered for Sunderland despite the snidish wisecracks from the Leeds brigade. When Ian Porterfield scored the winning goal you could have heard a pin drop, had I not been screaming my head off. To their credit, they took their team's defeat as well as they could, inviting me to go out with them. We all ended up in a small disco on Margate's sea-front and to our surprise it wasn't too full.

There, like any other self-respecting union delegate, I endeavoured to find a girlfriend. On the dance floor there were six girls all wearing tiny mini-skirts, just fooling around to an obscure dance track, when I, trying to be as smooth as I could be, walked on to the dance floor and started chatting one up.

Things seemed to be doing reasonably well, as I bopped along to whatever it was, not looking too out of place. Then the DJ played Stevie Wonder's classic 'Superstition' and suddenly all of the girls began dancing in a routine. They were the club's own dance troupe, and there was I right in the middle looking totally ridiculous.

My night ended as badly as it had begun, for in the early hours of the morning we were wandering back to our digs when we spotted a light from a building belonging, I think, to Butlins. There in the bay window was a pool table and an Asian lad was playing a huge fellow with bright ginger hair. Slightly the worse for beer, we decided to bet on the winner, all six of us staring through the window. I put my money on the young Asian fellow, while the others took the big lad. We cheered and yelled after every shot, making an awful noise at almost 2 a.m. Although I was right in the middle of the throng, something hit me from above. It was wet and surprisingly warm. I looked up and there at the window were about twenty men all looking down laughing. One of them was holding a bucket. Not a drop had missed me, it was in my hair, on my very best suit, yes that one, and soaked me through to my skin. It was only when I got back to the hotel that I realised that it was urine! They really had done the dirty on me, but it could have been worse I suppose.

I was then transferred to a new job in the Department of Employment as a clerk at Bede House on Sunderland Road in Gateshead. Once again on my first day I wore my only suit, the dark purple number, the flares, the lavender shirt and the huge shiny kipper tie. After the first day I tried wearing all kinds of outfits, and most got me sent home. Once, I went in wearing an *Oz* magazine T-shirt which bore the legend 'Micky did it!' and showed Minnie Mouse heavily pregnant, a pair of cord flares with hundreds of gold studs down each leg and a huge cross hanging around my neck. Before I took my coat off I was in the manager's office.

Despite my unorthodox appearance, I did manage to build a reputation as someone able to find people work. If there were no jobs available in a certain trade and the person in front of me was genuine, I would ring around on speck, trying to get an interview and often did.

Sometimes the wool would be pulled over your eyes by the conmen, particularly one fellow who was a radial arm driller. He was the only one we had signing on at Gateshead, and there were always vacancies on the Team Valley Trading Estate nearby. He would always come in immaculately dressed in a pin-stripe suit, clean as a whistle, hair slammed smartly into place with Brylcreem. How come he wasn't working? One day I arranged an interview at C. A. Parsons, a company I had a good working relationship with, and firmly expected a result. Two hours later, their personnel department asked why I had sent such a tramp down for an interview. What this fellow had done was go home, put on some dirty and smelly clothes, cover his hands and face with dirt and do everything he could to discourage the personnel officer from taking him on. This made me do my utmost to sort him. On explaining the full story to a big firm in Birtley, they agreed to play ball. An interview was arranged and he played his usual dirty trick, but was offered the job anyway. He nearly died! I heard three weeks later that he had signed on the sick and never returned. Still, at least I shook him up a bit.

Another of my disasters was with a driver, a really nice lad who always asked for me by name, or said, 'Can I see the lad with the big cross!' He used to boast to me that he could drive any vehicle in the world, and his licence testified to it. He had a heavy goods class one licence, a current P.S.V. licence for all buses, a badge to prove he could drive fork-lift trucks and in the army he'd driven tanks. His wife was pregnant and he needed a job, so one quiet Friday I worked non-stop ringing any company that employed drivers. Finally, a plant-hire company on the Scotswood Road said it had a vacancy for a steam-roller driver. I rang the man at once: 'Can you drive a steam roller?'

'I can drive anything,' came his confident reply. 'I don't know how to thank you. I'll go and get that job!'

I knew he would, and he did and after his interview on the Monday morning both he and his heavily pregnant wife came in to say a personal thank you. I wished them well, and off they went. That was the sadness of that job, if you do your job right, you never see the good ones any more. However, the very next day I was interviewing new claimants when I saw the driver in reception and called him into my cubicle for a chat. It seems that throughout his illustrious driving career he had never driven a steam-roller before. Within twenty minutes of starting with them, he'd thrown the huge thing into reverse by accident and flattened the company's portacabin office almost killing the boss and three of his pals. Two years after that, during a bus strike, I was walking to work along Scotswood Road in the snow, when a huge container truck stopped. It was the driver, who gave me a lift to work. We laughed about his adventures all the way. It is strange, but people do remember a kindness you have done them, and this gives you the incentive to do more.

My greatest success was when the office rearranged its files in order of keenness, selecting the men and women who we were more able to help. Because I had a reputation for finding jobs where there were no vacancies, I was given the 'Mission Impossible' files.

It was extremely frustrating when you found a really nice bloke, keen, desperate for work, but with unrealistic ambitions, because that normally equalled a long term of unemployment. So in he walks, five feet two, seventeen stone, tiny black moustache and no dress sense. He had hated his last job and had no idea what he wanted to do. Any suggestion of training was ignored, he really wanted work, he had lots of financial commitments and would go under unless some cash was forthcoming. I didn't have a clue where to start. He wasn't up to clerical work, he couldn't do heavy lifting, he couldn't work outside, he didn't like small spaces either, and at every turn I was frustrated. The rest of the team laughed at me for even trying, all writing him off as a waste of time. So after spending days trying everything I invited him in for a chat. I wasn't sure he'd bother, since all previous conversations had taken us nowhere, yet it proved how keen he was when he arrived at the office first thing the following morning. I said, 'Look, I've no idea what you're going to be doing but you're getting an interview today or neither of us is going home.' I decided to go totally off at a tangent: 'What kind of things do you enjoy doing in your social life?'

He thought for a while, mentioning sport of one sort or another. No matter what sport it was, he wasn't built for any, but I pressed on. 'Anything else that you have a passion for?'

'Oh, yes,' he said. 'I love antiques. I spend hours in galleries, old houses and museums and I study them at home. I can't afford to buy any but I do love them and know quite a bit about them!'

So right there I rang every antique shop in the North-East. There was not one single vacancy. I rang every mansion, stately home and National Trust property to see if guides were ever used but still coming up empty. Finally, I rang every art gallery and museum until Newcastle's Laing Gallery said it needed a caretaker/helper. It didn't pay much but the Gallery would be willing to see him. He got the job. I saw him twelve months later in the queue at W. H. Smiths book department. He was thrilled because he'd just been given responsibility for displaying a new collection. It may not appear to be anything major, yet it changed his life and was one of my proudest moments of my time in Gateshead.

There were others I wasn't too proud of. One was on a red-hot day in summer. I was trapped in the office on a very slow Friday afternoon, when in walked a beautiful blonde. All of the young lads reacted like dogs on heat, fighting to get to the front of the queue. I won and guided her into cubicle one, my place of work. As she walked around and took her seat I saw she was very attractive, wearing a small red halter-neck top displaying her chest and tiny waist, with tight red loon pants. As she sat down her zipper broke and a huge opening appeared. She swore as she covered the gap with her small beaded handbag. 'Have you got any safety pins?' she asked, her pale cheeks reddening with embarrassment. Being first-aid officer I knew where they were and brought four back. At first, I diverted my eyes while she tried to put them into place, but finally she said, 'Can you give me a hand?' Suddenly, I was all fingers and thumbs and found myself lying over my desk tugging at this girl's fly, trying to keep the material together while she pinned it. That was the precise moment my boss walked by. He never ever believed that story but it was absolutely true, sadly.

Within a fortnight of that incident I was in trouble again, in an episode that very nearly made the local papers. When you work with the public you often have to deal with people you don't like or conversely don't like you. Having very long hair, I was instantly at odds with one of Gateshead's biggest skinhead thugs, an animal nicknamed Murty. His records showed that he was in and out of borstal, remand centres and prison. He'd assaulted people, spat in our reception and we always knew when he was in because of the torrent of abuse and bad language in the air. Nobody wanted to see him and it usually fell to me to see and get shot of him, for the other clients' sake as much as anything. He hated me, and only answered my questions so he could get out. He'd say things like 'I'm going to fuck you, you hairy git!' as I persevered to process his claim. Sometimes I would make mistakes that delayed his claim for weeks – honestly, sometimes I could really be slapdash!

One day he was waiting for me in the underpass that links Tynegate Precinct with Gateshead High Street and I was kicked to the ground. I had two cracked ribs, a dislocated elbow and a black eye from the battering I took. My arm was in a sling for nearly a month, but as it was my left arm, I still was able to go to work. There I met Murty again and I had to interview him. Everyone had heard about how he had 'sorted the hairy cunt out', boasting how he'd been so big and tough. I remember noticing how he had failed to mention the two bruisers who held my arms while he hit me. Like most of these street buffoons courage wasn't part of his make-up. When I called his name, his friends laughed and giggled, taunting me, gesticulating and humiliating me in front of staff and public alike. So there I was sitting in my chair, leaning back out of reach from this caveman. Once again the tirade of abuse continued. 'I told you I'd chin you, you git?' I didn't reply, concentrating on my job in the hope of getting him out of my sight as quickly as I could. 'You're frightened, aren't you?' he grunted. I was, but I wouldn't admit it. 'You're shaking you yellow bastard. Well, we'll be waiting for you again tonight!'

The mentality of these hyenas is simple. The weaker you are, the more they get at you. Finally he aimed a slap at me, and I avoided it by leaning back in my chair, almost tumbling. It was instinct rather than intent that made me grab at the tufts of hair on his brow and slammed his head down on the desk. His nose was completely flattened and there was blood all over his case notes. The police were called, details taken and I expected to be prosecuted but never was. The local paper rang me, but I refused to comment, and the full story was never printed. I regularly had to be quick on my toes to avoid his mates from that point on. In one case seven of my pals met me from work, giving Murty's mates something to think about. They wouldn't ever get involved in a fair fight.

One of the girls in the office was a lovely girl called Hazel, a single mum and quite bonny. Not quite gorgeous, but as the only available girl she attracted my attentions. We never dated in any shape or form but did go for teabreaks together up to the tenth floor where the canteen was. After a cup of hot coffee and a slice of toast we took the goods lift down to the second floor again. Whilst in the lift we decided to play a trick on one of the nosey women in our office who always timed our comings and goings. We decided to unbutton our clothes and pretend we'd been 'at it' in the lift. When we got to the second floor, I pulled open the wire door and the main door, then stepped out zipping my fly and tucking my shirt in, while Hazel buttoned the top of her blouse and tucked it into her skirt. Out of the corner of my eye I saw the woman looking completely shocked, not noticing that the boss was standing behind her until it was too late. I got another official reprimand for that one too.

At one of the regular Sunday evening socials at the Salvation Army I met Elaine, who would become my first wife. I have to say I first thought her to be a giggly girl, full of daftness and mad as a hatter. She wore short skirts and was always smiling, but my attention had been attracted by two girls called Sue and Pauline. My mate went out with Sue and was badly hurt, but I was determined to get to know Pauline. She was about sixteen and I was two years older, yet she acted as if she was in her middle thirties. Despite being a uniformed member of the Salvation Army, she was anything but married to the church. A small pretty girl, she constantly complained about how one of her breasts was bigger than the other. I offered her the opportunity of an unbiased view but she ignored my offer. We did see each other for a while, once having a major date one Saturday afternoon when my folks were out. She had said that she was untouched by the male sex, and I certainly was a novice too, but I was, for once, totally confident that this would be where I would break my duck. She had even said, 'Buy some Tartan, it really gets me in the mood!' A Tartan-drinking Salvation Army girl in the mood – what a bizarre choice to be my very first sex-siren. Despite my fear I had purchased condoms and two six-packs of Tartan and in she came. She looked like every young boy's dream, I closed the curtains, put some Carole King on the stereo and began plying her with mood-provoking Tartan. All twelve cans were supped, I'd had none and she passed out. I spent every penny of my wages getting a taxi for her, and got banned from her house by her parents, both Army members, for leading their daughter off the right track. Honestly, she was leading me. I really wanted to follow but failed miserably as usual.

Sort of on the rebound, I found myself with Elaine, and we started courting in a very ad-hoc sort of way. At first it was just at the Torchbearer meetings, then it was very occasionally at my home, where my parents took a real shine to her. To be honest, the original teaming was mutually unsatisfactory but we were good friends and hung out with the same crowd. Eventually she tore my ear off because I wasn't being serious enough about the relationship and she called it off. I soon discovered what I had always known, that I hated being alone and felt quite desperate. All of my friends were courting yet there was I alone in Benwell, my folks were on holiday, I was on holiday too, just moping around the house.

For the first week I mainly drank myself silly, in the wild hope of making myself feel better. The truth about alcohol is that it may blur a problem for a while but it always returns bigger and more unfathomable the following day. At that time I felt that no one actually cared, women treated me like a toothless freak, my parents were away without me again, my friend Rob was too wrapped up with his girlfriend, I had been turned down for a promotion at work and we had very few bookings at night.

So I decided to do what I never thought I'd do, take my life. At the time it actually seemed the rational thing to do. After all, no one really gave a damn, I seemed to be achieving nothing with my life apart from being a burden. Perhaps I would be better out of the pain. So I gathered tablets of every kind from the cupboard beneath the stairs and a bottle of whisky and sat down in front of the gas fire to meet my fate. Although I had been frightened many times in my life I recall the calmness of sitting there in silence, watching the red heat of the fire element, feeling it almost burning my legs and face as one by one I downed the tablets, the whisky swilling it down my parched throat. It was almost as if I was watching it in a film. I felt my stomach regurgitate a foul-tasting mixture that I had to force myself to re-swallow.

The 30 or so tablets were half gone when I heard the doorbell ring. I was very dizzy but force of habit saw me wobbling down the passage to open the door. It was Rob who picked me up and took me inside, dragging me to the toilet and forcing his fingers down my throat. I remember spewing for what seemed years, as I watched the pan spattering with frothing tablets and capsules. I coughed and choked, retching even when there was nothing left to come, then fell into a deep sleep for almost two hours. When I woke Rob was still there placing cold wet sponges on my brow and pouring water down my bruised throat.

'Alan, if you really love her, go and tell her. She will come back to you.' His words etched themselves on to my mind. I didn't love her. I liked her a lot, but my world hadn't been shaken by her. I wanted that special love, that Robin Hood and Maid Marion love that Errol Flynn and Olivia de Havilland had created before my eyes on the television screen. Still I chose to be with someone instead of being alone.

11 Back on the Horse and Saddled With It

MY PRIVATE LIFE was in turmoil and I took refuge more and more in my career. I worked as hard as I could – I was determined not to be beaten by my woes. I needed to get on and get ahead so I galvanised myself into action. My first step was to talk to Rob to explore ideas with him and see if we could come up with a plan. One lunchtime, while we drank brown ale together, paddling a boat around the lake at Saltwell Park in Gateshead, we decided to get to grips with building up the mobile disco, and we began marketing ourselves. My agent had started giving me rubbishy gigs at the clubs that no one else wanted to play, and I knew that if no one was going to give me a break into showbiz, I had to do it myself. Deep down I thought that I stood only one chance in a million, yet I couldn't stop myself from taking it. So off we went into show after show. Martin Smith, one of my colleagues from Bede House, Gateshead, agreed to loan me some money to buy a bigger disco set-up. Martin was a scatty young man with a heart of gold. Had that gear not been purchased I have no doubt that we wouldn't have proceeded on to better things. We paid Martin off three months ahead of time and presented him with gifts as a thank you.

While I was dreaming of becoming 'a name', the realities of the club circuit were as far detached from stardom as it is possible to be. Once, we were given a show by Newcastle Council as part of their festival week, to bring communities together. We had been asked to put on a show at Cruddas Park Community Centre, so we got in and set up, as droves of pensioners came in for the afternoon tea-dance. I was getting them dancing to Al Martino,

Frank Sinatra and Glenn Miller when suddenly in marched about forty yobs. They promptly punched the old man on the door and stole his takings. Down from the hall dashed the gentleman who ran a martial arts class at the centre, and he was promptly kicked to the ground and his earring ripped from his lobe. Ever conscious that the show must go on, we kept the music going, despite glasses being hurled at my head. Finally, I shouted to Rob to close the curtains and this he did, as we proceeded to dismantle the gear and get it in the van as quickly as possible. I stood guard behind the curtain, the least movement and I would smack them hard with the heavy microphone stand. The equipment was hurled in the van and we made a narrow escape. As the van drove off, countless glasses and stones peppered the roof and sides.

Two days later, also for the festival, we were due to perform at Elswick Park, where a similar riot occurred. As we drove out at speed, I ran behind the van waving the mike stand at the gang of wasters who had done their utmost to spoil the day for everyone.

At this time, I found myself re-introduced to Elaine by Rob and Caroline, who were trying desperately to team me up. It worked, my parents were very keen on her, and before I knew where I was we were engaged. It is strange because in all honesty I never wanted to be, yet so hard and firm was that amazing example set by my parents, I felt that I had no option but to go along with it. I had a relationship, why should I question it? My mam and dad joyously happy together forever, wasn't that what I had to aspire to? Engagements are very strange things. I knew that Elaine wanted it very much, and I felt rather more like a spectator to all of the arrangements. But the pair of us were very much bystanders while the family machines did what they could to ensure our happiness. It was rather like dropping a bottle off a block of flats, the habit of some of the dumber kids in Benwell. You know it's wrong, you know it could cause misery but you still wait and see what happens.

Elaine and I were really good friends, we learned a lot from each other, but we never should have married. She had always wanted to be an air hostess and her time with me made me feel as if I was preventing her from seeking her dream. Yet still the family machines rumbled on. One lot made enquiries about a house in Westholme Gardens, Condecum Park Estate, just down from Newcastle's West Road. Within months it was bought, and all we had to do was sign the forms. I didn't just have cold feet, I was a block of ice about the whole thing, yet by this time we were so far down the road that I felt I had no option but do the decent thing. Unlike everyone I knew, I was the only man who had only had one single sexual partner in his life. Mind, it hadn't been for the want of trying. So perhaps it was the right thing to do? Deep down, I knew it wasn't, and even felt that Elaine was beginning to have doubts after earlier being most confident. Yet as my fears grew, so did the family commitment. My mother was talking to Elaine abut wedding dresses, talking about patterns, chatting to my sister about using my nieces as bridesmaids and organising lists of guests. I distanced myself from all of this, blaming the gigs or my day job for keeping me too occupied to get involved.

On the male side of my family my dad and his brother, my Uncle Jack, were stripping the newly acquired house, replacing all of the window frames, installing gas fires, gutting the house from top to bottom to give me my very own family home. I still had long hair and wore very bizarre outfits so the neighbours were most suspicious. Everyone had done so much, my mother had sewn every hour God sent for months on outfits, including a very posy black velvet suit for me, while the menfolk had rallied around and practically rebuilt the new house.

The wedding was three weeks away when I moved into Westholme Gardens, and I loved it. I had a room to keep all of my disco equipment and my records. What more could a man want? Then in the evenings Elaine would come around and it didn't seem quite so good an idea any more. I did love the girl, or believed that I did, and she loved me. That just deepened the tragedy of a marriage that shouldn't have been. My dad ordered me to go and paint well into the early hours, sanding down bannisters, grafting at every opportunity to get the house finished for the wedding. The wedding. I had forgotten about it, or certainly had wanted to.

Caroline, Rob's lady was thrilled that Elaine and I were going to get hitched. I felt she had just a glint of hope that Rob would follow suit with her. Rob was a few years older than me and was in no mood to be railroaded in the way I felt I was. A month before the wedding I had said that I didn't want to go through with it. This he interpreted as merely pre-nuptial nerves, and it was casually dismissed.

Still Elaine was a nice, fun lady and her heart was in the right place, so amidst such heated family activity I tried to summon up as much enthusiasm as I could. With little input from me the wedding, like the engagement, was arranged. It was a glorious day, my parents were so proud, even though I wore a white cheesecloth shirt that strained at every buttonhole with that velvet suit and stupidly high platform shoes. Elaine looked a picture of happiness, and I was happy that she was happy, happy that everyone there was happy, but I was more frightened than anything else. The ceremony took place at Newcastle's Civic Centre registry office, a swift and painless experience that led to a local afternoon buffet. The families chatted on well together and yet I was determined to leave early so I could watch the football, England playing Scotland in the final of the Home International tournament. It is awful to admit that during the meal I was trying to position myself for a swift get away. It was a good match and yet even then I was totally unaware of the situation I was in. We tried our best to put up with each other, me working all day, then out working in clubs all night, she working all day and with many family commitments.

Not having enough money to do much else, the honeymoon was to be a Hoseasons holiday on a barge on the River Thames with Rob and Caroline. It wasn't private in the least and it is a sign of the lack of mutual sexual appetite that we both later agreed the highlight of the journey had been when we bought a big birthday cake for Rob and pushed it in his face. The following day while attempting to dock I fell off and almost drowned.

It was a honeymoon that did accurately represent the topsy-turvy marriage we had. It wouldn't be long before we had row after row – in one case I hurled some of her clothes out of the upstairs window, following it with chucking her suitcase down the path. I recall vividly the day that she stormed out for good, finally sickened by my lack of interest and moodiness. My motivation was work, to get on and do well, and I was determined not to find myself back on the dole again. My life had to mean something, yet it didn't. Much as I tried to make a go of the relationship once we got into it, the sad times outweighed the smiles and inevitably someone had to make a move. I always thought it would be me, yet after the parting I found myself alone again and it hit me like a hammer.

In her tearful state Elaine had raced off to my parents, who now lived close by. My dad stormed around demanding to be let in, a weeping Elaine by his side. I refused to open the door, and the more he hammered the more I insisted that he wasn't getting in. I could feel the heat from the swelling blood vessels on his brow, but finally they were gone. I was glad to have the house to myself and yet it was as empty as I was.

I called Rob who wanted nothing to do with me, for both he and Caroline were rightly on Elaine's side. It was my fault right from the very beginning. No moral fortitude, I merely went along and caused a nice young woman a lot of pain. There was a high degree of bitterness particularly between Elaine's mother and me, for we'd never really got on. Knowing her feelings towards me, I had played several tricks on her. Once, during renovations to her old house in Robert Street, Scotswood, she dumped a load of rubble on to a council site. So I borrowed some headed notepaper from a friend who worked in the County Court and sent her a fake summons, telling her she was due in court to face a charge for illegal dumping. She was frightened for days. The best one was the last Christmas Elaine and I were together, when I was the ultimate swine. Elaine's dad loved his home brew, drinking it from a keg in his living room. Elaine didn't drink but her mam liked a glass of wine. So I bought her a bottle of strong laxative wine from the health food shop on Gateshead High Street next to Curleys bar. She was on the toilet until the first week in January and blamed a tummy bug.

Once again Alan was the black sheep. My sister in Germany had written me a terrible letter, my parents weren't speaking to me, my friends were firmly in her camp and so I decided to chicken out again. I remember walking along to her mam's home just up from Delaval Road to beg her forgiveness. I was horrified that she'd cut her hair really short just to spite me. I did plead with her to give me another chance, trying to ease her out of the house because her mother was earwigging every word. 'Why should I come back to that house?' she shouted. I couldn't think of a single reason so replied, 'Because I've just bought a cooked chicken!' It wasn't very convincing and Elaine knew better. Within days we were in the hands of a solicitor.

I returned to the house, brought down the disco equipment, set it up and played Rose Royce singing 'Love Don't Live Here Any

More' over and over again. I'm not sure it ever really had. Elaine was kind enough to say when asked by a journalist that 'We were just too young and didn't really have a clue!' That was the truth of it. She found her dream, got her job as a hostess, not in aeroplanes but on the cross-channel ferries, met Mr Right and now has a happy family living in the south.

I told Elaine that she could take from the house anything she wanted. One evening, I returned from work to find only the rented television left in the living room and only a bed and the disco gear remained upstairs. I will never ever forget that day. She took what was hers – I just hadn't realised that I had so little. I remember crying night after night, tears for the hurt I'd caused certainly, but selfishly it was mostly self-pity.

Whenever you're in trouble misery has a habit of piling down on you. My agent cast me aside because of unwarranted aggravation, I failed to gain promotion at work, the neighbours were having a go at me because the garden looked like a rain forest and the local worky tickets started. The house had an eight-foot wall at the back, but the problem was that on the other side of the wall it was only three-feet high. All the local 'scallies', local kids in search of trouble, would throw stones at the window, look in on me and climb down into the garden. I spent many nights whilst waiting to sell fighting with them and kicking them over my front hedge. It was a sad time that would lead to a catalogue of errors.

12 Moving Into Another World

ISN'T IT STRANGE how so many of us need stability, need a firm foundation to build from? I suffer from this dreadfully. Like most, I fear the unknown yet strive to face it as often as possible just to see what will happen. I recall a particularly unpleasant evening attempting to make love to an early girlfriend. I can remember my feelings vividly. It was so embarrassing and humiliating and caused me even more hang-ups for years to come. She and I were good friends, certainly not really in love, just both inquisitive and curious when I decided to make a play. I was in my downstairs bedroom in my parents' house, sitting on the tiny single bed covering the damp patch. The walls were bedecked from floor to ceiling with pictures and posters of rock stars, movie stars and day-glo art from Newcastles' trendy Kard Bar. We had kissed before, in a harmless way, and earlier that day I'd been talking to the male slag Eddie, who had been winding me up about still being a virgin. So partly out of that embarrassment I decided to go for broke, and ended up achieving nothing.

She was very sweet about it, trying to be understanding but falling some way short of making me feel better. After walking her to the bus stop and waving her goodbye, I turned to the wall at the bottom of Ethel Street and punched it, turning the skin on my knuckles to pulp. I walked home, dejected, alone and a total failure. I had failed to be a man, those seemingly primeval emotions that culminate in an erection were lost within me. Although every morning it was up before me, the lads all joking about what they called 'morning thickness', yet, when it really counted, I couldn't cut the mustard. My inexperience was verging on stupidity, and that night whilst not being able to sleep I convinced myself that she was pregnant. The very next morning I insisted that she go to her doctor for the 'morning after pill'. But how could she be pregnant when nothing had happened? And even then it was common sense to wear a condom, though it was rather like covering a mouse with a continental quilt. To her credit she went through this most undignified of procedures and I felt very guilty about the whole thing. This was one of my very lowest ebbs and because of my ineptitude I stayed away from her, not having the courage to face her.

One day whilst interviewing people for jobs at my office in Gateshead I met a lad who had moved to the North called Allan. A fellow long hair, he didn't know anyone. So I suggested that we hit the town that Friday night and I'd show him around. This happened and we eventually struck up a close friendship. We'd visit all the rock clubs in search of a woman or a DJ who played 'our' kind of stuff. This was the beginning of a tricky phase in my life when I found myself lost in a hippy world of free love.

During the sixties I had been too young to really know what was going on. I certainly didn't think it was a particularly lovable time, for most of it I was being kicked around and having my nose broken. Yet Allan introduced me to the people that he lived with in a commune in Joan Street, Benwell. What a crazy bunch they were, all hippies with long hair, beards and most of them several years older than me. They couldn't quite work me out because I was a hairy doing a 'straight' job, but I would stay there on a fairly regular basis and my eyes were opened wide. The leader of this house-full, at times up to twenty people stayed in two two-bedroom flats, was a man in his thirties called Rick. He was a quietly spoken man who everyone paid attention to. He was the glue that kept the group together. In real terms nobody had anything, yet between student grants, Saturday jobs and bar work the bills were always paid and everyone was reasonably well fed. It was Rick that I turned to after spending many evenings soul searching about my sexual problems, and he helped more than I could ever say. Without ever judging or making me feel stupid he listened and really understood. We sat on the floor in front of a smokey coal fire, the others weren't around and it all just poured out.

'Everybody has to go through that,' he said. 'It happens to every man. You just keep trying and everything will work out. Laugh about it, it is funny that your own body plays tricks on you. Your mind is telling you to be frightened about something that is perfectly natural. Just let it happen!' Their lives were so simple, and I wished with all my heart that my tangled existence could be anywhere near as straightforward.

Within the week, I had worked everything out and my relationship with Elaine had been cemented. She never knew how much these people had helped sort out a difficult situation. Most teen courtships were fairly short lived and such was the case with Elaine. My parents really liked her a lot, still do, but something was telling me to look for something more. The topsy-turvy relationship ultimately ended over nothing in particular, and I was free to stumble towards my destiny again.

Time and time again I would be drawn towards the commune where I would experience things that were totally alien to me. Some of the girls would walk around the house topless, sometimes even naked and to my surprise no one seemed to even notice. I would walk into the bathroom to find a couple in there together, yet they both had a different partner normally. On one occasion one of the girls suggested that I go to bed with her. I politely refused, and regretted it for the next month or so. It was as if I was an explorer lost in another culture, every day discovering something new.

It was in this weird company that I first sampled drugs and their varied effects. First it was marijuana, then Mandrax, speed, LSD and various capsules. None of the crowd was a particularly heavy user, but there was a regular throughflow of substances. Now I didn't even smoke, so smoking a joint was an effort, and I really didn't like it. It didn't calm me down, it just made my chest tight and my head swim. Although when in with the group I would smoke it, I knew that it could give me nothing I wanted. I had enough trouble coping when I had my wits about me. I didn't need anything that would steal them away. There were countless different types of designer drugs of their day, some I used in the same way that people use drink but they were all just trendy at the time and ultimately discarded as a waste of money and time.

Even though I had never given them any real credence they were almost my undoing. One wet Wednesday afternoon I had taken a half-day off work from the Department of Employment and was sitting on the floor in the commune. We'd been drinking, and some were smoking dope. Then there was a knock on the door. Looking down from the upstairs window we saw that it was the police. While I rolled around the floor in a lager-induced haze, added to by the cannabis smoke that filled the room, the others raced to flush their stash down the toilet. By then the door had been kicked open and the police were marching in both the front and back doors.

One by one we were taken out into the street, but the police had underestimated the numbers, having brought only one van and a car, when there were about eighteen of us. Allan decided to run, and as he did hippies ran in every direction. The police gave chase while I sat on the wall still in that purple suit that had lasted me almost three years by this point. I remember calmly walking down Joan Street towards Armstrong Road. No one tried to stop me and I headed home. I realised later that had I been arrested for drugs my job would probably have been forfeit.

In my mid-to-late teens every Friday night would be rock party night at Newcastle's Mayfair ballroom. No matter who the band was we had to be there. Brian Johnson's old band, Geordie, was a huge favourite, along with Nazareth, Ted Nugent, The Sensational Alex Harvey Band, Roy Wood's Wizzard, Free, Motorhead, Girlschool and many others. I had hosted a few shows there and it was always heaving, a great atmosphere to have a laugh. At the time I was going through a melancholy phase. I had stopped singing live, I had stopped all my shows as a comedian and was trying very hard to establish myself as the North's top mobile disc jockey. We weren't getting many gigs, our agent wasn't much good and I was there to drown my sorrows. What just about every lad did was spend the early part of the night trying to find a girlfriend. If you weren't successful by the time the main band came on you'd get drunk. It was almost 12.30 a.m. and through the drunken haze my mate Phil found me sitting on the floor in the corner half asleep. Next to me a couple were making love underneath a great coat, but I was too blitzed to care. Phil had met a girl and she had a friend with her, and he wanted me to occupy the friend while he worked on the latest love of his life. I was totally pie-eyed and after far too many brown ales with whisky chasers I would have found Freddy Kruger pretty. I was dragged to a table where I saw a girl with long blonde hair sitting in the corner. She chatted away telling me her name was Angelique, talking about this party that was happening the following night in Birtley.

That's about all I can remember about that night, but the very next day Phil told me that I was supposed to meet her outside Newcastle's Fire Station on Pilgrim Street at 6.30 p.m. to take her to the party.

At first, I thought he was sending me up, but he swore that I had agreed to stay the night! My heart was thumping like a brass gong. My record with the women that I knew was pathetic, yet it looked as if I'd be spending the night with a total stranger. I had no idea who this girl was, and I would certainly never be able to recognise her.

So once again, like a lot of weak men, I decided I would go to the pub that lunchtime, then see if I felt like a party. After a few bottles I was certainly game and rolled up to the rendezvous. I tried to stand where I could escape if she wasn't good looking. I admit this was not in the slightest bit gallant but I was only about eighteen years old. Then, at barely twenty past six, I was tapped on the shoulder by a girl with long blonde hair. She wore a tiny pair of square glasses and had a heavy black coat fastened high at the neck. She was only about five foot tall and was about a size sixteen. At that time I was only attracted to the skinnier girls and this was a serious shock.

But there was no way out, and before I knew what had hit me we were on a bus in Worswick Bus Station, waiting to go to Birtley for a party with nobody I knew. I kept looking at her, trying to make polite conversation, finding out what bands she liked. She was pleasant but wide, taking up most of the double seat. Although we had never kissed, as soon as we reached the party she was all over me like sweat. Under her coat she wore a tight white dress that showed every bulge. I began to worry that if all of that flesh was allowed to escape she could've filled the room. She would talk to her friends as if I wasn't there, telling the most outrageous lies: 'Oh, we've been seeing each other for some time now!', 'Oh, we were just going to go back to his place, but we just had to check out the party first!' and the blackest of lies to the girl whose party it was, 'Oh, he's great in bed!' I was to the art of love what Marcel Marceau is to radio!

So after trying to mix, I consoled myself by giving the kiss of life to a bottle of Pernod. I really didn't enjoy the taste of alcohol, but it seemed an escape at the time. The small terraced house was ablaze with lights as these other rockers danced, sang and caroused into the early hours, not giving much thought to the ginger character who sat on the sofa all night listening to Uriah Heep's 'Demons and Wizards' album.

Eventually the party began to evaporate, until there were only about ten of us left. Boyfriends took girlfriends to bedrooms for fumbled passions and I said that I'd just crash out on the couch. The hostess, a girl whose name I never knew, insisted that I sleep in her little brother's bedroom, a tiny room barely big enough for a single bed. Her parents had taken her brother on holiday and the house was all hers for a fortnight. I collapsed onto the spongy bed, tearing off my shirt, jeans and boots in roughly that order. I buried myself in the bed, wearing a small pair of undies, oblivious to the coldness of the sheets. I had inner warmth, and a fervent desire to be asleep and then to get myself home first thing in the morning.

It was then that Angelique arrived, quietly closing the door behind her. At first, I thought someone had just looked in, perhaps to see if there was a free bed, but I soon felt an unwanted presence. Opening one eye I scanned the twilight to see the unmistakable bulbous shape that was her. I remember feeling that she was so large had she taken a deep breath she could suck in all the oxygen in the room and I'd suffocate. I was a spindly young man, my ribs there for all to see and I was intimidated by any woman, let alone one who weighed at least double my weight. She sat on the bed and kissed me, the kind of kiss given by someone who knew what it was all about. Not only was I trapped, I was about to be taken advantage of by an experienced mountain of a woman. I was more than well aware that it took my body all of its time to be aroused by someone that I liked let alone by someone I was scared of. I wanted to scream as she began to take off her dress. There was enough material in that to make a sail for a tall ship. She fell on me like a sack of potatoes forcing a kiss into my mouth, and I was wriggling, trying to break free. It was like some sordid Swedish film with a storyline that no one believes, given the assumption that men always want sex. I didn't, I really didn't! Then in my drunkenness I felt that she was forcing my hand into her pants, covered by what must have been a pantie girdle. My hand sunk into what felt like fleshy marshmallow, and gripped by this heinous garment I was totally trapped. My head was swimming, I felt quite sick and I had my hand wedged in the girdle of a nymphomaniac barrage balloon. Her hands were all over me, presumably looking for my private parts which were hiding at the time. At that very second, and proving that there really is a God, a voice shouted from downstairs, 'Angelique, are you still here?'

'Shit, it's my dad,' she spluttered, rising to her feet and carrying me with her, my hand turning purple half-way down her pantie girdle. She threw me aside like an unwanted teddy bear, my hand rejoicing to feel blood coursing through it again. She replaced her dress in seconds – it must have been a well-rehearsed manoeuvre – and disappeared, leaving me to have turbulent dreams, but only after I'd wedged a wardrobe in front of the door.

It was at this time my agent got me fixed up with a couple of really fun gigs, travelling on the ferries from the River Tyne to Denmark and back as a DJ. The North Sea has a most unreliable character, and because of this the twin turntables were hung from the dance-floor ceiling, so the records didn't jump when the ship rolled on the waves. It took a bit of getting used to, but as a professional it was my duty to overcome any problems. I visited Denmark about twenty times in all, yet never got off the ferry.

Most trips were fun and without any major incident, but my second last journey was right out of a *Carry On* film. It was some Danish holiday or other and in the disco area they had placed a huge buffet, with open sandwiches, trays full of huge prawns, cakes and a huge punch bowl as a centrepiece. It was all free and everyone aboard was in party mood. It was the trip out to Denmark and the ship was full of holidaymakers bursting to have a good time. They were bopping away when the Captain sent me a message warning that the sea was rough ahead. Over the microphone I suggested that passengers took their seats, but they thought it was a great joke and insisted that I continue. This I did as best I could, when a second message came down ordering me to stop. The Captain's word was law, so I waited for the record to end before shutting down. The dance floor had maybe fifty folk dancing away when the ferry hit a huge wave. Suddenly, everyone was on the floor and rolling under the buffet table which practically disintegrated under such force covering everyone in food. Then the ship righted itself, sending all the sliding people back in my direction, knocking the legs out from under me and dropping me to the ground. As I tried to get up, I was caught in the chest by the swinging twin turntable cracking a rib. On reaching Denmark many of the people exited the ship looking as if they'd just finished a Keystone Cop custard-pie fight. I performed on the return trip, then was replaced by another jock whilst my rib knitted together again.

At this time I left home and set up in a tatty and rather disgusting flat in St George's Terrace in Jesmond, one of the posher suburbs of Newcastle. It took me every single penny just to keep the place and I ended up with no money for food. My entire week's intake was two loaves of bread and four tins of Campbells condensed soup. I bought that because if you were careful you could eke out seven meals over a week, sometimes adding the odd potato or carrot. It filled you up if you took it with enough bread. The only other meal would be if I visited my mam, who used to stock me up with home-made fancy cakes, corned beef and potato squares plus the odd pastie.

This was my first time really alone, surrounded by the sounds of strangers. I lived in a first-floor flat and had neighbours beneath me, on three sides and above me. I had no furniture apart from a small put-up camp bed and a primus stove that I purloined from my dad's outhouse – fortunately he never missed it. The toilet was old and chipped, it didn't have a seat and was in the corner of the room, next to a sink that didn't match. The bed was in the opposite corner. Four cardboard boxes contained all my personal stuff at that time.

Had my parents known the conditions, I am sure they would have whisked me out of there very quickly indeed. But I needed room to start to understand myself. I was in total confusion, I had no real direction and felt as if my life was in tatters. Work was not progressing well, and others less capable than me were promoted over my head. My love life was in its usual disarray, I was still very conscious of my gap-toothed smile and it was nearing Christmas, the first I would ever spend really alone.

That Christmas was very miserable. I spent most of it with my parents and my flat seemed more uncomfortable than ever each time I returned to it. The flat didn't even have a proper carpet, just a strange-shaped piece in front of the fire. It had obviously been cut to fit a small bathroom and lay sadly on top of the bare floorboards. The place was damp, the people unfriendly and I was cold and miserable. I had been offered the chance to go to Paris to work in a nightclub called Le Chat Noir, just off the rue de Clichy. As I was trying to carve out a career for myself with the Department of Employment I was reluctant to go, however exciting it sounded. So I'd made my mind up not to take the chance, concentrating on persuading my employers that I was promotion material. The reality was that as long as I had long hair there was no way that my career was moving anywhere, irrespective of my abilities.

Back in the flat I was plagued by tiny blacklocks, black beetles that each evening crawled *en masse* out of the cracked old fireplace. I had seen the odd cockroach too, but had put down Borax powder to see them off. It was time to return to work following the New Year break and my loud brass alarm clock rattled into action, echoing throughout the barren flat. I slammed off the bell and stood up.

It was then that I heard a crunch and a loud crack underneath my right foot. I lifted it up but there was nothing on the floor. Yet I could still feel something stuck to my sole. Turning my foot upwards I saw that I had stood on the biggest black cockroach I had ever seen. What made it worse was that its back was broken, but it was still alive, and all of its legs were wriggling in mid-air. I slammed my foot down so hard its shell cut into my flesh, as I struggled to scrape it off. I knew then that I had to take up that chance to work abroad – anything was better than this!

Doubts flooded my brain about the French trip, my friendships had all suffered and yet things kept happening that made me just want to get away. At work they had agreed to let me have up to six months unpaid leave. The contract was only for three months but there was a clause saying that I could have the option of another three months.

Three weeks passed by and I was on the verge of my scary trip heading once more into the unknown, when the Employment Office asked me to play football for them in their annual Sports Day.

This I did and whilst trying a spectacular overhead kick, I suffered a most awful groin strain. One of my testicles grew to football proportions, and on my last day at work I suffered such agony that they insisted that I go straight either to hospital or my doctor. They insisted that a member of staff accompany me, because I could hardly walk. They nominated the new girl, a very pleasant but naive youngster called Gill. We didn't know each other particularly well, which made it all the more embarrassing.

On reaching my doctor's surgery on Ethel Street, in Benwell, we discovered that it was being rebuilt. It was in an ordinary terraced house and they'd ripped out a wall, so all that divided the doctor from his patients was a sheet of hardboard. You could hear every single thing that either doctor or patient said. When my turn came, in I went, with this girl I hardly knew waiting for me among strangers in the makeshift waiting room.

'Oh, Alan,' said Dr Kumar loudly, 'what can I do for you?'

'Not so loud, Doc,' I whispered.

'Why?' he asked. 'Have you a sore throat?'

'No, not my throat,' I whispered, crouching as near as I could without invading his personal space. 'It's my groin. I reckon I've strained it.'

His face beamed with delight, for he was a rare and special man, with a real gift to heal, and he chuckled, 'Drop your trousers.'

I heard giggles from the waiting room. 'Please Doctor, keep it down!' I implored.

He started to giggle and I started to get a little shirty. 'Look, it's sore and you shouldn't laugh at it!'

Once again there were roars of laughter from behind the hardboard screen.

'It's not as big as I thought it would be!' said Dr Kumar.

This time I heard a woman screaming with laughter from next door.

As the doctor felt around the very painful testis, he kept asking, 'Does this hurt?' I inevitably said 'Yes' in varying levels of distress, much to everyone's amusement.

'Yes, it is a groin strain,' affirmed the good doctor.

It seems that inadvertently my testicle was the highlight of the waiting room's day, as more giggles rose to meet our every word.

'So can you give me something for it?' I begged.

'Oh, just leave it alone. Don't play with it,' came his reply. If I hadn't known him better, I would have sworn he was playing to the gallery.

Still trying to whisper, I said, 'I don't want to play with it. It really hurts!'

The doctor had seen me arrive with Gill, a platonic friend of less than three days, and jumped to the wrong conclusion. 'Well, don't let your girlfriend out there play with it either!'

Well, everyone roared, except Gill who suddenly had a face like thunder.

'Just take it easy. Don't do anything too active for a week or so. If it hurts, take an aspirin!'

'That's it?' I barked. 'I've gone through all this just to be told to take an aspirin?'

'That's all you need!' said Dr Kumar, always keen not to prescribe anything unless it was really necessary.

I thanked him, however ruefully, and walked into the waiting room to suffer the indignity of an impromptu round of applause. Gill grabbed my arm and dragged me out into the street. The way she tugged at me made my pain worse, yet I suppose I deserved it. She fired a volley of impolite phrases and stormed off to the bus. Work wasn't going to be too friendly, so France here I come, still walking with a limp for a while though!

13 Then Was the Winter of My Discotheque

THE DAY ARRIVED for me to leave for Paris. I was petrified. To all intents and purposes I was off to stay with friends. This may have been true, but these were friends I had never met! My stomach spun like an overloaded twin tub as I walked to the bus stop, then to the coach station, then bus to London, train to Dover, ferry to Calais and the final leg by train to Paris. I had only been abroad once before to visit my sister in Germany and then by my parent's side. They carried the responsibility, and I had merely followed, as usual, a yard behind.

I didn't have any suitcases, just a huge pack filled with the very few smart shirts and trousers I owned. I also took with me a small pup tent in case the promise of accommodation fell through. All I had been told was that it was a tourist nightclub frequented mainly by English speakers. So I was confident that I'd be able to do my job.

My first shock was the body search at French customs at Calais. Anyone with hair as long as mine should have expected it, yet I was appalled by the entire experience. I was still far from confident about my body, yet here was an eighteen-stone Frenchman with a beard helping to remove all my clothes. The room was sparse, with only a small table and a plastic coat hanger attached to a wall hook, and there was a smell of Domestos. It reminded me of those Second World War films – I half-expected a member of the SS to strut in carrying electrodes to fit to my quivering genitalia. There was a screen and I half-hid behind it, yet the entire wall opposite was a mirror, so no matter where you stood, the customs man could see everything.

Once my clothes were off, I stood there, my hands tightly clasped around my amazing disappearing small parts. He turned my pack inside out, searched my clothes but thank Heavens did not reach for a rubber glove. I had heard stories of them looking in your bottom, apparently some smugglers used their buttocks rather like a wall safe. Fortunately I was spared the further indignity. As he threw me my clothes I saw him open the door, allowing two female officers the chance to stare at me in my nakedness. It was obviously done on purpose and made me feel even more intimidated than ever. But eventually my passport was stamped and I was on my way to Paris.

I had been told to say that I was just on holiday, as the club didn't want the hassle of sorting out work permits, etc. The agent told me this was quite normal, insisting that 'everyone does it'. The naive nugget from Benwell believed them and innocently headed off inadvertently to break the law.

It was almost lunchtime when I finally found the club, lost in a maze of side streets. Its sign, in tacky neon, was switched off and it looked cheap and ugly. Handbills peeled off the outside along with the paint. I had expected something along the lines of the Crazy Horse or the Moulin Rouge, a ritzy nightspot with the sort of clientele that could give me my first real break. If this was my passport to international stardom, it wore a very convincing disguise.

About forty yards down the shaded street strode a man in a crumpled linen suit, a small chap with jet-black hair and a friendly smile: 'Bonjour Alan.' Then came a hearty handshake, as he dragged me along to a crowded café to introduce me to the rest of his staff.

Every Monday all of the club met at the café to take care of business, any punishment and praise would be dished out, all shifts would be assigned and overtime payments agreed. There was no way that I would remember the names, for almost thirty people were there, ranging from cleaners to dancing girls, bouncers to accountants. A few of them did come up to greet me personally, and I was grateful for that. I bolted down my first *bâton* filled with Gruyère and some *café au lait* and tried to steady my nerves.

Siggy was the name of the owner. That tiny man in the linen suit was in fact their Mr Big. Later I would discover that rumours abounded that he had been involved in organised crime, yet I always saw him as a hard working 'hands-on' boss. He took me in his car to a small side street off the rue de Clichy where there were apartments. This was to be my new home. All Paris was the same to me, I didn't know one area from the next. I was given a tourist map and a key to my room, then Siggy left saying that he'd see me for my first night at about 6.30 p.m. I stared as his car sped off round the corner, the exhaust rattling over the cobbled street.

I was on the first floor of a three-storey building. There were eight other doors in the long corridor where I finally located room 111. As I fumbled with the long silver latch key a mop of ginger hair with a woman under it poked out from along the corridor. She shouted something in French, it sounded friendly so I gave her a lip-locked smile, still ever conscious of my gapped teeth.

I slammed the door behind me, sliding down on to the polished wood floor. It was a one-room apartment with a toilet and minute bath behind a curtain in the corner. There wasn't such a thing as a fridge, but there was a cupboard filled with soups, vegetables and fruit. Siggy had even arranged for fresh bread and milk to be waiting on the small coffee table along with a wad of French francs. I brought with me my entire fortune from England, £28 in travellers cheques and about £2 in sterling. I lay down on the cot bed and it was then that I felt what would become normal in my life, abject loneliness.

Rather than waste the day, I decided that I would check out the obvious tourist destinations. The first just had to be the Eiffel Tower and I started walking towards it, following Siggy's map. It looked close enough, yet I had walked miles and it still seemed forever far away. Eventually my courage gave out and I walked back, uphill nearly all the way.

I was at the club at about 6 p.m. and was shown how to operate the set-up, then taken into a huge record library in a small room behind the stage.

Having selected more than enough music for the night ahead, I had a Coca-Cola with the barman, a Belgian student called Adrian who could speak very little English. My French centred mainly around my auntie's pen so we didn't get too far, but as it was his first night too, we gave each other as much support as we could.

To my most pleasant surprise, at night the club looked really hot. It was dark and sweaty, but when the music bit and the light stacks spun it looked very fancy indeed.

I started rather cagily, but soon gathering confidence to get up among the action and hurl myself about. I had always hated DJs who hid behind their turntables at live shows, believing they should get among the people and make them enjoy themselves. This was totally alien to this strange mixture of tourists and avant-garde French students, who treated the club as their property. I had no choice but to do it my way, and by the end of the night they were loving it.

At eleven o'clock I got the shock of my life. Suddenly, from each corner of the club, the walls began to turn and four huge birdcages appeared. I was instructed to start a cassette tape and the show began. The tape featured four national anthems with a disco beat. First came Britain and a girl marched across the stage in front of me wearing a long black coat, a bowler hat and umbrella. When she got to the cage she tore off the coat to reveal herself naked except for a tiny Union Jack G-string. There were similar scenarios for America, Germany and France, then I was told to carry on. No matter what I played these girls danced to it. Very occasionally, they were given a few francs through the bars of their cages by leering men. They did about three different spots in various costumes until I started slowing things down as it neared two in the morning. I was lathered in sweat, I had danced non-stop from 7 p.m. when the first people came in until 2 a.m. and felt quite exhilarated by it all. Once the last drunken tourists, always English, were guided to the door, everyone gathered around me and applauded. I felt thrilled that I had proved myself in a foreign land.

Once the main lights came on I discovered that those very plain girls I had met at the café were in fact the erotic dancers. They were well painted and looked immaculate under the lights. While everyone scurried about to clean the club, I washed myself down and proceeded to file away my records, before heading to the apartment. I arrived there no earlier than 3.45 a.m. and found the entire street looking as if it were rush hour. Cars were pulling up, couples walking to and fro, groups of men laughed on street corners and I was quite non-plussed by the whole situation. It was then that I learned a most uncomfortable truth, that the other apartments in my building were occupied almost totally by prostitutes. It was their busiest time. I was propositioned by a couple as I walked to the stairs, but kept walking until I could lock myself in. All my young life I had been seeking to try out that wondrous experience, failing miserably each time, yet here I was surrounded by it and I was hiding!

Even though I was exhausted, I was surrounded by noises of a most intimate nature, discussions over money, laughing, giggling, grunting, groaning, panting, anger, exhilaration and insincere farewells. The night was their working day, and ended with the clanking and grinding of the antiquated plumbing system as everyone tried to bathe away the sins of the night. It was agony and ecstasy. Girls as young as fifteen to women well into their forties plied their trade and were exceedingly busy. Had I not been totally spent the sheer volume of noise would have made sleep impossible.

The following morning around ten I awoke in a strange bed, just as a cricket scurried across the floor, its tiny feet tapping a path to a nick in the skirting board. To my surprise a small French woman was in my room opening the windows and putting chemicals down the toilet. Her name was Paulette and she never spoke. It was as if I was invisible. I later found out that she cleaned for all of the working girls and discretion was her best protection. I filled the tiny bath and dived in, my legs hanging over the edge, then slid into a clean pair of jeans and set off in search of breakfast.

I didn't have far to go, for there on the street corner opposite was a café bustling with trade. After buying a two-day-old English paper from a barrow, I took my seat for what would soon become my daily cheese sandwich and coffee.

It was at this café that I met a most remarkable woman. As I sipped away at this huge cup of coffee, there was a sudden hush and a woman dripping with fur strode purposefully across the busy road, the cars seeming to fall away on her approach. The sun was glinting through the café window, yet such was her presence that I even shielded my eyes to stare. She walked into the café, people nodding respectfully as she made eye contact with each table in turn. From a distance, she could have been mistaken for a Hollywood star or a famous model. Beneath her long brown fur coat, her thin shapely legs fitted snugly into brown leather boots, and a high-fashion woollen mini-dress completed her outfit. She dripped with jewellery, obviously real, most blatantly expensive. Her piercing blue eyes continued their tour of the tables as she made contact with mine. I nodded as if I knew her, she was certain I did not and she made her way to the table. I nearly gave birth to kittens as she stood before me, hypnotising me and speaking French simultaneously.

'I'm sorry,' I stuttered. 'I can't speak French.'

'Ah, an English baby so far from home,' came a husky voice. The faces at the other tables smiled. The faces belonged almost exclusively to women. Much as I hated being described as a baby, I was transfixed by this incredible woman. At first I thought she was a girl in her twenties, yet close up it was obvious she was almost certainly 50, possibly older. Her name was Eve, and she was the madam in charge of practically every prostitute for miles around. From the outside at least she still had an amazing body. She walked away from my table leaving me shaking, more with fear than attraction. Every day this scene was re-enacted.

All the girls had stories about Eve. How she'd been in a brothel during the Nazi occupation and had killed an officer who had raped one of the girls. According to the stories she escaped death because she had been the consort to one of Marshal Pétain's ministers who had bribed the Germans to get her out of trouble. When the Germans marched into Paris on 14 June 1940, she watched them march down the Champs-Elysées, smiling, though gritting her teeth. She had no choice but to go with this most unsavoury flow. Eve's parents were two of almost 200 French Resistance fighters raked with gunfire in a battle next to the Place de la Concorde three days earlier. Even worked from that day on trying to put a stick in the spokes of the German war machine. Her more recent exploits included having a man thrown out of a second storey window for refusing to pay one of her girls. From my conversations I built up a picture of an incredible woman who had made a career out of a degrading life, yet you could do little other than admire her. Siggy, my boss, said that she was well connected and that no one dared invade her turf.

I was too young to really understand but accepted that she was a formidable lady. Life is so complex. My opinion of prostitutes had been so one-sided, that they were all sad, disease-ridden women who were to be pitied. The truth was far from this. Here was a flock of attractive women who did a job. If they did it well, they earned a lot. They didn't really enjoy their job, but how many people do? Each one strove to earn as much as she could, some for their children's education, others so they could retire. I met many who were in their forties who had done so, thus setting a precedent that the others strove to follow. Many of the local shops were run by women who had earned a stake to settle into another career. The restaurant, florist, newsagent's, bakery and patisserie were all headed by ex-working girls. I felt proud of them. I had expected to be there only a month in that apartment, but no moves were made to find another. Deep down I was glad. There was an amazing amity about everyone, so very protective, and I felt a part of that. Within two months I had already written to the agent accepting a second three-month stay.

The wonders of Paris carried me into another world. I had left behind the grubby back lanes and the fights, and here I was in the romantic capital of the world. Yet all I had witnessed involved the buying and selling of sex. It was as far from romance as you could possibly get. Each day I visited another place, ambling around, mixing with the tourists, very occasionally striking up a conversation with someone from home. Walking down the Champs-Elysées on a spring day, just watching the people gave me such a thrill.

My first two months were amazing; how I loved that city. My second two were good, I still had so much to see, yet by the fourth I was beginning to feel homesick. I was starting to look forward to getting back at the beginning of September.

My luck with the ladies was still as bad as ever. Despite several flirtations at the club, by closing time these girls had left, leaving me to get on with my filing. My only female friendships were with the dancers, all married or in relationships, or the prostitutes back at Clichy. Two girls were particularly good pals of mine, Mae and Annette, both roughly my age and very keen on the same kind of music. They were frequent visitors to the club and I'd always played rock for them.

I tried to channel my friskiness into cultural activities, and spent much of my time gazing at statues and paintings in the museums and galleries. However, even Mona Lisa's enigmatic smile didn't make up for a hug given by someone who really means it. My immature curiosity often made me wonder what the difference between sex with a girlfriend and sex with a professional would be like. A couple of girls did offer, but I didn't want to cheapen what was a good, platonic friendship, so I kept my curiosity locked in my trousers.

It was four in the morning and I was barely asleep when I heard screams from along the corridor. A girl I didn't know was being thrown around. Half of the rooms emptied into the corridor, so I pulled on my jeans, my pale, skinny body looking particularly gawky at the time. Yet along with another man, presumably a customer, I pushed my way into the room and removed the girl. Her mouth was bleeding and her left cheek all the colours of the rainbow. The man responsible was a blustering, overweight Iraqi who not only had refused to pay, but had inflicted a range of savage indignities, including buggery upon the poor girl. I didn't know this at the time, but was later told. The Iraqi and I half-wrestled, half-fought our way down to the street where he punched another girl in the face, knocking her into the busy road. A taxi clipped her arm shattering her elbow, and the driver had to take her off to hospital. A night's earnings would be lost to her, maybe more depending on the arm. The dark-faced man grinned at the trouble he was causing, and sent a stream of incomprehensible curses across at the group of us who swore back in French and Geordie!

The girl was taken to a big house in Montmartre where Eve lived. Later that night Eve went out with two cars filled with her 'friends' to hunt for the man. The following day's evening paper told of the vicious murder of an Iraqi tourist. He was found stabbed in a back alley that morning. I have no doubt that this was direct retribution, a warning to everyone that Eve's girls must be treated with respect. The following days involved police interviews for everyone in the block, as they sought to find the truth.

Because of the daily disturbance, Siggy decided to move me to the other side of the river into more of a family hotel near the Eiffel Tower. My affair with Paris was now almost over and I would be glad to come home. My club shows were no longer a challenge, my friends were miles away and I was lonelier than ever.

Two days before I travelled home, I returned to the rue de Clichy to say my goodbyes and be hugged by the girls. It was like saying goodbye to family, the replacement family I had shared in my brief period of exile. I didn't see Eve that day, but sent my respects in a 'Thank You' card I had bought for her. Her determination, guts and no-holds barred loyalty taught me a lot. She had faced more than I ever would, yet had risen above indignity, war and perhaps even murder. She protected her own.

My final show was treated as a party by everyone. To my amazement half the prostitutes of Clichy were there with their 'Johns' and Siggy gave everyone half-price drinks. I played music that I am sure was more my taste than anyone else's, yet no one gave a damn. The few genuine customers were swept happily along with the throng. Speeches were made and then, as the room fell silent, in walked Eve. She looked like Zsa Zsa Gabor, a white fox fur sweeping along the floor, her steely eyes touring the room, then fixing on mine. It seemed to take forever for her to carve her way across the packed dancefloor, people melting away, almost dissolving as she neared them. She glided up to the side of the stage and clicked her white-gloved fingers. Siggy snatched the cable microphone from my sticky grip and passed it to Eve. She spoke in fast French, finally instructing everyone to give me three cheers. She beckoned for me to bend down towards her and she kissed me on both cheeks. Lipstick as thick as gloss paint etched itself on my face. When I stood up and said 'Bien merci' the crowd all cheered and I cried. I always have been a sentimental so-and-so, and could never understand it when people genuinely gave a damn. Yet here in a club known for villains, prostitutes and voyeurs I had found real friends.

At two, Siggy locked the doors and everyone drank and danced for about another hour, then he gave me a lift home with three of the Clichy girls. I invited them all in and we talked to the early hours, then Siggy, despite having had no sleep for about 36 hours, drove me to the Gard du Nord to catch my train for home. It was such a bittersweet leaving, I so wanted to get back home, yet I wanted to bring so many people back with me. I was coming back to the rather staid world of the Employment service, to pick up the pieces of old friendships and to the real world. It had been a huge culture shock to leave home, but how glorious it felt to be on that train passing Durham Cathedral, then seeing the magnificent Tyne Bridge as the train made its way into Newcastle Central Station.

I half-expected a band to be playing, friends and family waving handkerchiefs, yet there was no one. The only people who I had told where I was were my commune friends. My welcome home was a fish-and-chip dinner at that tatty communal flat in Joan Street. Half of the residents had changed and once more I was surrounded by strangers. From being lonely in a foreign land I was suddenly lonely at home, and had to begin to rebuild my life again.

14 Crumbs of Success

NO MATTER HOW PAINFUL my personal life was, at least I had my work. I used it as a prop to carry me through situations that were nothing short of a living hell. When the world turned against me I knew that I had friends to rely on, friends I hadn't met – the audience. There was no way this was profitable, for every penny was pushed back into paying off hire purchase, to buy the latest hit records or to keep my first vehicle, a tatty and battered Ford Transit van, on the road. From the age of 19 to 25 there were so many adventures and all impossible to pin down to a particular year, so instead I'll just pour out some of the magic and some of the tragic.

To the outsider, the entertainment business is one long party, filled with glamour, fame and applause, but when you're at the bottom looking up it is a far cry from Beverly Hills. Those freezing cold nights when the van wouldn't start, getting lost in a rainstorm on the North Yorkshire Moors, watching people slash the speakers with knives and the relentless chore of carrying all the gear in and out. It was a time when every club had a dodgy fire-escape that hung loose from the wall, yet still you had to climb it carrying bass bins or heavy scaffolding. Often it looked like a round from *It's a Knockout* and led to many accidents and unnecessary expense.

Most of the club chairmen of the time were drunken egocentric idiots who didn't give a damn who was appearing. To them it all seemed about power, to keep the act working or to pull it off. As a singer, I had certainly been paid off. As a comic and a DJ it had never happened. Once you've experienced it, you work harder to make sure it never happens again. After many shows I would have to collect my fee from the club's office, yet this was more often than not a nightmare in itself. By this time the concert chairman was inevitably stotting drunk and usually belligerent. On seeing the length of my hair I'd get all of the remarks: 'Are you a boy or a girl?' or 'Come on pet!' I wanted my fee so I would just swallow hard and try to pretend that this man was as witty as Oscar Wilde. They used regularly to try to rip me off, saying things like 'So you think you earned all this money?' or 'You made us late for the bingo so I'm docking your fee!' It was all bull, as they sought to line their own pockets. On top of the cash many of them would skim from the domino cards, the bingo, the door and not forgetting the free drinks from the bar. There were honest concert chairmen, but they were certainly in the minority in those dark days between 1973 and 1980. Once, a gang of nine drunken club men insisted we bought them a drink after a show. We had only made £16, our hire purchase agreement took £10, and the round was over £7.

So why did we do it? Money wasn't a consideration and it was really hard graft. For Rob it was his passion for music but it was more complicated for me. I didn't realise for years that I did it for love, because if I did my job right those strangers would love me. Not in a physical way, but they clapped and cheered and filled an empty space inside me. Believe me, we had enough disasters too, times when I swore that I wouldn't accept any more work and I didn't until the next gig.

During this time, I was finally transferred from Gateshead Employment Office to Plummer House on Market Street, Newcastle, to join the Employment Information Centre, a specialist section providing whatever information was required for all of the offices in the North-East. I thrived there, gaining the rank of executive officer and guiding the darts team to winning the National Civil Service Trophy. It was at the EIC that I got my very first airing on radio, bringing job news to BBC Radio Newcastle, reading out the Joblink slot on Metro Radio and writing *Where The Jobs Are* for Tyne Tees Television. It was my only claim to fame in those days. It may not have been anything too exciting but I prided myself on doing a decent job.

Many years ago I had written an underground newspaper at the Ministry of Agriculture calling it *QUATERMAFF*, with gossip and

Above, left: My plastic Beatles wig was an essential accessory when playing the mandolin

Above, right: The 'Wor Gang' line up outside headquarters – 203 Hugh Gardens. I'm second from the left

Below, left: At nine years old I caught my first fish – a roach
Below, right: With my Mam on a day trip to High Force when I was eleven

An early shot of the Flashing Blade (*Turners Photography Ltd*)

Under starter's orders for a horse race through the streets of Newcastle

With Gazza and Steve Colman after a charity football match. Gazza was the star, but I scored the best goal

Hundreds of children entered the Lord Mayor's Charity competition to draw an owl. As the country's most famous Night Owl, I flew in to give them a helping hand

The 'Brave and Fearless Leader' takes his life into his own hands again – here I am abseiling down the L D Mountain Centre in Newcastle for charity

I was joined by a strange spirit at the Marsden Grotto during my first ghost hunt in 1987 (*Ian Dobson*)

One of my more dramatic entrances in *The Revenge of the Lambton Worm* at the Newcastle Playhouse

With Dame Hilda Bracket, Derek Hatton and Norman Wisdom – an all-star line-up for a programme in my third series of 'Robson's People'

The cast of *Sherlock Holmes*, another pantomime at the Newcastle Playhouse

Hosting a Bryan Adams concert at Gateshead Stadium in summer 1993
(*Doug Hall, Stewart Barney Press*)

Me with my Mam and Dad

With Rosie and Sarah after my investiture at Buckingham Palace

cartoons, so I decided to do something similar at the Information Centre. They already had a very dour news-sheet called *Construction News*, so I transformed it into a very simple and fun *EIC News* with a simpler format, a few one-liners and more useful features. It became a great success and was my main task until my promotion moved me on to a Crown Agency in charge of press and publicity.

By this time I had been bombarding Metro Radio with countless cassettes in a desperate attempt to get that all-consuming break. The demo tapes were always wrong, for like most 'live' performers I had created a tape designed to get them dancing, yet on radio you have to get them listening!

Eventually, I heard that the presenter who did a one-hour rock slot was off on holiday, so I was determined to push my name forward. I wrote to one of the senior presenters who also acted as producer, John Coulson, who ripped my demo to pieces. He insisted that I go into a studio with a sound engineer and learn to talk. It was a humiliating but necessary experience. We recorded about five or six shows then he told me he was going to unleash me on *Mal Herdman's Spot*, the one-hour segment on Saturday night between 11 p.m. and midnight. I hated calling any show a 'spot', so called it the *Hot'n'Heavy Express*. By the time Mal returned from holiday my two weeks had generated heaps of letters and his days were numbered. Mal wanted to be a journalist rather than a presenter and subsequently served his apprenticeship before becoming one of Metro's top newsmen, then moving on to Tyne Tees Television. To his credit, he never held it against me and is still a good friend, but having taken over someone's show like this made me far too paranoid to take a holiday myself for almost six years. I refused to take any time off, working seven days a week, twelve months a year. I had to consolidate, to build a foundation that would allow me the freedom later on. At this time Metro offered me two weekend shows, the *Hot'n'Heavy Express* that would soon be extended to two, then three, then four hours due to its accelerating success and a lighter rock show for four more hours on Sundays called *Bridges*.

All the while the day job rumbled on, I was 25 years of age and the only live work I would do were the shows that sprang out of the rock shows. Everything suddenly had to be much bigger and better. For almost two years I was caught between two stools, on the one hand I knew that I had a safe and secure career, where at executive level I could build a life for myself without any prospect of redundancy. Yet all the while the rock show made me hungry to do more.

Finally, I wrote to Metro Radio's programme controller, a gentleman called Mic Johnson, who had tried me on a Friday *Night Owls*, a show that consisted purely of callers singing, playing musical instruments and telling the full gambit of dodgy jokes. It had been quite successful so I decided to plead my case. We had a long discussion about my capabilities, and frankly I didn't have many. The rock shows were still doing very well, but I knew that soon I would have to make some hard and firm decisions about the day job. I was due to be given another executive posting which could take me as far afield as Sheffield, so I needed to know Metro's intensions. The reality was Metro didn't really have any, other than the freelance contracts I already had under my belt. I hadn't applied to any other radio station, I wanted to work for Metro, the local BBC had some nice people but was too small and had no pizzazz, and I wanted to stay in the North. I insisted that I could do a good job for Metro if given the chance. Although Mic Johnson's poker face accepted all I said, I went off feeling none too confident. It was going to take another couple of months before I was given my posting, and I felt totally deflated, knowing full well that if I left the North-East my radio days were over. Some incredible things had already happened through the show, including one that brought Newcastle city centre to a standstill. The *Hot'n'Heavy Express* was becoming a cult show, it played radical music and the dialogue was totally outrageous. The jokes were rude at worst, bawdy at best and the audience loved it. Rock stars of all kinds would tune in and actively partake, often doing the show with me whilst I took the mickey out of them all night. In the early years the national rock press voted me top independent rock DJ in five publications within two years. Things were happening, yet it was a fragile success that could so easily end, depending on where I was sent with the bill-paying day job.

To my surprise I then got a letter summoning me to another meeting with Metro's programme controller, and I was swift to attend. Totally out of the blue, Metro offered me the early evening show, then running from 7 p.m. until 10 p.m. I was absolutely delighted and accepted readily, then discovered that the amount they were willing to pay me was £2,450 less per year than I was getting from the Employment Service. Had I taken the promotion I would be on at least £3,000 more on top of that. Could I really take a salary drop of £5,000 on the gamble that I could make it? But I'd already accepted, so however big the gamble, it would give me the incentive to make sure that I made it. I didn't have a choice.

At work everyone seemed glad that I was at least a pace nearer my dream. As the word circulated, phone calls poured in and people visited the section to wish me good luck. An afternoon leaving party was arranged, I bought as much drink as I could and friends weighed in with crisps, nuts and sandwiches. They bought me a stop-watch to time discs and a barometer, presumably so I always knew which way the wind was blowing. I had many great memories with those people, yet once again I was off into the unknown.

On my way home I was dragged into a pub called The Portland for a few drinks when a young lad at the bar suddenly screamed out in pain. His glass had smashed in his hand and with each beat of his heart blood spurted out of his palm. So grabbing some clean tissues from my pocket, I covered the wound and guided him outside to the taxi rank to whisk him up to hospital. On getting there, we were shown into a cubicle. After a few minutes an Asian doctor in a white coat swept back the green curtain and stepped inside. I explained what had happened and he asked for a look. I told him that if the lad moved the tissues the blood would spurt. 'I have to see what is wrong, so move your hand please!' The man did and two heavyweight spurts of blood spattered the doctor's white coat, shirt and tie. We both laughed but the doctor didn't.

The lad needed a couple of stitches so I said my goodbyes and ran back to the West Road to catch a bus back to my own leaving party at the Portland. On getting back just over an hour later everyone had gone.

15 First Outing for a Would-Be Star!

SO JUST EXACTLY HOW do you become a celebrity? I had been broadcasting on air for barely three months. Nobody really knew who I was. Granted my catch phrases at the time had caught on. I was 'the brave and fearless leader' and 'the flashing blade', but hardly a household name! The rock audience that listened to the irreverent *Hot'n'Heavy Express* were completely sold, but my very first invite to 'open something' was from a health club in Northumberland. Nothing to do with rock music. What I didn't know was that they had asked everybody else and they had all refused. I was merely the booby prize. The booby as it happens!

Being just a snotty-nosed kid from the back streets of Benwell, I didn't have the faintest idea what I was supposed to do. Whenever you are least prepared that is always when your services are called for.

Having worked the intimidating northern clubs, I decided to treat it as such, putting together a string of decent jokes and learning them. This was the very first live appearance I had ever made as a representative of the radio station. It had to be right!

My debut was to be on a Saturday at 10.30 a.m. and I didn't know what I should wear. I had taken a drop in salary to join Metro FM and couldn't afford fancy clothes. Then I noticed in the local paper that superstar David Essex was opening a shop in Newcastle city centre. This was exactly what I needed to see. What would he wear? How would he act? What would he do? Not having a car at the time I caught the bus into the city and waited for the star to appear. That Thursday lunchtime the crowds gathered.

About twenty or thirty committed fans and forty or fifty passers-by curious enough to hang around. Then slowly along the street came a big Rover car that slowed outside the shop. A huge square-shouldered chauffeur in a uniform far too small for him stepped out and opened the rear door. There he was, eyes sparkling like fireflies on a dark night. David Essex. The crowds began to clap and cheer as he shook hands with the shop's proprietor.

I was taking a mental note of everything.

He was wearing a white suit, a black shirt open at the neck and he had a red rose in his buttonhole. Amid the crowd who wore mainly blues and blacks, he looked stunning. After a short introduction he took the microphone in his hands, said 'Hello' and everybody cheered.

'You all right?' he asked.

Everybody cheered.

He then took hold of a pair of scissors handed to him by a promotion girl in a white T-shirt and white pleated skirt. She was obviously the girlfriend of the man who provided the PA because she had a face like a bulldog, jowls dripping down her cheeks, cellulite pouring down her legs like fudge on a sundae. She said nothing but tried hard to giggle in all the right places. It must have been embarrassing for her, she didn't have a clue, but I can only hope that the money would be a compensation to her.

Then the star said, 'I now declare the store open!', and in he walked, followed by the hordes of teenies that wanted to grab him.

Not having any money in the bank, I persuaded my mother to make me a suit. White of course, so I could look the part on my launch into the minor celebrity scene. She did a great job. The huge lapels tended to curl up a bit, but I was happy with it. I borrowed a black shirt, decided against a red rose and polished my least scuffed pair of shoes.

Having persuaded one of Metro's technicians to drive me, I set off to do the business. He had taken with him a Uher, a mobile Alan Whicker kit to record anything that I could use on my show. I was very chuffed that he'd offered, because I didn't want to get on the bus in that suit. I felt very poncy indeed. I remember praying that nobody from Benwell would see me like that.

The journey was fairly straightforward. The radio blasted out some thumping chart hit, my stomach gurgling to the beat. No matter how many times you've been to the toilet beforehand, it never seems enough. Then there it was, an entrance shrouded by trees and protected by a huge iron gate. And there a yellow sign, paint flaking off it in the autumn sun, bore the legend 'NATURIST CLUB'. The technician looked at me. I returned his glance. We'd both been set up!

Before we drove in, my mind tried to rationalise that in chilly Northumberland there couldn't be that many nudists. Twenty, thirty, no problem. Then driving in the first gate I saw beyond a small gatehouse a car park that had at least 250 cars in it!

My heart was playing tom-toms in my chest as we closed the door on the battered old Ford Escort and walked up the three steps towards the reception area. There I was in my mam-made suit, looking like a star, but certainly not feeling like one.

What I did feel was the need for the toilet again.

The man behind the reception desk was a man in his middle fifties, wearing a fluffy terry-towelling bathrobe.

'Hello, you must be Alan Robinson!'

'Robson,' I corrected.

He looked at the poster that was cellotaped to the wall, picking up his glasses to check. It read: 'Metro Radio's brave and fearless leader Alan Robson opens our new sports hall Saturday at 10.30 a.m.'

'Robson, Oh aye. So it is,' and he handed me a large metal contraption. It looked very similar to the clothes' frames you often get when you go swimming.

'What's this for?' I asked. My heart already beginning to sink.

'For your clothes, of course,' came the terse reply. 'Nobody gets into our club with clothes on.'

At this, the technician tugged my sleeve. 'I'll wait in the car.' And before I could stop him he was gone.

The station had hired me because I had the gift of the gab, so I decided to try reasoning with the craggy-faced Northumbrian who stood before me.

'I am not a naturist myself, so I'm keeping my clothes on, if that's all right?' I gave him a weak smile. It didn't convince me and it certainly didn't work on him.

'Sorry, but it is the first rule of the club.' His expression gave no lea-way for negotiation.

Once again I attempted a half-hearted grin, adding, 'I'm sure if I can talk to Mr Graham who invited me we could sort this out!'

'No can do,' said the man.

'Please go and get Mr Graham,' I insisted. 'I arranged all this with him. I'm sure he'll be able to get around this!'

Gritting his teeth and giving a heavy sigh, the receptionist said: 'If you've got a shovel you can see him, but he'll not get you in here with your clothes on, son!'

I hate people who call me son. It's tantamount to saying they've slept with my mother!

By this time my nerves were fraying to the very last strand.

'Why can't he help and why do I need a shovel?'

The man chuckled, 'Cos they buried the bugger on Tuesday!'

The chicken that clucks inside of all of us at times showed its feathers. 'Well, I'm sorry it's obviously one big misunderstanding. I can't go in there. Goodbye.' Then I turned to join the other candidate for the white feather club in the car.

'You're not very brave and fearless,' came the man's taunt that stopped me dead in my tracks. He was right. What is the point of the nickname if you didn't live up to it? I snatched the frame and walked into one of the narrow cubicles. It had a curtain on it. I never understood why.

Whilst I was removing that suit, the man stood outside talking to me all the while.

'My name is Billy Swan. I'm the caretaker here as well.'

I had never ever wanted to take my clothes off in public and my innards were gripped by terror. I wasn't really listening to what he was saying, although he had sensed my anxiety.

He started cracking awful jokes to try and relax me.

'There's a bloke at a bus stop with no arms and legs –'

I was already not interested because I'm not keen on sick jokes, but he continued. 'The driver stops his bus and says "How ye getting on?" '

Billy Swan roared at his own joke, while behind the curtain I just shook my head.

He was just getting into his stride as I was getting out of my clothes.

'Man with no arms and legs and a bloke comes up to him and says, "Got the time on ye cock?" '

Off he went again with a loud chesty laugh.

He was just about to start another story when I stepped out from behind the curtain, using the full clothes' frame to cover my nakedness. I felt so vulnerable. It isn't like being in a room with an equally naked woman, it isn't like being equally naked with your team mates in the showers after a football match. It is terrifying!

So once behind the counter we stepped down into the main courtyard, me following Billy the caretaker who to my chagrin had kept on his warm and fluffy dressing gown. The path across the courtyard to what I presumed to be the new sports club was gravel. The well-calloused feet of my host never felt the thousand sharp edges on this surface, but my wimpy tender feet thought they were walking on razor blades. I jerked and danced across it like an epileptic go-go dancer. It was then that I noticed my penis. The cold wind had transformed Sammy the Snake into a tiny mushroom lost in a ginger field of pubic hair. Trying not to be noticed my hand slapped at it, trying desperately to stir some life into him. I began walking so that my leg could rub against him. It was beginning to work. Then it hit me – what if I'd gone too far?

If I get an erection now, my career is over! So I started thinking about awful things, road accidents, ripe tripe and feminists and that soon brought it to a halt.

We didn't enter the sports hall from the main door, instead we walked to the back, entering at the side of the stage. Despite the car park being filled, I had set my mind to there being only a handful of people willing to remove their clothes *en masse*. However, having worked with audiences for years, I could tell by the hubbub that there was a lot more than that. As we both stood quietly at the side of the stage behind the curtain, out of the darkness a huge naked man appeared. My bowels almost exploded in shock and I jumped almost a foot off the ground.

'Hello, Mr Robson, my name is Sam Figgis.' This human barrage balloon shook my hand with a grip as soggy as a wet fish.

'I took over from Mr Graham,' he added. 'Did you hear about him?'

I nodded as he continued. 'It was awful. We were all at his funeral this morning, so let's hope you can cheer us all up.'

I felt sick. I wanted to run away.

I was now being ushered to one side as the curtains opened and Sam Figgis stepped out into the spotlight.

'Hello ladies and gentlemen, boys and girls. First of all, can I thank so many of you for coming. It's been a very sad morning, but I am particularly glad that Mrs Graham and her family are here. After we have the launch of the sports hall, we've provided a buffet and we can all pay tribute to John Graham who was a good man and a very special friend.'

While I was listening to this, I was watching a five-foot-five tennis-ball of a man, with rolls of fat on his stomach hanging so low that they obscured any clear view of his genitalia. I began to wish that my belly was that big, or that I had brought a speech on paper. At that moment a very small speech would've just about covered it.

Not only was I naked in front of strangers, I was also the warm-up man for a funeral party. As the new chairman's speech droned on, my imagination started planting even more seeds of doubt in my mind. What if this was a total set-up? Maybe when I walk out there everybody in the audience will be fully dressed? Then suddenly I heard my name. I'd been introduced and instinct started me walking like a moth into the light.

The Sumo wrestler of a chairman shook my hand and wobbled off, dragging his buttocks behind him.

There I was alone in the spotlight and I started talking. To this day I can't remember what I said. It was probably the well-rehearsed jokes, though I can't remember hearing much laughter. I was standing in front of a table which, had it been eight inches higher, would've hidden my tackle. As it was, it provided almost a picture frame for it.

As my eyes began to adjust to the spotlight, I saw a most amazing sight. At least five or six hundred men, women and children of all ages, all completely naked. Women with large breasts, small breasts, no breasts, breasts that resembled spaniels' ears, breasts that pointed north and elder ones that had begun their migration south. Men's privates that were so big they looked deformed, so little they could've been women. Fat men, thin men, tall men, short men, my mind was suffering an overdose of flesh. My brain was now off my repartee and all I wanted to do was stare! It wasn't sexually appealing, just intimidating in the extreme. I gathered myself and started working the audience. This you do by looking them straight in the eye and making them warm to you. As I tried to do this, I noticed that none of them were actually looking at my eyes! I panicked and looked groinwards, just in case he was playing up. He wasn't. I decided that retreat was the most dignified way out of this gig from hell, so I thanked everyone for giving me my very first guest appearance and declared the new sports hall open. At that moment there was a flicker of lights from a variety of camera flashes. I'd never thought of that. Now these strangers would have pictures of the naked Robson for ever more. As I walked down the stage steps into the crowd I thought, 'Serves the buggers right!'

I stayed there almost an hour, trying to avoid rubbing against anybody. I felt like the outsider I was. Everybody knew everybody. I just smiled a lot and tried to avoid staring. As I was leaving the sports hall, the disco started and on a Saturday lunchtime they were dancing naked to Wild Cherry playing funky white boy music. Several of the throng were black but proved that they were at least as funky as the various shades of white folks who tried to strut their stuff. The first thing you notice about nude dancing is that not everything stops when the music does.

I was guided back across the barbwire-style gravel, around to the outside football pitch where there were about forty or fifty stalls, all raising money to help support the club. I wondered where everybody kept their cash?

They insisted I have a go on some of the attractions, all manned or womanned by naked people. The man on the hoop-la had no sense of humour.

Various sports were taking place – volley ball, five-a-side football, archery and various races. I smiled to myself, imagining the 4 × 100 metres relay, where runners put their hands behind them and grab the baton without looking. I could see myself running in that, all four of my team crossing the line together, the back three all digging their heels in!

Just as I was beginning to loosen up, I said my goodbyes and made my way back to the reception hut, into the cubicle and on went the suit. I got into the car and was glad to get back into the real world. Some may consider that it would be a joyous fantasy to be among that much nudity, but believe me it was scary!

The stories went around the building for a while until replaced by some other gossip. Then one day three weeks later I got a phone call at home saying that a photograph of me had appeared in a naturist magazine. At that I raced around all of the shops in Newcastle City Centre, buying every single copy I could. I didn't want my mam to see it, and Heaven forbid that the mob at the radio station should catch a glimpse of it. That Saturday I arrived to do the technical work for my show at about five in the afternoon and there behind the reception desk, blown up to about five feet tall was a naked Robson. I ripped it down and raced upstairs, being lampooned all the way. In the canteen was another nude poster of me and one of the other jocks had placed a sign that read 'SPOT THE BALL'.

The Flashing Blade really was an appropriate name now.

16 The Rock Party Nights

THE LATE NIGHT shows on a Saturday evening really pulled rock fans from all over the North together, so more live shows had to be hastily arranged. If you do a way-out, totally over the top radio programme, your live shows have to be totally outrageous, and eventually it gets quite tricky to think of something that is over the top without being sick.

One show I will never forget took place at Sunderland Mecca. I started the show to the Art Garfunkel song 'Bright Eyes' from the movie *Watership Down* when I scurried onto a stage with a country setting dressed as a rabbit. The Hot'n'Heavy ladies were scantily clad as provocative bunny girls. All the obvious rabbit innuendo concluded when they ripped my suit off to reveal an enormous carrot covering my cheekier parts. They loved the mucky jokes, though I refused to swear on stage, feeling that it cheapened the performance. Instead I was very much near the knuckle. The second half of my show that night was co-hosted by an inflatable woman who had been punctured. This led to the ugly plastic thing falling to her knees in front of me every couple of minutes, with me screaming, 'Not now, can't you see I'm busy!' At these shows it was my job to get the audience wound up as far as I could, and this Christmas extravaganza really was the business. Three days before on the radio show my guests had been David Bryant and Tico Torres from Bon Jovi who had presented me with an entire set of signed Bon Jovi albums, a T-shirt and silk tour jacket. So I said to the sell-out auditorium, 'This entire stack of Bon Jovi goodies I will give to the first person to streak around this room!' I thought maybe someone would be daft enough to do it. As it was

I have never seen so much flesh in my life. About 40 per cent of the audience tore their clothes off and started running in all directions. I was left with an audience screaming with laughter and I was on the floor. The staff were less than happy though, petrified that the local police were there in undercover because they would have shut the place down.

The East Coast Hell's Angels invited me to Carlisle to entertain at a bike rally. About 1400 bikers from all over the country attended to watch about four local bands. I took over at 11 p.m. on the Friday night to provide the music and the stunts until morning. At about 3.30 a.m. the police arrived answering complaints from houses almost three-quarters of a mile away about the noise. They realised we were just having a good time. After all, we had permission and three officers assigned to the event had had no trouble from anyone, so off they went. The entire area was a mass of bodies dancing away, fuelled by the gallons of cheaply made home brew that was raising money for a hospital in the Borders.

Suddenly there was a loud revving of a car engine and over the field roared a Ford Escort, charging straight through the crowd, clipping some and knocking them to the ground. How no one was seriously hurt I will never know. The car pulled up in front of the stage and the driver in a ski-mask handbrake-turned the car in a circle, then leaned out of his window screaming a torrent of abuse at all the leather-clad bikers. As he did so, one of the beefier Angels hit him and the car spun out of control, crashing into the generator running the show. Sparks fired in all directions as the car slowly came to rest up against the edge of the stage.

Although it happened slowly, its final impact threw me off the back of the platform. The music and lights came to an abrupt halt. The police arrested the car thief and I shouted my apology to the bikers who staggered off to their tents to sleep off their disappointment. Despite the event being totally peaceful, the local press chose to blame the bikers. One paper said: 'To allow these scum into our own backyard to steal cars, disturb residents and have drunken orgies is totally reprehensible!' It certainly wasn't the best review I have ever got, but the truth has a habit of never appearing in the press. Instead you get one journalist's opinion, and that is a very different thing!

The biggest travelling fair in Europe visits Newcastle's Town

Moor every year for 'The Hoppings'. The Hoppings is an old tradition, but it doesn't always run smoothly. When it opened one year, on the first afternoon a number of people were beaten up by skinheads who had decided that they were going to take over the event. That night every person with long hair going to the Hoppings was attacked. I had a dozen or so calls to Metro about this before I took the *Hot'n'Heavy Express* on air. So I warned everyone that this was happening and within ten minutes the security man had rushed up with a message from Kurt, the leader of the East Coast Angels, to say that they would 'police' the event. The following afternoon about 150 bikers drove across Town Moor, chasing out any troublemakers that they saw, staying there until after the fair closed down for the night. There were no more attacks for the rest of that week.

There were many things that rock show managed to achieve, including striking a blow for my friends in their wheelchairs. I received a letter from a young man who said he was a rock fan, but after a nasty accident was in a wheelchair for the rest of his life. He explained how he still loved to go to concerts, but even when he managed to get a ticket he very rarely ever saw the band. It is well known that when the headline band comes on everybody stands up, so if you are unable to stand you miss the show. The practise at the time was to put people from 'wheels of steel' into seats. I contacted all of the halls and they instantly changed their policy, creating special front areas so that in future those in chairs got value for money too. I had been aware of the difficulties of being in a chair after spending one Sunday in one, as a helper at a school for physically disabled children. It was an education. Simple things like going to the toilet, going into shops, picking something up, all had extra difficulties added to them. I wanted to even things up whenever I could.

One of the first shows that I was able to change was when AC/DC did two nights at Newcastle's City Hall. The tickets were all sold and it seemed to be too late to create that extra room for half-a-dozen young lads in wheelchairs. However, I contacted the band's management company who said, 'We'll sort something out.' Rather than leave it and hope, I decided to chance my arm saying, 'Why not meet these people?' The band was asked and within the hour I was checking to see if transport could be arranged to bring eight young lads and lasses to Lumley Castle where AC/DC were staying. It was and these gutsy folk were able to sit face to face with their heroes, Angus Young and Brian Johnson, and just chat. I grabbed some interviews and arranged some local press for the band, keeping out of the limelight myself. It really felt good, it made a difference to these young fans' lives. Most fans who are persistent enough can wait by the stage door, or traipse around the hotels to at least catch a glimpse of their favourite stars, but for these friends it took a bit more careful planning. That night they were in the front row of the gig, treated like royalty and piled high with T-shirts, badges and sweatshirts. It seemed to me that to make things happen, all you needed was the will to try.

At this time I was always looking out for new bands to introduce to the listeners and I was sent an album by an Australian band called Cheetah, two sisters who really sounded tremendous, and I agreed to interview them even though they were complete unknowns. They were sharing the bill with Saxon who I'd also grab a chat with. The sisters were staying at the Holiday Inn and I turned up with my little tape recorder to get whatever material I could for that Saturday's show. On knocking on the door I was greeted by Lyndsay Hammond, the blonde sister, who wore a pair of blue jeans and a red T-shirt. We exchanged greetings, then she shouted goodbye to her sister Chrissie and left for the restaurant to meet one of the crew. It was a hot summer afternoon, and the sliding patio door was slightly open, allowing just a hint of breeze to disturb the pulled curtain. The smell of steam and soap wafted from the bathroom then out came Chrissie Hammond, a pretty brunette wearing only a white shirt over a tiny pair of briefs. I almost passed out with shock. It is the kind of story that you dream about but just know it is never going to happen to you, yet there I was. I stuttered an introduction and noticed that her hair was dripping wet. I actually turned away, saying, 'I beg your pardon, would you like me to wait in reception until you're dressed?' In a friendly Australian drawl she said, 'Naw, just grab a seat let's get it done!'

The only seat was covered with clothes, so she motioned for me to sit on the bed.

'Would you like a drink?' she said, as she poured some clear liquid out of a bottle on the dresser. I shook my head, and felt myself staring at her. We made casual chit-chat and then we started the interview. Things were going really well when she lay back on the bed next to me, her shirt almost transparent, clinging tightly to her wet tanned skin. We laughed and joked away in a fun interview, and all the while my head was screaming 'She wants you'. Deep down I knew she didn't, but I liked to kid myself. She certainly did make a big impression on me, and that I feel was exactly what she was trying to do. I still had a lot to learn about interviewing, but it was coming.

By the time I tracked down Whitesnakes' David Coverdale, I had interviewed some 300 rock and pop stars and knew what I was doing. Having been a fan of the man for a good few years I knew everything about him. During the interview I even corrected him about a song he provided for a project called 'The Wizards Convention' and he said, 'How come you know more about me than I do?'

I had two ways of interviewing. If the star was huge, I'd research them for days; if not, I'd go in totally blind. The latter technique usually worked, because they would tell you everything about themselves as they worked to build a following.

However, my biggest cock-up over research occurred at Metro's studios when I was due to interview the rock band UFO. They had recently reformed so I learned who was in the line-up and researched their backgrounds. Yet unknown to me the line-up had changed again, and three different people were in the band. So there I was, live around the table, when the sound engineer said, 'Go around the table, Alan, telling me who is sitting where and what they're called.' As I started, I looked around and I didn't know who was who. I recognised the vocalist Phil Mogg and Pete Way, but I had no idea who the others were. Finally, I just blurted, 'Just who are you, then?' To their credit, they just laughed but I felt that I hadn't shown them the right amount of respect. It was a humiliating experience to be found out, and following that I was never caught out again.

One of the rock world's favourite bands was Thin Lizzy. I managed to interview them on many occasions and had the sad privilege of interviewing frontman Phil Lynott days before his tragic death. He had made little headway since disbanding Lizzy, trying various projects with no major success. He told me how tired he was and he looked very haggard and worn. He said that he was thinking of asking the band to get back together, believing that many of his new songs needed the old line-up to make them come alive. His words were optimistic, yet behind his eyes there seemed to be a sad acceptance that things would never be the same again. The previous meetings with Phil had been full of fun, his wry sense of humour pouring over everything we talked about. Yet this was a very different man. I came away from the interview very sad and upset, and the following weekend I read that he had died. He was one of rock's great stars, a genius who created magic.

It is a rock fan's dream to be able to interview those stars who you've played for years on your record or CD player. You may only meet them once, yet they have briefly touched your life, as you have touched theirs. When they die, you feel helpless at the waste of so much talent.

I first met Led Zeppelin's drummer, John Bonham, whilst working as a support DJ at Knebworth rock festival, yet it would be years later before I was able to interview him. He seemed to me to be a complex man, far more intent on enjoying himself than making music, yet he was easily one of the world's finest percussionists. His life would end less than a year later, choking on his own vomit after a serious drinking session.

I remember talking to Dave Byron, Uriah Heep vocalist, and he told me how awful his life was, how every day he felt the pressure on him to prove himself. No matter how successful he had been in the past, he had to keep being successful or he was nowhere and nobody. He was right, the business chews up talent, often discarding it long before it has reached its full potential. It is easy for those trapped in the full glare of publicity to seek refuge in drink or drugs, escaping for at least a while. The press often hounds people to such a degree, building people up just to knock them down. It cost Dave Byron his life and a few years later fellow Heep member Gary Thain was lost too.

My own massive insecurity has always been hard to carry since leaving the 'safe' day job. My only dream and ambition is still the same as it was on that day – to have the privilege of being able to keep working until I reach retirement age. Yet my worries were fuelled after a conversation with Atomic Roosters' keyboard star, Vincent Crane. We met for a drink in Newcastle and chatted about how his life had turned sour. He'd been part of massive hit records like 'Fire', part of 'The Crazy World Of Arthur Brown', with Rooster, top-twenty hits with 'Tomorrow Night' and 'Devil's Answer' and he spoke of how he'd recently done some session work with Dexy's Midnight Runners. He said, 'If you do well in this game, your life is over, your friends just take from you and you're never free to just live your life.' At the time I felt he was overreacting, yet I would learn many harsh lessons as the years went by. By the end of the year Vincent Crane too was dead.

The end for the *Hot'n'Heavy Express* was inevitable when I was asked to take over the *Night Owls* phone-in show. It was Metro's flagship programme and could it really be hosted by the madman from Saturday night's rock package? I was hauled into the bosses office and told that the rock show was too vulgar and that complaints had been made. This was inevitable, because it was designed for the wild brigade, and anyone casually listening in would certainly have been shocked. The gag that killed it wasn't too bad, yet as a final straw to snap the camel's back, it was effective. I was doing a sketch on nicknames, suggesting that Shakin' Stevens could've been called that because of what he does in the urinal stall when he's finished, then I asked if it really was true that Elvis the Pelvis had a brother called Enis? Before I got off air I knew that I was in trouble, for the security man informed me that the show was being recorded by the boss. Admittedly, I had received countless warnings, but the success of the show had been based on its 'rag mag' or *Viz* appeal, and to ease back would change its nature and emasculate it. Instead it was pulled altogether. The station didn't kill it, but due to my refusal to sanitise it, we lost the only show of its kind in Britain. I am still very sad about it. It had *every* big star interviewed or co-hosting, rare live concerts, rock charts and music mixes of the latest rock albums obscure or not. It was my baby and I couldn't believe that it was dead. Its string of awards failed to save it, although they still hang on Metro FM's hallowed walls.

17 Carving a Reputation

TWO WORLDS HAD collided, one that of being a radio phone-in host and the other a near-the-knuckle, zany radio DJ. Although my sense of humour remained totally intact, being outrageous wasn't in keeping with building people's confidence. After cracking the ultimate in bawdy jokes on a Saturday night I was then called upon to give the most personal advice on Sunday. It was a strange mix that could end in no other way than in conflict. The nicknames I had built up on the rock show certainly didn't seem suitable for a mixed audience programme. I had been called 'The Ginger Ninja', 'The brave and fearless leader' and the 'flashing blade'. These names had originally come from my great love of the old movies of Errol Flynn. Many years earlier Rob, my roadie, had bought a birthday card that featured a black-and-white shot of the sword-wielding Mr Flynn. The message read 'Happy birthday Oh brave and fearless leader' and in tiny print the photograph was captioned: 'Errol Flynn's flashing blade in the film *The Sea Hawk*.' Both had stuck and yet those in power at Metro Radio were having difficulty getting such an unorthodox look accepted by the mainstream radio audience. All through this time my long flowing ginger locks were way down my back, so those at the radio station had real problems marketing me. Most people didn't have long hair at the time, so how could they make it acceptable?

Finally, after they had had a brainstorming session, it was decided that they would 'sell' the image of a 'Flashing Blade'. So on a very cold and frosty morning I found myself taken to Lumley Castle, near Chester-le-Street, where I was handed a cavalier's outfit of very heavy embroidered velvet, topped with a huge felt hat exploding with plumes. The leather boots were so high I could hardly walk and a sword was thrust in my belt to complete the devastating effect.

It was very early on a Sunday morning to avoid being swamped with people, and as I began walking through the grounds a couple of photographers snapped away. One merely wanted close shots around the castle, but the other chose to be more adventurous. Suddenly, from around the back of the castle walked a young girl in jodhpurs clasping the reins of a huge brown horse. The photographer wanted me to hold the beast, then walk it and finally to mount it. It may surprise you, but in the west end of Newcastle there aren't any horses, and this is the nearest that I had ever been to one. The cameraman joked, 'If ever anyone had left a horse outside their front door, when they came out they'd have found it on four bricks.'

Tentatively I climbed aboard, guided by the young horsey lady who walked me about as I slid all over the saddle, haphazardly trying to find my balance. The horse seemed certainly better behaved than I was, so when the photographer suggested that I walk the horse myself, I felt confident enough to give it a try. The woman grimaced at the thought of her beloved pet being placed in the hands of someone who obviously couldn't ride, but she agreed and the photographer ran about 600 yards to the main gate of the castle and set up his tripod.

My instructions were just to stay aback, perhaps waving my sword about, and to take off the huge hat as if bowing and generally ham it up for the camera. Gently the woman released her grip on the horse and said, in an authoritative tone: 'Walk!'

I thought she meant me, so I shouted 'Yah' in my most convincing John Wayne fashion. The horse began to trot and was off, while behind me the woman in a blind panic was screaming for the horse to stop. At the gate the cameraman was yelling for her to get out of the shot.

The horse by this time was in a gallop and I was hanging on for dear life, yet remembering my orders I tried to wave my sword about, ultimately dropping it, then my hat blew off and before I knew it the photographer was almost trampled as the horse raced past him, catching his tripod and sending almost a thousand pounds' worth of camera into a mud puddle.

I could still hear his blasphemous curses as the horse failed to stop at the gate and clattered out onto the road, over the path and then raced along a narrow grass verge. If you've never sat on a horse it is quite a shock to see just how high you are off the ground, so any thought of diving off was soon forgotten about. The cars hurtled past as I tried to jerk at the reins, trying to stop the horse in the same way I'd started him. 'Whoa boy', it always worked for 'The Duke', then 'Whoooa', then finally 'Stop you bastard! AAAARGH!'

Almost half a mile from the castle gates two other riders were able to stop the horse for me, leading this quivering wreck of a supposed bold cavalier back to the grounds of Lumley Castle. There I was met by the cursing cameraman and the hoarse horse lady who both gave me a thorough earbashing before heading on their way. She was patting the horse, checking its legs and exchanging moans with the then thoroughly belligerent cameraman.

None of this was my fault, nor my idea, yet I was to blame. He was going to send me the bill to have his camera cleaned, and if the horse was injured she was going to sue. The photographer ignored my apologies and tried to wipe away the oozing mud that had found its way into every nook and cranny of his expensive Japanese camera. Then the horse lifted his tail and did what I had felt like doing on my gallop to hell. He deposited about a carrier-bag full of steaming droppings on to the ground, one huge cannonball inches away from the photographer's bag. Whilst they continued their animated conversation, I stuck my recently retrieved sword into the dung ball, deposited it into his canvas bag, then zipped it up. I apologised again, without any response, then proceeded to walk up the long path towards the castle to get changed.

It was still barely 7 a.m. on a bright but nippy Sunday morning and the castle was host to a conference for Levi Jeans. One of the reps, still half-asleep, was ambling down the road reading a *Sunday Mirror*. I was within about a yard of him when he looked up from the headlines. There in front of him in the castle grounds was a cavalier! He turned white and dropped his paper. I realised what he was thinking so chirped, 'Good morrow fine sir, hast thou seen where Cromwell is hiding?'

'Err . . . no' was his terrified reply, as he turned and ran back inside the hotel.

18 Episodes in the Life of a Flashing Blade

TRYING TO LIVE up to the name of the Flashing Blade certainly wasn't easy, as I ended up being roped in to every kind of dangerous stunt imaginable. I had already abseiled from the Tyne Bridge and from two huge buildings in the centre of Newcastle, and parachuted out of a balloon. Following that I was approached by a man called Tony who was a student belonging to 'The Dangerous Sports Association'. Live on the show, he had challenged me to take part in an event happening early the following Sunday morning. He wouldn't say where it was, or what it was. I was very intrigued so said that I would meet him, carrying with me a portable tape recorder so that I could use whatever it was on the show.

We met at a pub on the sea-front at Roker and they explained they were going to do something called a bungee jump. I had never heard of it, yet after their explanation I did vaguely remember seeing a David Attenborough documentary about some African natives climbing to the tops of trees, tying vines to their legs then jumping off. It seemed the height of stupidity to me, but they were determined to do it.

Just as the sky was transforming the land from black to a beautiful hazy red the van pulled up close to Sunderland's Monkwearmouth Bridge. Along it and by the Wear various groups of students had gathered to watch, all cheering me on. It seems that at Sunderland Poly they had been plugging the event for weeks, and without proclaiming it to the public it was one of the cult happenings. About 200 people were there, most of them badly hung over and wrapped up in heavy coats. They were a very vocal crowd, shouting constructive comments like 'What kind of flowers would you like?', 'Do you want to be buried or cremated?' or 'Don't worry about a funeral, they'll probably never find your body anyway!' When an audience is watching you have no option but to try to live up to their expectations of you. Actually you do, but I was far too stupid to realise that I did have that amount of control.

They fitted me into a harness very similar to the one climbers wear. Tony the leader wore exactly the same and instructed one of the team to run across the bridge and take as many photographs as possible. Down on the River Wear there was a tiny motorboat that they had borrowed, belonging to a man called Philip Edwards who lived in Whitby. It was his job to unhook the jumpers. This really didn't seem like a good idea at all, firstly I couldn't swim so if the cable snapped I was dead, secondly I had so much to live for. Yet by this time it was down to stupid pride, and I couldn't back out. In the early days of the bungee jump you weren't ever going to be upside down, the harness would keep you upright. So the bungee cord was affixed securely and Tony climbed up on to the rail of the bridge and made a speech as to how this was the fourth bridge he'd conquered and then he was gone. I peered over the edge to see him dropping like a bomb then suddenly he stopped, screamed and then seemed to bounce back into the air only to fall again, slowly bouncing to a halt. The boat positioned itself beneath him and he was lowered down into it, yelling his glee for all the world to hear. A rather fat, podgy-faced student wearing a Smiths' T-shirt said, 'Come on Alan, it's your turn now. You'd better make it quick before the police come!'

I'd never considered it, yet I supposed it must be illegal to jump off bridges without permission, so toyed with using that as an excuse. Instead, I slowly climbed on to the edge, swinging my legs out into nothing. The pit of my stomach was thumping as if I was carrying sextuplets all wearing Doc Marten boots. I can't remember jumping, but I can remember falling, looking along the river, glancing at the water that rushed up to greet me. The harness held my chest and a hard leather strap went between my legs and up my rear clipping on to the belt at the back. Within seconds I'd reached the bottom, my full weight hitting this strap and almost cutting me in half, totally squashing my tenderer parts and then sending me bouncing back up into the air. As I started to fall again I was squealing like a pig in a bacon factory, for any second I knew my testicles would be pulped again, then again, and again as the bungee rope bounced to a halt and I was swinging free. Try as I might I couldn't release the pressure from my groin, and it felt as if a horse had kicked me in the tackle. My underarms were also chafed and sore, but it was over. To describe it as exhilarating was certainly true, but how I wished I'd had that cable tied to my leg. As I was lowered into the boat I yanked and pulled at the harness trying to get it off me. Tony was grinning widely, and I saw that his outfit had huge waddings of cloth and padding to protect him, while I wore only boxer shorts with jeans over the top. I never considered my privacy at all and stripping almost naked in the open boat I found that my thighs and that area between testes and bottom badly cut and bleeding. Mr Edwards the boatman said, 'Serves you right, you bloody idiot.' It was fair comment, but I was indebted to him for the plastic bottle of Savlon and the cotton wool he dug out of his crude first aid kit. He took us to a landing nearby where we were picked up by the van and I was taken back to the car. I walked with bow legs for almost a month and the wound between my legs caused untold agonies rubbing against the tight trousers that were fashionable at that time. Once, whilst wearing a pair of cream trousers at a roadshow, I began to bleed and was made aware of it by a member of the audience. Embarrassing to say the least. Yet once again the Flashing Blade had succeeded in rising to a challenge that to my knowledge no other presenter had done at that time.

A few calls were made on air from those that had watched, including a very impressed Tony who spoke of courage and bravery. To be quite honest, I was desperate to build up a reputation and had pursued that objective with a total disregard to common sense, and there were more adventures to come. For the label of 'Flashing Blade' would lead me to have constantly to prove myself.

Even now, I feel the pressure weighing on me as acutely as I did then. To prove to my parents that I am as worthy of their love as my sister, to prove to my employers that I am worthy of a place in their ranks, to prove to the people that I have something to offer. Maybe a psychiatrist would put it all down to a deep-seated insecurity, a fear of rejection, yet still I seek affection, any affection.

Back then in my quiet times I would be so desperate to impress that in my social life I would put on an act. I would suddenly 'entertain' instead of being myself, to try to get people to like me, afraid to show them the real me. That person hid in a dark corner, waiting for someone to attack or take from him. Someone always did!

I was working hard every day, not having a day off in months, no holidays, no nights out, and I failed to realise just how exciting life actually was. My name was beginning to be known, and although not everyone liked me at least they were beginning to know of me. I was determined to win over as many people as I possibly could.

I had fallen for a student from Lancaster University and was very keen on her pursuit. She was a lovely girl and I was aware that things were moving very quickly as rather than studying she was spending time in the North. There were many complications in my life, as there always are, yet I did feel that we stood as good a chance as any. I had promised her mother that I would do my best not to hurt her, yet by fouling up her education I was doing precisely that. I told her to complete her studies and then we would pick up the pieces. She took this to mean that I no longer wanted anything to do with her, and I received a most unpleasant letter. I felt that I had a huge obligation to her, as I had been the first man to be close to her. Yet she couldn't understand I was doing this so that she could gain the qualifications that she needed for her career. She did obtain those qualifications, yet when I contacted her again I was rebuffed firmly. My protestations were ignored, and I believe that she was probably wise to build a new life for herself. Around this time I felt as if the curse surrounding my love life was back with a vengeance.

In situations like that it is pointless feeling sorry for yourself. You have no choice but to fill your mind with less painful things. In my case it is always with work. I had decided to spend a week on the phone-in attacking criminals, wiping the floor with them and allowing the audience to have their say too. Having lived in an area where crime was now flourishing I was already angry about it. I heard from a woman in her seventies who had been hit in the face with a brick as she slept so a twelve-year-old could steal her purse, and a woman who despite being 63, was subjected to rape and sexual assault lasting almost five hours by a gang consisting of boys as young as ten. Such violent crimes, as well as the burglaries, car thefts, armed robberies, ram raids, shoplifting, etc. sickened me, and I vowed I would never back down in my fight against it.

Over the following years this stand has caused a vast number of difficult situations, some physical, some just unpleasant. On my way to host the North Shields Fish Quay Festival I was bombarded with abuse from a group of lads, who openly admitted to being burglars. However, my view is that if you tell scum that they are scum and they don't like it, then they should stop being scum and get a life! On a few occasions I have been followed by car thieves wearing ski-masks yelling and gesticulating from some stolen car. Whilst they are doing this I'm calling the police to get them arrested, but they're too dumb to realise. Amazing gadgets these hands-free phones. Travelling home after doing a radio contest called *The Bladerunner Superquiz*, I was giving the scorekeeper, a canny lad called Ian Brumwell, a lift when a car filled with these half-formed dipsticks, lights flashing, car weaving all over the road, threatened us. Ian had never witnessed anything like it before and was very upset, but I was well used to the games these dopes played.

It was Christmas time and once again *Night Owls* was crusading against crime. I was walking through Eldon Square in Newcastle, heading towards Percy Street to pick up some videos to be used as prizes on the show. At the back entrance to Marks & Spencer, there were a number of men selling Christmas paper, party poppers, decorations, etc. but having no wish to purchase I walked through the throngs of people who were oblivious to me, intent only on their last-minute shopping.

At that point I heard a gruff voice bark, 'Hey, are you Alan Robson?'

I turned to see a squat man, a wall of muscle and fat, who had more in common with Jabba the Hutt than with anything really human.

'I'm afraid I am,' came my reply.

He walked up to me, his nose less than an inch off my face as he poked a finger into my chest: 'You said on your programme that burglars are slime!'

This was one of those moments when you're tempted to say, 'No, not slime. I said slim, so they can climb in narrow windows!' However, you owe it to yourself to stick up for what you believe, so with the conviction of your average Kamikaze pilot I replied, 'Yes, that's true!'

He was quite surprised that I was as blunt about it, then I started to sink in my shoes when he added, 'My brother and my best friend are both in prison for burglary. Are you saying that they are slime?'

My mind whizzed about trying to find anything I could reply without getting my face broken. Finally I found a straw to cling to.

'Imagine that you get home tonight and someone has wrecked your house, paint-sprayed across your wall and used your fireside rug as a toilet. What would you call these people?'

Without thinking, he answered, 'I'd kill the fucking bastards!'

So I finished him off saying, 'So you think your brother and best friend are both fucking bastards?'

'No, but . . .'

Interjecting, I added, 'Well that's how the people feel about it. Merry Christmas!'

Then I walked away as he began to flam, and hopefully realisation was dripping into his head like treacle spills down the side of its pot. I was out of Eldon Square, walking, fairly quickly, down the metal steps outside when I heard the door swing open. With all of the grace of a hippopotamus with a club foot, I felt the stairs vibrating under his clatter. He was coming for me!

I had spent many years being frightened of that noise, having to battle and face up to this type of unpleasantry. Realistically you have three choices:

1 Run like hell.

2 Hit him as hard as you can, then run like hell.

3 Let him hit you, then do him for assault!

The law prefers you to do the third one, but it involves you having to prove it, and also gives you broken bones, gaping wounds, bruises and slack teeth. So I decided on choice number two. As he approached me, I started winding myself to throw my full weight behind my right hand to flatten his already squashed nose. As he put his hand on my shoulder, I prepared to swing around. I was a split second away from actually assaulting him, when I noticed that he was handing me a carrier bag. I looked inside and it was full of Christmas paper, crackers and stuff.

'All the best, Alan lad!' he said, and clanged his way back up the stairs.

I spent the rest of the day thinking about this, choosing to believe that he might be on the wrong side of the law, but at least he respected me for my stand. Within the month, I had decided that I would start a visit of prisons and remand centres. Practically everyone in there listened to *Night Owls*, and if I attacked crime there would be what they described themselves as 'The Robson Rumble' along the wing. At these meetings I would tell them just what I thought of them. They would treat me initially with contempt, but after telling them stories, jokes and anecdotes, I'd normally win them around. Once, after accepting an invitation to HM Remand Centre Acklington, I talked for over an hour, and one very strongly built black lad hadn't said a word, nor laughed once. At the end of the gig, he came up to me and said: 'It was brilliant, you bastard, and I still fucking hate you!' On asking him why, he explained that if I had my way and sentences were drastically increased he would never be out of prison.

To me, this proved that the biggest deterrent to crime of all kinds is longer sentencing. It is unlikely that corporal or capital punishment will be restored, yet regularly the majority of people in the North seem to support that. One of the most fascinating conversations I ever had on the radio was with an Arab gentleman who had sliced off the heads of murderers in his homeland. There, he proclaimed, that to slice off a rapist's penis or to cut off a burglar's hand was decisive action that led to them having a very low incidence of serious crime. Many described him as barbaric, yet in his homeland men, women and children can walk safely through the streets day or night, and can still leave their doors open, the keys in their cars knowing that no one will take them. Is that the result of barbarism? Yet in our beloved homeland we have a small hardcore of worms who make life very miserable for as many people as they can.

Following what others described as my 'tough and relentless stand against crime', I involved myself in many police campaigns, helping to publicise Neighbourhood Watch and Shopwatch, often representing ordinary people in negotiations with the police to clear up a variety of difficult problems. The boys and girls in blue were always very fair, trying to sort out situations ranging from assaults to suicide attempts, fraud to noisy neighbours. This close working relationship sometimes would lead to some very strange adventures.

I was working seven days a week, at the cost of my social life, yet still the breaks weren't coming. Around every bend there seemed to be a disaster, and the next would be in the form of a secret lover. One evening I was opening my post at Metro when I found a paternity suit beckoning. A girl called Julie claimed that I was the father of her newly born child. I racked my brain for any girl that I'd ever met called Julie and wasn't able to come up with any remembrance at all. Much of my sex life had been easily forgettable, but I am not so much of a cad that I couldn't name the very few women that I had been close to. I wrote back to the solicitor saying that I didn't know this girl and was absolutely positive that my sexual organs had never even seen her. At first I did think it to be a joke, but on ringing them I was invited in to talk about it, face to face with Julie. This I readily agreed to, because if she had given birth to my son, I felt we really should have met! So on getting there, I was in the reception sitting next to a girl with a young baby and nervously decided to sort her out before it went any further. I said, 'Now listen you, I have never met you before, and I have never had sex with you, right!'

Astounded by my outburst in the silent solicitorial waiting room, she answered a shocked 'Yes, that's true!'

Feeling that I had her on the ropes, I continued my thrust: 'I'm not giving you a penny and if you're going to tell lies about the baby, I'll have to prosecute you!'

I felt great. I had sorted out the entire matter without even needing to hire any legal representative.

When I was at the very peak of my pride over my handling of what is an unpleasant allegation, a door opened, and out stepped a man in his early thirties wearing a sharp grey suit.

'Hello darling', he said, kissing the young mother on the lips.

She looked shaken and when he asked, 'What's wrong?', I realised that she was the wife of one of the solicitors. I crumbled into my seat and put my hand over my eyes. They went to lunch and what a story she had to tell. The receptionist tried very hard not to laugh, but couldn't stop her face contorting as she tried to stifle the giggles.

About five minutes later, another door opened and I was called in to face a very pug-faced woman who had a baby that suffered the same facial affliction. I certainly hadn't entered into any sexual relationship with this woman, if that was in fact what she was. She wore black trousers, a heavy black smock and white shoes. The solicitor listed when the sexual encounter was alleged to have taken place and as it was a work night I could easily refute her claim. While she was in the throes of passion I was on air, doing a live phone-in, and could easily prove it. I offered a blood test, she refused, then I never heard from the solicitor again.

However, Julie did contact me almost eight months later, apologising to me. She had been dumped by her 'one night stand' boyfriend, yet had been telling her parents that she had been seeing me on the quiet. The lies and stories were getting bigger and bigger and eventually she was bound to be found out. She didn't want to admit to her family and friends that this incredible love tryst was all a fantasy. Like many fantasies, if given an ounce of truth, it seems to be quite believable. Her mother had insisted she go to a solicitor to make sure the father, who she believed was me, lived up to his responsibilities.

To my chagrin, this was not the only paternity suit that I would receive during this period. Another got to the verge of court, yet on meeting me this young woman said, 'That's not Alan Robson.' It seems she'd been dating a lad who used to leave her house at 9 p.m. every night 'to go to work'. She believed he was Alan Robson when in fact it was another man with ginger hair and moustache. I was beginning to feel that not only was my actual love life in tatters, I was also suffering for other people's too.

Then I met Lynn, a charming and pretty lady who seemed to be as confused about love as I was. After we had been seeing each other for a short while, she insisted that my gap tooth was fixed. The nightmare I believed that dental process would be happened, and after a few minutes' discomfort, the tooth was capped and I had what I hadn't had since I was thirteen, a real smile. I was thrilled by it and within a wink of an eye we were engaged then married. After having been devoid of any real affection for so long, I was glad to be with such a nice, genuine and sincere lady. But in less than a handful of years we found ourselves growing apart, and then divorced, as work stole the thunder of the relationship again. I apportion all of the blame on myself. I worked all day and all night allowing little or no time for the things that she felt were special. She worked hard during the day and was successful at her chosen career too. As a result, we rarely saw one another, and at times it seemed as if we were passing strangers. My selfish pursuit of work ate away at everything we had, then finally when we sought for love to cement the cracks in our relationship there wasn't enough to do the job. Never was there any intent in my heart to hurt her, yet I had and I felt very badly about it. Deeds, not words, are the proof of love, and I never gave enough. I met Lynn after the divorce on a few occasions and it was then that she showed me the ultimate kindness of treating me as a friend. A friendly wave, a flash of her headlights on the road seems so very little after two people were once wed. Yet I sincerely thank her for that, for my entire life seems littered with those people who have, at one time or the other, shown themselves to be false friends. My friendship and subsequent marriage to her was not false, yet it didn't fill our lives in the way it should. We were always an odd mixture, and I will never forget the day that she left. I cried non-stop for almost 48 hours. It was not so much because the marriage had ended, for in real terms that had happened almost five months earlier, it was because once again I'd be starting from scratch. I had reached out for someone, yet failure was mine yet again. So once more I charged headlong into work, my perpetual escape.

When you witness death, you can't help but quake at the realisation that your life could turn down the same road at any time. Each year I prided myself on trying to visit as many people in hospital, believing that it made a difference, but I'm not sure that it ever did. I still do it, yet can't help but think that my visits are merely a distraction, a novelty, and never really do any genuine good. When I first started visiting, my objective was to lift the spirits of the patients, by being there for them. More often than not I'd take in a couple of books, magazines or tapes. As the years rolled by I saw that these people may have been pleased to see me, yet their pleasure was quadrupled by the sight of their families, that was the only source of any real tonic. This would lead me to target people who specifically requested me to visit them, or who were on their own. These visits taught me a great deal, particularly my times in hospices or the cancer wards. It is there that you really learn the meaning of courage and spirit.

Once, I was invited by a woman called Margaret to visit her during her chemotherapy, as her family all lived down South and she hadn't received a single visitor. My visit sent the other women into a panic. They were all totally bald, but knowing that I was going to be there gave them an excuse to get dolled up and they phoned their families to get them to deliver their smartest outfits. Make-up was applied, head scarves placed over some heads and wigs over others, and it was posh frocks and suits all around. I had found out how many ladies were there, in total 11, so I had gifts for all, jokey things like combs, polish and dusters and lollipops (à la Kojak), plus some genuine goodies ranging from chocolates to books.

My private life at that time was suffering, and I was feeling pretty miserable about things, particularly that day. When your schedule is that full, it's hard enough to get through it when you're feeling chipper, but when you're not it can become a hard slog. Always having to smile, when inside you feel more like crying. Over the years I have learned to cover my feelings, put on the clown's mask, and get through it. No one would ever have a clue. People have listened to me on the radio, watched me on television and said 'My, you're in good form!', yet sometimes I had never felt lower. But I knew that my only escape from reality was to dive headlong into work, so with my smile wedged firmly in place, off I headed to fulfill all obligations.

These valiant ladies looked wonderful, and I stayed there for about two hours, just chatting and meeting the visitors as they arrived just prior to my exit. They laughed, they joked and Margaret chased me around the beds threatening to shave my head. I was screaming and laughing, and so were they, and I left that hospital feeling twenty feet tall. I had gone there to cheer them up, yet the reverse had happened. Whatever grief I had to face at home, it would take only an ounce of courage, yet these ladies were showing tons of guts every moment of every day.

The anti-smoking debate brought me face to face with a man who in reality killed himself. I received a phone call from a tearful lady who begged me to visit her husband who was seriously ill in hospital. She said that he had listened to the show for years and his one big regret was that he had never ever met me. This was something I could and would easily sort; it really was so very little to ask for. We had been talking on the *Night Owls* phone-in about whether cigarettes should be banned, with vociferous protests from the various lobby groups. Personally, I have always believed in people having the freedom of choice, yet what I saw has inevitably coloured my views. On walking into the ward I saw a man lying on the bed with tubes attached to every orifice. Both his legs had recently been amputated. He was as white as a ghost, very weak indeed, and yet he did respond on seeing me. I shook his hand yet felt there was no strength in it. His wife explained how after countless heart and bronchial problems, his doctor had insisted that he give up smoking. His reply was 'It's the only pleasure I get out of life.' That was where it was taking him, out of his life. He thanked me for coming, and we chatted for a while, yet I knew that he was close to death. He seemed to know that he was beaten, and was going gracefully. The face of his wife watching helplessly will be etched in my memory forever. She walked me to the end of the ward and said, 'He can die happy now. This was the last thing I could do for him!' I hugged her and she broke down, and tears rolled down my cheeks too. Yet I fought back the sobbing. Even at such a time I knew that she needed me to be the rock to cling to, although the rock was leaking badly. Once away from her I broke down totally, sitting on the grass outside totally inconsolable.

I still don't fully understand why. Was it really for this stranger who I had just met who had allowed his life to fade away? Was it for the woman who would soon be a widow and couldn't cope? Was it to be honoured in such a way by a dying man? Perhaps it was all these things, but my thoughts were so tangled I couldn't break it down so clearly at the time. I have never understood why people should consider me to be any different. I am the same as they are, my job is merely more in the public eye! Yet these people loved me, a real honest love without any strings attached. Maybe it was that fact alone that hit home. So often people claimed to be friends then their true mercenary purpose would be revealed. Once again, I had discovered more pure emotion from strangers, whilst my 'friends' often circled like vultures just waiting to pull another piece off.

To list all my faults would take a book far bigger than this, but one is certainly impulsiveness. And if I decide to do something, I see it through no matter what, even if, as was once the case, it almost gets me arrested for assault.

I'd received a call from a young woman. She refused to give me her name and said that her boyfriend was beating her up and had been abusing her five-year-old daughter. I suggested she ring the police to deal with the scumbag, but she was far too frightened. This man had her petrified and even though she was sobbing her heart, the hold he had over her was obvious to all. It was plain that she wanted to get free of him, and moreover she wanted her child to be safe. He had 'touched' the little girl and stubbed cigarettes out on her tiny body.

I was on the verge of getting the police round, but she said that if they did her beautiful baby girl could be taken from her, and none of it was her fault. She was a victim too. I was swift to point out that if she left her child at risk in that house with him, *she* would be guilty of child abuse. If anyone stands back and lets this happen, that is tantamount to being an accomplice. I investigated every option, whether she could go and stay with her parents, seek help from friends or even go into a women's refuge until a safe haven was found. She was far too scared to do anything like that. Her boyfriend was in bed, sleeping off another night on the beer, and she needed someone to take the lead and break this cycle of apathy and the brutality it inevitably led to. The longer I spoke to her the more I knew it was going to have to be me. I told her to pack up everything she could, all of her clothes, and her daughter's things, and I would send a taxi to pick her up. This I did and got the youngster to safety. A bed and breakfast place offered her free accommodation for the short term and the following day the police were brought in and the social services took over. The image of that tiny child's face will never leave me: pale, unhappy and sad, with eyes like saucers and tears beginning to grow in each corner as her mother, frightened and confused, snuggled her in, as much to help herself as the child. Just below the child's right eye was a deep cigarette burn. No one was going to harm her again, wasn't it everybody's duty to protect children? To everyone's credit the 'authorities', often chastised for being uncaring, handled the entire matter swiftly and effectively.

Those next two days I saw that woman leave everything behind, her home, her possessions, her friends, neighbours and ultimately her family. She wanted to be miles away from her boyfriend, who had several convictions for violence and being drunk and disorderly. The tiny girl had to suffer internal examinations and spoke to the police about the indignities that her mother's boyfriend had put her through. To imagine how this would affect her in later life didn't bear thinking about, yet at least she was free of him now. I spent most of the day with them, trying to act as a bridge between them and all of the people they needed to speak with. This woman was close to the edge and it would be touch and go whether she could hold on to her sanity. Wherever I drove them they scanned the paths, stared at every red Ford car, because that is what 'he' drove. They were still trapped in this man's mesh of terror, and yet now they had never been safer. A place had been found, but it would take a couple of weeks to fix it up. The boarding house who had been so kind was ultimately paid by the social services to allow the two of them to stay there, almost twenty miles from him, and they began the slow road back to living a normal life again.

I wish I could write of the immense satisfaction that being involved in something like this gives me, but really it doesn't. It continues to eat away at me like an unhealed sore. A few days of involvement and then you release the reins of their life and hope they 'make it' safely. I always feel that it's never enough. However, two days later, in a car park in Newcastle city centre, I was confronted by the boyfriend who was out on bail and looking for vengeance. I was unpacking my gear from the boot when I was hit hard between the shoulder blades and fell to the ground. A woman walking past saw the fight and phoned the police. By the time they arrived I was kicking this drunken bastard all over the multi-storey. I must admit I had lost it, and he was so drunk he was unable to really defend himself. All I remembered was that youngster's face, sexually abused and burned by this swine, yet he had the cheek to feel hard done by. He was screaming that he would kill them both and winding me up even more. I wasn't going to let him, and each time he tried to get up I'd punch him down again. The policeman pulled me off, while the woman was screaming that I had started the fight, having only arrived after it had begun. My brain was ablaze, I had never fully understood what it meant 'to see red' but that afternoon I did. My right hand was skinned practically to the bone, there was an inch-long wound in my right wrist, torn open by a sovereign ring, that needed stitching and I was shaking with anger. Maybe I was in shock, I really don't know. The policeman was certainly going to charge me for assault, and the boyfriend was demanding a solicitor to get me 'put away'. All I remember was being taken to the hospital, stitched and cleaned up. Then I drove back to the police station to explain myself. My back was black with bruising and I'd been so badly hit in the kidneys I was urinating blood for almost a week.

His case against me dissolved thankfully, as he began defending himself against his girlfriend's allegations. He wasn't the child's father and vigorously denied any assault on her. He claimed her mother had done it, although she didn't smoke, and no sexual interference could be confirmed. The child said that he had burned her and had touched her 'down there', but for whatever reason she never gave evidence. He walked free from the court.

The show has been involved in many cases of this kind and each one is a minefield. The only hope I've got is to have sufficient nous to call it right. Anything less is a disaster for all concerned.

No broadcaster had ever been part of a black magic ritual, so I managed to persuade Metro FM to at least see how far we'd be allowed to go. Once again Jim Brown was to be the outside broadcast producer, and before we could find out if it could go ahead, we had to ask for permission from one of the country's leading witches. Television had sought such a thing, but was always turned down point-blank, as the bubble of secrecy would be burst. Faces would be seen, identified and whatever secretive association would be lost forever. Live radio had a far better chance, but no one had the foresight to give it a try. So off we went to Manchester.

It was a very sunny day as we drove through the neat suburbs of red-brick buildings with tidy trimmed lawns and radiant flower-beds brimming with blossoms. Yet there at the end of the roadway stood one house on its own, and despite the strength of the sun it looked perpetually in shadow, as if a dark cloud hung over it. We all knew it was the very house we were seeking. We didn't need to check the number. The house was a fairly ordinary-looking four-bedroom detached, but it gave the same kind of feeling that you would get were you visiting the Addams Family. The sound engineer decided to wait in the car whilst Jim and I ventured inside.

We were greeted by a large portly lady in black with piercing eyes that practically stripped you to the bone with a single glance. When someone has eyes that different, you would note their colour, yet the only prevalent colour I could see was black. Having had many discussions with those involved in the dark arts, I knew that hypnotism is often a stock in trade, so I only made eye contact when absolutely necessary. We talked through how we saw the programme going and asked what our chances were to cover a Sabbat, a black magic gathering. At first she was shy to discuss anything in any depth, but eventually she realised that we wanted to treat the entire subject with respect.

In the front room of the house was an altar with black candles and a pentagram on the floor. Into the room they all filed: a wine waiter from a bistro, a kitchen porter from a hotel, two Canadian students, an American lawyer and three tall shipyard workers. They sat around the pentagram chanting, when in walked the Witch Queen with her daughter, a staggeringly beautiful girl, aged about fifteen, with a gypsy look to her. They chanted, talked in a strange tongue, then placed a huge python in the centre of the star and fed it a live white rat. So bulky was the white furred creature that the snake had to detach its lower jaw to swallow the rat as it wriggled and writhed in terror. Following that short sacrifice they were swift to agree to give me permission to attend a 'gathering'.

To say we were glad to get out of that house is an understatement. The people were fine, and had not given us any major cause for concern, other than the fact that most of them carried daggers. As a man, I showed tremendous interest in the daughter, who had the shape of a young Bo Derek and the intelligence of a graduate.

In laters years she would be quite a force to bargain with. It was easy to see how people could be drawn into such a fascinating group. Those who say that these 'covens' are set up by ignorant people, led like sheep, are way off the mark. Whether there is any firm basis for their own strand of faith, I don't know, but their creed has existed since long before Christianity.

Several phone calls were made to firm up details of what would happen. The Queen Witch told me she did not worship the Devil but the god and goddess of nature, the power that gives everything life.

A month later, the appointed time arrived. I was taken in a car, a Ford Sierra, driven by a stony-faced man who pulled into a lay-by, after driving through the Tyne Tunnel, on the road that leads to South Shields. There I was met by a tall man, built like a weight-lifter and wearing a black ski-mask. He asked if I had been followed, I swore that I hadn't and he ordered me to get in the back of a dark blue Transit van.

Inside was a young girl, aged about seventeen, who told me that she was going to blindfold me, then remove all of my clothes. Under normal circumstances the thought of a good-looking girl removing my clothes would have been more than acceptable, yet in this case the blindfold caused me a great deal of concern. There is something about being in total darkness that makes your imagination run wild. I felt embarrassed, humiliated and more than a little frightened as I rolled around in the back of that van, my skin scraping along the cold metal-frame of the vehicle. This young girl was very gentle and she told me that she was putting my clothes, keys and money into a kit bag, and that I would be given everything back on the return journey. When she had finished I was totally naked, even to the degree that my small chain and watch were both confiscated too. All I had with me was a metal case filled with outside broadcast equipment.

At that point, she instructed me to put my hands behind my back. She tied them together tightly with a cord, then I heard her leave the back of the van to go and sit in the front with the driver. I strained my ears to hear their conversation, but it was no more than a mumble over the roar of the ageing van.

The journey took no more than about half an hour, and after driving over what my backside told me must be rough countryside, the van ground to a halt. As the young girl helped me out of the van and I was standing naked beside her, feeling the wind blow the bottom of her long skirt against my legs, it crossed my mind for a second that this would be one hell of a stunt on *Candid Camera*. But I was completely vulnerable. They could have done anything to me. I had placed my life and my naked body into the hands of witches, in a way I wouldn't even trust my closest friends.

My hands were untied and the blindfold removed and there before me was a blazing bonfire in the centre of a dense wooded area. The night was jet black and around the fire sat about thirty men and women, all naked. I was greeted by a man who called himself 'Edge'. He introduced me to people, not giving me their names only their occupations. I had expected a number of immature students, keen to latch on to something different, the 'ravish a virgin at midnight just for kicks crowd', but nothing could have prepared me for the actual truth. I met businessmen, accountants, police officers, bank managers, heads of companies, tradesmen, secretaries. All professional people, well educated, aged between 17 and about 60. The girl who had stripped me was now also naked, yet all of the tingles that red-blooded men are supposed to feel refused to kick in. My brain kept yelling 'Now what?'

The ritual was over in seconds. A chicken was slaughtered by a woman wearing a tall hat and mask, its blood was smeared on her body before the carcass was passed around the others to do the same. They began a chant that started quietly and built in volume until it filled your head completely. They grasped each others hands and did a sort of pagan 'Ring a ring o' roses' until finally they hugged and caressed each other. They then sat around eating from a pot that was cooking on the fire – a strange mulch of some unrecognisable flesh, hopefully animal. They drank wine from wooden goblets then they disappeared into the undergrowth, returning fully clad. I later discovered that all of their cars had been parked at the edge of a farmer's field, out of sight of the road.

All the while I was gibbering into my microphone, each word being recorded at the radio station. I was invited to sample the food, and did so, hoping it wasn't anyone I knew or anything still actually alive. It tasted not unlike undercooked pork and you had to chew for almost an eternity before you were able to swallow. It was fatty and far too raw for my particular palate. Still I forced it down and then a flagon of the wine was handed to me. I looked inside expecting blood, but instead it was a pale yellow liquid, looking too close to urine for my liking. It was very cold and despite looking fairly disgusting it tasted of lemon. I asked what it was, only to be told it was 'the ale of the earth'.

It felt as if I had been there only ten or fifteen minutes, yet when I got my watch back I found it had been almost an hour and a half. I said my goodbyes, was blindfolded again after being allowed to dress for my return trip. I had planned to take the registration number of the van, but the plates were obscured with rags. On my journey home they gave no clues as to where I had been, nor as to where I would be dropped off. The girl was willing to talk about her favourite television shows or pop music, and it was as if what had gone on that night was second nature to her. Rather like how going to church is for Christians. She had been, and now she wanted to talk about other things. This all opened my eyes and made me even more wary of dismissing the so called magical and mystical out of hand. These had been highly intelligent people, no mugs, who had devoted their lives to a creed that very few accepted as the norm. They were totally sincere in their beliefs. They seemed to wish no harm to anyone, yet stood apart from society, despite living amongst us. I never set eyes on those people ever again, save one exception. I was visiting a Night Owl who was in hospital at Newcastle's General Hospital and there, dressed as a nurse, was the young girl who had accompanied me in the van. She pretended not to know me, but her eyes gave away that she did.

My preconceptions of phone-in shows were much the same as everyone else's, believing them to be nothing but endless streams of drunks, hordes of pre-pubescent teenagers wanting to swear and the mind-numbingly boring depressives droning on about the latest part of their anatomy that is causing them distress. Getting rid of the drunks was easy. The telephonists can tell how 'together' they are. If they sound like fun, they're welcome and we'd share a few laughs. If they couldn't string a sentence together they were politely advised not to go on. Within two months we had no drunks at all.

The only gadget that any self-respecting phone-in host has is a digital delay system, a clever piece of software linked to your recording desk that delays what you broadcast for up to twelve seconds. Therefore if someone says something offensive you can, if you want, cut it out of the broadcast altogether. Usually, if someone does make an outrageous statement you leave it in. There is nothing more likely to have people racing for their telephones in droves. There was the lapsed Catholic lady in her sixties who caused dozens of complaints when I had a visiting clergyman in the studio answering calls. He had pontificated about how no one could possibly get into Heaven unless they accepted Jesus Christ as saviour. Instantly we had calls from Jews, Muslims, Hindus, Buddhists and a particularly uncool member of the Hari Krishna Temple in Newcastle. They despised this Christian's seeming un-Christian arrogance that unless everyone believed what he believed they would burn in hell. Finally this little old lady, Vera from Consett, called in to explain how her life had been changed by religion. At first the guest clergyman paid her polite lip service as she waded into how as a child she'd been forced into Catholicism by her parents, made to recite the creed, declaring that the Catholic God was the only God. It was when her marriage didn't work that she finally found herself an outcast for seeking a divorce. Her priest had visited her home, where she was trying desperately to raise her five young children on her own, to try and win a reconciliation. This was a total waste of time as her husband had run off to Manchester with a younger woman. They had been married only seven years and had five children. This all happened in the 1950s when more Catholics adhered to the rules against contraception, so despite being a low-income family they ended up with more children than they could afford to look after properly. Expecting sympathy and help from her Church, Vera received only a lecture on how bad a wife she must have been. Vera carried on explaining how that priest had made her feel cheap and dirty, making it understood how she would not be welcome in his church if she continued to try and end her marriage. She was the victim, yet here was the Church that she had supported for all of her 37 years putting the boot in!

She never did return to church, not any church, and instead she had given great thought to people's beliefs over the following 20 to 30 years. At this point the quietly spoken lady asked if she could talk to the clergyman, and I was happy to sit back and let her subtly take the pompous man apart. First she asked if he believed that the

Devil was a cunning creature, capable of immense Evil? He accepted that as a fact. Then she quizzed him if he believed in both the Old and New Testaments? Once again he affirmed his total belief in both of those sizable tomes. As delicately as a surgeon this lady began tying him in philosophical knots. Having stressed his belief in the Bible, she asked him what he thought of a man who could murder little children. The clergyman began droning on about man's inhumanity to man, how this all came about because of 'free will' given to man by God. Vera stopped him dead in his tracks saying 'God made man in *his* image. Therefore if man is evil, God must be evil too!' From that point the clergyman reacted rather like a man on a lake with a leak in his dinghy. He flapped and flustered, he tried to keep going but everyone could hear he was sinking. Finally Vera carried out a complete hatchet job on God and Jesus Christ adding, 'God killed those little babies, the first born of every household. He drowned those people following Moses, he killed millions of men, women, children and animals of all kinds in the Great Flood. We hate Hitler yet he hasn't killed half as many as God!'

The clergyman tried desperately to calm her, as she began to overwhelm him. 'Surely you can't be well,' he said, his voice as sickly as a treacle sandwich. 'God loves us all. He loves you too!'

Unperturbed, Vera carried on. 'What kind of man would torture his own son, claiming that it would stop us sinning! It didn't stop us, did it? So at very best God is an abject failure!'

I watched this rather cocky clergyman turn white with fear, knowing that his congregation and his superiors would be listening to his utter and complete destruction. Vera ended by suggesting that if the Devil really was as cunning as the clergyman had amitted, perhaps he was calling himself God!

'Turn back to God,' croaked the weary clergyman. 'Only then will your life be fulfilled!'

By this time the caller was in no mood to be condescended to.

'Alan, listen to this brain-washed baboon. It is as if they are deaf to the truth. While I was a staunch member of my Church my sister was raped, my mother died of cancer, my father died soon after of a broken heart. I suffered two miscarriages, my eldest daughter lost her leg in a car accident, my only son contracted leukaemia and due to the breakdown of my marriage I lost my home, my business and my car. Each time I prayed to God for help. He's not there, he's not anywhere. Only someone cruel could possibly ignore prayers so desperately delivered!' Vera thanked me for giving her the chance to speak and disappeared into the night, leaving me sitting next to a clergyman looking ill and visibly shaken.

As is the nature of *Night Owls* the following calls were not directed at the guest. We had a young man saying 'Alan did you hear about the blind prostitute . . . well, you had to hand it to her!' quickly followed by a woman complaining about how male drivers never indicate. So my guest sat quietly sipping a hot cup of coffee provided by Alice who was in charge of the telephones that evening. It was getting closer and closer to 2 a.m. and the end of the show when my next caller was a young girl called Julie. I had actually met this girl at several guest appearances. She had entered competitions and once had taken part in a beauty pageant I was involved in. On realising who it was, I smiled, because she was a real firebrand of humour, happy go lucky and game for a laugh.

'Alan . . . is that you . . .'

She sounded different, and my guts turned like a tumble drier as I waited for her to speak again.

'Alan I've just been raped!' Her voice disappearing into nothing.

Although I had been doing the show for almost three years, I had never been confronted with someone who had been the victim of rape, least of all someone that I knew. It seemed that Vera's earlier call where she had mentioned her sister's assault had acted as the catalyst for Julie's call. Now it was my turn to be terrified. There was this huge responsibility and it had been presented to me. All I had ever wanted from the show was light and bright entertainment mixed with the occasional serious debate, yet already it had grown far beyond that. It seemed that people trusted me, they had faith that when the chips were down that I would be able somehow to help. There at my right was a clergyman, his mouth agape at such a desperate call, and there somewhere out in the darkness was this girl, alone, abused and hurting!

What could I do?

How could I help?

I was a man, and it was a man who had attacked her, yet above all others she had come to me!

Sometimes in all of our lives we need something to cling to, someone to hold on to, to pick up pieces and point the way ahead.

At this moment I felt as if it was inevitable that I would let her down. No matter what I did or said she still had been raped. I couldn't undo it. I have always had a fierce hatred for those that carry out such atrocities, and have always said so, yet nothing had prepared me for this. The coward in me started seeking refuges, ways to move the pressure elsewhere.

'Tell your parents. They will help you.' It was a pathetic sentence, but all my feeble mind had to offer.

Through the tears Julie replied: 'My family live in Suffolk, I'm a student at Durham University!'

Still panicking for a way out, I tried another total cop-out. 'What about your friends? Surely they can help you?'

'I can't tell them. I'd just left my boyfriend ten minutes before. I can't face anybody. I can't!' Once again she broke down and sobbed.

As there had been no escape for her, there was none for me.

Yet it was the clergyman who kick started me into action. He gesticulated that I should let him speak to her.

'Julie . . . it is Julie, isn't it?' enquired my guest.

There was a noise similar to that of 'yes'.

'What you must remember Julie is that no matter what has happened you must be strong!'

Finally, the clergyman had made a statement that I actually agreed with. Then he spoiled it all.

'We must pity the man that has done this to you and seek to forgive him in our hearts. In life we all suffer so many things . . .'

At this I interjected: 'Pity him, forgive him . . . You stupid fool, what have you suffered? Blisters on your backside from doing nothing?'

Julie was crying so much she was gasping for air.

'Julie, listen to me.' At last I was talking with conviction. 'We need to get help to you. Do you understand?'

While I waited for her to reply, I switched off my microphone and shouted through to Alice on the switchboard. 'Get the police to trace this call. She needs help!'

'We can't,' came Alice's response. 'I forgot to take her number!'

'Shit!' I barked. 'Get on to Telecom. They must track her down!' I tried to hold on to that call as long as I could to give them a chance to find her. She had phoned me whilst drowning in a sea of trouble that men couldn't in their wildest dreams imagine the full horror of. I was the rock she had needed to cling on to. I had to be strong enough to hold on to her until she was helped. The clock seemed to whir around. It was a minute to 2 a.m. and I ended the show but begged Julie to hold on.

After the news, Alice helped my guest to reception and out of the building. I must admit that I didn't even say goodbye. All of my attention was with Julie who was still alone and frightened. By this time I was in the telephonist's office, separated from the main studio by a huge soundproofed glass screen. By this time two officers from the local police force had heard the broadcast and wanted to know if they could help. Other women who had suffered similar attacks flooded the switchboard offering their help. Finally, I said, 'Listen Julie. Where are you? I'll come and get you right now!'

'Just you though, no one else . . .' came her squeaking reply.

'All right. Where are you now?' and I scribbled down the general area where she was in a phone box on the outskirts of Durham City.

The police officer tried to read my scrawl, insisting that he could have a car at her location within minutes. It would have been the easy way out, the escape that I had been seeking, but I couldn't do it. I had given her my word, promising that I would go there alone. My young telephonist, Alice, warned me against going saying, 'She could say it was you. Take a policeman with you!' She was right, but I felt that I had to be true to what I had said. Within seconds I was dashing from the building having asked Alice to ring Telecom and the Durham police to call off the search. I begged them to go on hold. I might need them later that night.

At the time I drove a silver Honda Prelude. It featured on the publicity photograph I had signed for Julie only months earlier. Hopefully, she would recognise the car as I was worried that I wouldn't be able to follow the scant directions that I had been given. Leaving my case full of letters, records and CDs in Metro Radio's main reception, I tore away from the car park, along the dual carriageway towards Durham. Fortunately at that hour in the morning there weren't many cars on the road, and I really put my foot down. Within twenty minutes I was driving as instructed past Durham's Dunelm House, up the bank and around a corner and there fifty yards along the road stood a phone box. I expected her to still be there, but it looked empty. Several of the street lights were broken, casting long dark shadows across the street. There were half-a-dozen cars parked haphazardly along the roadside as I stopped the car some twenty yards from the box. I put my headlights on main beam, hoping to catch some glimpse of Julie. I seemed to sit there for hours, yet in reality it could only have been moments.

Although I had only ever met this girl on half-a-dozen occasions, I could remember her quite vividly. At a rock party at Sunderland Mecca she had taken part in a comedy version of *Gone with the Wind*. I had given her the part of Scarlett O' Hara. She had been the perfect stooge, as I entertained the crowd by reading out my rather mucky story version, asking members of the audience to act it out. It had been hilarious. She had also turned up in a competition to find 'Miss Hot 'n' Heavy Express', not winning, but enjoying a funny night and helping selecting Mr Wimp at the same event.

In much the same way that people feel that they 'know' a phone-in presenter, I felt that I 'knew' her. If I could possibly help her I would, whatever it took. It was then that I spotted something moving to my right. There in the very bottom of the telephone box sat Julie. Her hands clutched her knees tightly to her chest. She could barely see through her tangles of brown mousy hair that hung over her arms and knees. I left the keys in the car with the engine still running and raced over to her, opening the heavy red door. Nothing could possibly have prepared me for that moment: there on the ground was all that was left of Julie, her eyes crazed and frightened, staring up at me as if I was about to hurt her all over again. She wore a dark grey fluffy jumper over a pair of washed-out jeans, and stayed huddled in the corner of that filthy phone box, sitting on a floor covered with dirt, saliva and drunken urination.

What do I do now?

Should I lift her up?

Do I sit there with her?

My mind flooded with possibilities yet none sat right with me. Instead of reaching out, I simply said, 'Julie come with me'. To my surprise she got to her feet. I wanted to hold her, I wanted to squeeze the very life out of her, I wanted to take on just some of the pain that she was carrying. I wanted to make a difference. She stepped out of the phone box, her hands completely covered by the long arms of that pullover and her jeans all muddied and wet, and slowly stumbled towards the car. She almost jumped out of her skin when I ran past her to open the passenger door and guided her into her seat. This wasn't how it happened on television, where the girl's bright chiffon dress is torn away, the almost romantic quality television and films give to even the most violent of attacks. I thought that they could only have been directed by men. What the fuck do they know?

I was angry, totally and utterly, as I saw what a man had done to her. She never spoke a word. She just sat there, accepting that I would know what to do. I didn't!

This laughing chatterbox of a girl, always full of joy had become an empty shell. She was now the opposite of what she once was and couldn't help herself. Once she had been like a leaf on a tree, full of life, full of colour, strong and healthy. Now, the least touch and she would disintegrate before my eyes. Purposefully, I drove to the outskirts of Durham, as if I knew what I was doing, until I saw a parking area with a bright spotlight up ahead. As I pulled up I noticed a look of panic on Julie's face. Her mascara had run in every direction and under the light I saw that her eye was badly swollen and the entire inside of her bottom lip was bleeding.

Gradually the story came out. 'I've known him for three terms,' she whispered. 'He's in my lecture group. I'd just been up to my boyfriend's house and he was there. When I started off home he said to Chris that he'd see me home safe because he lives just along the road. When we got to the door of my flat he asked if he could use my toilet. So I showed him where it was while I put my coat away. I've got a little bedsit . . .' The tears started to fall and it took several minutes before she picked up the thread again. 'I was waiting by the kitchen door for him to come out of the toilet, and when he did he put his arm around me and kissed me on the cheek. It's the thing that everybody does. It's just friends, nothing more. Then he said that he'd always fancied me, that I should go out with him instead of Chris. Then he said that he was staying the night and he pushed me on to the sofa and started grabbing me!'

She was inconsolable for almost fifteen minutes, crying and

retching by the roadside, vomiting all over the inside door of the car. The only cloth I had was a yellow polishing rag and it left tiny yellow fluff on her mouth and face after she had wiped herself.

Then she began to shake, not violently at first, but it built up more and more and more as she stumbled from the car onto a grass verge. 'He raped me,' she sobbed. 'He's in my house and he raped me! He said that he'd tell everybody that I was begging him for it. He said that Chris knew that I fancied him, that Chris wanted me to do it!' She was beginning to show more uneasiness. 'But they'll let him off. He'll say I let him and he'll get off with it. He will, and they'll blame me for leading him on. I didn't, Alan. Honest I didn't . . .'

I explained that normally the police would prosecute, and if they didn't *she* could prosecute him herself. I wasn't sure how much she fully understood, but knew that she had to get this scumbag off the streets if she possibly could.

'We must get you to a hospital,' I said, realising that the injuries to her mouth must be serious to cause that amount of blood to leak out of her.

As her head cradled deeper into my armpit, she said almost sleepily, 'Please let me get a bath first. I feel dirty. I just want a bath first!'

I wanted so much to say that she could, but I believed that perhaps there were more horrors to come that night. The police might need samples of what was inside her so they could prosecute the sod who had attacked her. I tried as gently as I could to broach the subject of getting him arrested. It met with fierce rejection.

'No I don't want to go to the police!' she screamed.

'That means this man will think he can take you whenever he wants. Let's you and I sort him out once and for all!'

A huge tear was appearing from her eye as she finally nodded. After a few moments I kissed her gently on the top of her head and guided her to her feet. We walked to the car as if we had been fused into one person. As I turned the car around and headed to the hospital I remember talking to her, calmly and quietly, about thousands of things, trivial things, trying to make her look beyond that night, anything to stop her from thinking about what the rest of that night would have in store for her. As we approached the accident and emergency unit of the hospital she latched on to my arm saying, 'You won't leave me will you?'

I wanted the nightmare to end almost as much as Julie did but was determined to see it through. 'We'll do it together!' As we left that car I felt really proud of her as she headed into the unknown. I could understand how 30–40 per cent of rape victims don't report their assaults, choosing to try and bury the hurt inside themselves rather than face up to such a harrowing ordeal. At the desk I tried to do all of the talking until the cold but efficient receptionist asked for full name, address and other details that only Julie could answer. To my surprise she rose from the chair to stride up to my side and calmly helped complete the red tape. As we sat there for almost fifteen minutes waiting for a doctor to appear, I asked if she would allow me to contact some of my friends at the police. 'Will my mum find out?' asked Julie, going off at a tangent.

'Not if you don't want her to,' I answered, 'but can I get the police to pop here for a chat?'

Julie gave a brave little half-smile, making a gooey drip of thick blood slide from the corner of her battered mouth.

An Asian doctor appeared and took Julie to a cubicle, swishing the curtains closed behind them. I asked the receptionist to phone the police, only to be directed to the public telephones. I had to run out to the car to scrat for what little change I had in the glove compartment. Finally, the police arrived, having already been placed on stand-by, thanks to their colleagues at Whickham who had called at the radio station.

When the doctor examined Julie, he found that not only had she been raped but the man had inserted something inside her that had ripped open her insides. She needed fourteen internal stitches and eight stitches in her lip, had fractured her jaw and one of her teeth had been snapped in half. She would have to stay in hospital that night, making a statement from her bedside. It was almost 6.30 a.m. when she asked me to go to her flat to collect some things. It was just along the street from where she had phoned, so she gave me a Yale key from a key fob on her jeans and off I headed.

I was half-way there when I remembered what she had said about the rapist. How he was going to stay the night. He might still be there. Fear ate away at my insides, mixing with a huge proportion of anger. After I had parked I took out a tyre lever from my boot and walked up to the door. It was a heavy wooden door that opened with a dull creak. In the half light of early morning the brown carpet was almost invisible beneath my feet. I walked up to the bedsitting room. It was empty. What I would have done had he been there, to this day I still don't know. I like to believe that I would have had the courage to kill him!

I returned to the hospital with a plastic carrier bag full of underwear, toiletries and the only night gear I could find, a well-worn pair of striped pyjamas. I wasn't allowed to see her because she had been given an injection to help calm her and she was asleep.

By the time I got home it was almost 9 a.m. and I had promised to be back that afternoon. There was just enough time for a shave, a bath and a change of clothes before I was on the road back to Durham once again. When I walked in to see her, clutching a bunch of mixed flowers and a huge bag full of fruit, I almost walked past her bed. She was unrecognisable. Her face was swollen and shining all of the colours of the rainbow. Her lip jutted out like an open till, the black stitches visible for all to see. She tried to talk, but could only slur her words. I sat next to the bed only to be asked to leave by the police, who wanted to take more statements from her. Screens were drawn around her bed as Julie remonstrated against my removal. Finally she got her way, so instead I stood back while they asked a variety of very intimate and personal questions. Not only did Julie convince the police that she was telling the truth, she even added, 'If you don't prosecute him, I will!'

To explain how I felt isn't easy. Maybe it was like how parents feel when their child passes their exams.

I visited Julie for the three days she was in hospital and even took her boyfriend in to see her. She finally had the guts to tell him about the entire episode and rather than dump her as she thought, it brought them closer together. They attended counselling for almost a year. I kept in touch by telephone until the case was brought to court. The rapist was found guilty and sentenced to five years. It should have been fifty. Apart from the rape he admitted inserting a sharpened metal comb inside her that had caused horrendous internal injuries.

This one call generated hundreds of others from women who had also been assaulted, leading to many having the courage to prosecute their attackers.

Usually when you've got involved with people, as soon as their lives begin to get back as close to normal as is possible you lose contact with them. Yet some six years later in 1991, totally out of the blue and live on air Julie told me that she had married Chris and that four months previous she had given birth to a fat and healthy baby girl. She was in the North-East to spend time with Chris's family and had decided to give me a call. I'm glad to say that even the most awful stories can still have a happy ending.

I know it changed Julie, and I would never ever be the same man again.

One of the more sickening so-called sports is the vicious practice of dog fighting, and I found myself aware of this very early on in my *Night Owl* career. Often we'd hear of vans cruising around estates picking up stray dogs and cats, and taking them away. On many occasions we could track them as they headed across the North acting like unofficial dog/cat catchers. Some callers said it served the owners right for allowing their animals out, yet I am sure that none would have wished these animals the fate that would befall them. Sometimes cats were stolen and killed and their skins flown to Germany to make coats, but more often than not it was dog fighters stealing dogs. These people want and need to give their fighting animals a taste of blood, so what better way than giving them a pet dog to rip to pieces? Some family's friendly spaniel and even labradors trained to be guide dogs were used in this barbaric way.

On one night alone over 200 pets were snatched. The smaller dogs were killed and used as meat, as were the bigger animals after they had been shredded by the vicious fighting animals. One dog fighter said on the show: 'We can't afford expensive steaks to feed our animals, so we pick up the unwanted pets from the street. It's a public service really. The cats we skin and then microwave. It's a good diet for the dogs. Remember, if our dog wins it can earn us up to £200,000!' It is not just a sport for dumb bumpkins down a back alley doing it for a depraved laugh. It is big business, backed by seriously wealthy sickos. I did everything I could to find out more, including tipping off the police on several occasions as to the whereabouts of the fighting pits, and the precise times of fights. Some were on the banks of the River Wear, others in North Northumberland, South Durham, the North Riding of Yorkshire, and across in Cumbria. I was causing quite a stir, having received some vile letters and some straightforward death threats. On one occasion I returned to my car to find it covered in animals' blood. Behind the windscreen wiper was a typed note: 'This blood could easily be yours!'

It took me a few days to calm down over that one, but soon I was back hammering out warnings and asking for information to stop them in any way I could.

That following weekend I was the guest of honour at a country fayre near Alnwick. The hunting, shooting and fishing brigade were out in force and I'd performed on stage for two hours, spending a further forty-five minutes solidly signing autographs. Feeling really good about the day, I started walking back over the fields to my car. Halfway across the field a Land Rover pulled alongside, and from the passenger window the twin barrels of a shotgun were pointed directly at me. A man in his forties with a flat cap pulled low over his eyes barked: 'Listen you cunt, stop messing with us dog fighters or we'll fucking kill you.' As they drove away I heard them both laughing, while I took the Land Rover's registration number.

To say I was frightened is an understatement, but at times like that you must defend yourself as best you can. My only hope was to get them arrested. Before the vehicle was off the field I had reported this to a police officer who had been standing less than thirty feet from me during their intimidation of me. I pointed to the Land Rover: 'Look, there they are, stop them, arrest them, they've got a shotgun!'

The policeman grinned. 'Look, half the people here have got shotguns. It's a country fayre!'

'But they threatened to kill me!' I yelled.

Some members of the public still lingered around, so I controlled my anger, as he explained how he would take the vehicle registration number and follow it up. He said someone would come and take my statement, yet they never did.

Two weeks later, I tipped off the authorities about a dog fight in Redcar. Over thirty people were arrested and eight dogs seized and destroyed. To this day I still get threatening letters from the same people. I like to feel the numbers have reduced because we're watching out for them.

* * *

Ever seeking a new angle for the late night phone-in, I decided to tap into the phenomenon of UFOs. Having heard of burn marks in fields in Hexham, cattle rippings in Northumberland and sightings across the North, I decided to put the entire subject under the microscope.

My first foray was to arrange a regional UFO hunt. On hearing from a local observatory that there was to be a major meteor storm the following month, everything was arranged. The place for our search was to be Penshaw Hill, a mound with a huge Victorian folly standing on top of it. A few miles outside Sunderland, it was the perfect viewpoint and gathering place for the thousands that would turn up.

Jim Brown, the outside broadcast producer, drove the Espace filled with sound equipment up the precarious and steep slope, then extended the huge aerial from its roof. He also positioned a small tent at the edge of the incline to act as a wind break. Jayne Steel, that evening's telephonist, accompanied me on foot along with hundreds of people who were thronging to the site. It was a bitterly cold night and cars from as far afield as Sheffield and Leeds were heading north, while vehicles from the Scottish borders headed south. By the time we reached the summit we estimated about 3,000 people to be on the hill, with hundreds more jamming roads in all directions. This was our great UFO hunt. The call went up to 'Watch the Skies', we all did, but couldn't see a single thing for clouds. We had other smaller observation points all having the very same problem. We knew that of all nights that would be the one with certain results, for if all else failed hundreds of meteors were going to pass overhead. This they did, but not a soul actually saw one.

As an event it was never going to happen, because unbeknown to us, the top of Penshaw Hill was used by drunks, drug addicts and glue sniffers and we found ourselves surrounded by about 90 of them. They hadn't a clue what was going on, but just kept drinking, using and sniffing until they reached the obnoxious state. Then all they wanted was trouble. We kept the programme running, despite getting the odd kick in the back through the tent. I went out to sort them out on three occasions, when they all pretended not to be guilty. Finally, as it was getting really rowdy, I made the executive decision to get the hell out. I couldn't keep attracting people to a place that I no longer considered safe, particularly as many people were bringing their small children with them for a 'fun night out'. That's what my target had been, but this really missed by a mile.

Instead, we drove at speed to our other UFO sky-watch site on Newcastle's Town Moor. The show sounded all right, but much of the excitement was still happening at Penshaw Hill where the huge 30-foot aerial had been snapped off the van, some sound equipment was stolen and the tent full of our gear had been kicked down the hill.

This was my biggest disaster and every subsequent outside broadcast would be scrutinised down to the most minute detail. Yet another lesson had been learned. The people that had taken part understood that we had tried our best, but it just hadn't worked. Another direct example of what we see around us every day: out of the 5,000 people who visited that hill to have fun, it was spoiled by a handful of wasters.

On many occasions callers to *Night Owls* have witnessed strange lights in the sky and in as many incidents as possible we have uncovered all kinds of fascinating things, more usually emanating from earth. We were told by several people that UFOs regularly flew down the Tyne Valley in the early hours of the morning, always at the same time between 1 a.m. and 3 a.m. So I recruited the listening hordes to follow them, watch them, photograph them if possible. The results were like something out of *Close Encounters of the Third Kind*: helicopters leapfrogging each other with spotlights aimed earthwards, strange flashes from the sky and a deep heavy rumbling noise that some callers said 'shook the house'. I started digging, despite a great deal of secrecy and a few people telling us things like 'We know what it is and it's nothing to worry about!' That was like waving a red rag to a bull. Surely if there was nothing to worry about, then they would be able to tell us exactly what it was? Finally, we were informed that nuclear waste was travelling through the region, and it was being watched closely to make sure it was safe. This was strenuously denied, as government ministers had sworn that the practice of taking such waste through built-up areas had been stopped. Well, coincidence or not, since we announced it on air, it never happened again.

One of the more amazing stories involved a bus mechanic from

Morpeth in Northumberland called Steve, who used to regale us with really funny tales, yet he had a run-in with a UFO. He told us how one night his car was actually pursued by a 'bright light' and eventually his engine cut out. He was petrified by the experience and once the craft had vanished, he discovered that so severe had been the heat the boot of his Granada was all blistered and burnt.

I hate to admit this, but one night I decided to see just how far I could go to create what I can only describe as 'mass hypnosis'. We'd had a couple of really heavy nights on *Night Owls* discussing various gynaecological subjects, mixed with politics and child sex abuse, so I had to find something to change tack. I decided that I would invent a UFO sighting over the Scottish border country. There never was any sighting – I merely said there was and asked people to look out and see it. I described it as a 'long thin craft with blue and green flashing lights'. I said it could be clearly seen and asked callers to ring in and tell us the direction so we could keep tabs on it. We were completely flooded by calls as we monitored this 'alien craft' from Scotland to Yorkshire, back up the North-East coast, then finally out to sea and away. Some women in a block of flats in Newcastle insisted that it was level with their windows and they could see brown-skinned aliens looking in. They did sound truly terrified and I was beginning to worry about this monster I had literally created. In every call, without exception, they described the exact type of spacecraft I had etched in their minds. One lorry driver stopped his truck near Scots' Gap to ring in to say his wagon had been buzzed by it. Airports were phoned, police stations had numerous reports and by the end of the show I was asking, 'So have we been visited for the very first time by beings from another world?' The audience regularly wound me up with stories, and this time I had turned them over good and proper. This rebounded on me slightly the following day when I received phone calls at home from all of the local papers and most of the nationals. Some used it as a front-page story about how thousands of people had witnessed this craft from beyond the stars. We let the press use the story, then after they'd sucked all of the juice out of the tale I came clean on air. By that time we could all have a good laugh about it. The very next caller after my confession said, 'You rotten bugger, I've never believed in that type of thing, but you had me convinced!' It was interesting to note that not one of the newspapers ever printed that it was a hoax, choosing to kid themselves and their readers that it was genuine, rather than lose face.

I have always had an open mind about outer space, and as to whether there is life on other planets, yet some months later I did witness something very peculiar. I was still living in a small two-bedroom semi in Cramlington, and on driving along the bottom road from the Holiday Inn I noticed something in the sky heading towards me. As Cramlington is on the main flight path in to Newcastle Airport I thought nothing of it until I was driving up the slip road. On getting to the top I saw a huge craft with four wings. It wasn't just flying ahead, but spinning around too. I actually stopped the car, got out and stared at it as it seemed to fly very slowly overhead, no higher than 300 feet. I remember looking around for anybody else to say 'Hell's bells look at that thing!' There was no one about, and I knew the following evening when I mentioned it on air that I would be classed as just another loony! I was. Thinking back, maybe someone/something somewhere had been aware of my hoax and decided to pay me back.

In amongst all of these wacky tales, I was racing out after shows to talk down suicidal men wanting to leap off the Tyne Bridge, zooming out to remove abused children from their homes, helping battered women escape from brutal husbands, and anything else that was asked of me. I seemed to be everyone's last option, a huge weight I often found it difficult to carry. There never seemed to be any time for me to deal with my own sackful of worries and stress.

19 The Metro Years

WHEN I FIRST STARTED doing the *Night Owls* phone-in, I tried to make sure that I had read every single newspaper that I could, watched every documentary, studied each news report and checked with our journalists to see what was happening locally. Then one evening in 1986 I received a call from a young man who wished to remain anonymous. He explained how a particularly vivid dream had frightened him. He said: 'Alan, I know that somebody famous is going to die. I know he is. Don't ask me how, but I do!' I treated this with a fair degree of scepticism, but he did give some specifics: 'He's a huge Hollywood star and I know he's 82.' Six days later, on 30 November, screen-idol Cary Grant died aged 82.

Dozens of callers bombarded the switchboard, each one shocked at the accuracy of this prediction. I rang this so-called 'seer' back, but there was no answer. It was the following February before he returned to the show with a bigger horror that he'd dreamed: 'I can see hundreds of people in the water. They're all trying to swim, but it's freezing cold. They're shouting, screaming. What can I do?'

He wanted to warn someone, but didn't know what ship it would be, nor where in the world it was. Because of his previous success we were less inclined to doubt him, all we could do was hope that he was wrong! Several callers rang in to say that he hadn't actually had a vision, he'd merely dreamt about the movie *The Poseidon Adventure* as it had been on television the previous night.

Imagine our horror then, when eight days later on 6 March

1987 the *Herald of Free Enterprise* ferry capsized outside Zeebrugge harbour killing some 200 people.

Then in October 1987, in the middle of a particularly funny *Night Owls* programme, the mood was brought down with a bump when the seer returned. 'I've had another dream,' he said.

He had been right on the nose with his previous two – who would take odds against him now? 'I see a big procession,' he whispered. 'I see flags flying and soldiers marching. I see Mrs Thatcher and Mr Kinnock standing together. I see the Queen with a wreath. There is a huge flash and bodies lying everywhere!'

I quickly asked if the Queen or any of the politicians would be injured.

He replied, 'No, they're not even there!' This confused me, so I asked what else he saw?

'Bodies of women, little children cut and bleeding, arms ripped from bodies. It's sick, it's really sick!'

This self-proclaimed visionary had a faultless record and we steadied ourselves for the headlines to come, and come it did! On 8 November 1987 during the Remembrance Day parade in Enniskillen in County Fermanagh an IRA bomb exploded, killing eleven innocent people and badly injuring 63 others. The prophet of doom had been exactly right again. The 'seer' only surfaced once more, claiming that a star with the initials FS would die early in the New Year. We all jumped to the conclusion it was Frank Sinatra, but no star died and the 'seer' vanished without a trace.

The Zeebrugge ferry disaster would lead me into a war of words with several people including Boy George, who was on the verge of one of his comebacks. A record was cut to raise money for the victims and I promptly refused to play it. I had some very good and sound reasons why I had made such a decision, but the newspapers never even asked me, instead they slated me. One, the *Shields Gazette*, never even spoke to me. Instead, they put on their front page: 'VILE ATTACK BY LOATHSOME DJ'. Within the week Boy George gave a quote – 'He must be sick!' – and all of the other newspapers followed suit with similarly cutting articles. Yet *not one* actually called me to allow me to give my side of the story. The families of the victims of the Zeebrugge ferry disaster were all being given an interim settlement by the ferry company, with a final figure to be decided upon later. Even so, no amount of money can ever replace a life lost. What many didn't know was that another man lost his life that night off the North-East coast. No helicopters could search for his missing boat because they were at Zeebrugge helping with the rescue. One of his friends had called the show telling me how his wife had no insurance, because his occupation was too risky. She had nothing, she was left to look after her family without her man, and could lose her house. She would get nothing from anyone. Surely this was unfair? Do you have to die in the sea in the South before anyone will help you? This man was also a victim of the Zeebrugge ferry disaster: who knows if he could have been saved, had those helicopters been available? All I wanted was that the monies raised over and above the final settlement figure should go into a fund to be used to help the families of those lost at sea, wherever in Britain that happened. My intentions were not 'vile' nor 'loathsome', yet journalists enjoyed their savage attack on me, and it hurt me very much. I had discussions with the Dover ferry fund co-ordinator, explained the situation to him, and he promptly agreed with me. Within a week it was all in place. I notified the *Shields Gazette* and they never printed a word. To their credit, the other newspapers proclaimed 'a great victory for justice and common sense'. It was a complete turnaround for them, but at least they covered it. Once again, the press had shown a disregard for the truth. Instead of seeking it out, they had merely made it up as they went along.

The huge phone-in audience latches on to every major news item and discusses it in depth. Such certainly was the case following the Enniskillen bomb. The North has a huge Irish population and both Catholics and Protestants were swift to declare their outrage at yet another massacre of the innocents. Call after call they criticised and slagged the IRA and all the other terrorist groups on both sides, and I must admit I waded in with my two-pennyworth too. Having spoken to the relatives of two of the people who had died on the night it happened, I was angry and bitter over such moronic stupidity. I continued my tirade describing the bombers as 'pathetic cowards' while callers went even further. A Catholic man from Sheffield called them 'murdering bastards who would rot in hell!' The week that followed was a waterfall of direct attacks on the killers and it led to a very frightening situation. On the Sunday night on air a caller with an Irish accent said, 'I've given your girl the code word. In ten days' time I'm going to blow your knee caps off!' I took it to be a crank, yet following the show I discovered that the code word had been given. I contacted the police who told me that it was most likely just someone trying to intimidate me, and that I should ignore it. So I tried to, but the very next evening the switchboard received another call: 'In nine days' time we're going to blow his kneecaps off.'

Each evening this happened, sometimes on the switchboard, other times a message given to the security man downstairs, as the countdown to my crippling continued. Finally, as the last day neared I checked my diary: I was opening a charity shop in Byker in the morning, that afternoon I had a roadshow at a hypermarket and I was on air that evening. It wasn't hard for someone to plot my movements, the radio and newspapers were all advertising them. Trying to control what was, by that time certainly, very genuine fear I rationalised that perhaps being in public was my very best defence. So on checking with the police that morning, they promised that they would keep a close eye on me. If they did I wasn't aware of it, but maybe that was part of their plan. Maybe their men and women were part of the crowd. The charity guestie went very well, about 400 turned out to help launch a charity shop, and I left to make my way to the hypermarket. There the show was out of doors and a bit chilly, but it was fun, and I managed to keep my mind on my performance rather than the nagging doubt that someone was waiting to do me great harm. I had suffered a thousand threats in my time, but very few from such a dangerous source. I reached Metro FM at about 6.30 p.m. and stayed in, knowing that in five and a half hours their deadline would have passed. Maybe they were just trying, successfully, to frighten me. It was a Tuesday night and I phoned the police again, who said, 'See it was a hoax all along!' I asked if they could see me home safe later that night and they promised that they would, so all I could do was sit tight.

After preparing the show, I spent the rest of the evening in the canteen with the light off, staring through the window watching for any movement, any strangers, anything untoward. The moonlight fired streaks of light through the open blinds as I watched rabbits hopping around the car park and the occasional man walking his dog. I watched the night shift DJ arrive, and saw a few people drive up for stickers or signed photographs. My imagination began to run away with me. A man and woman parked a blue Sierra next to my car, and walked menacingly towards reception. He carried a parcel, she had her hand in a carrier bag, held tightly to her chest. Was that parcel a bomb? Was her hand clenched tightly to a gun? I didn't know who they were, yet they left the building within moments and drove off at speed. One of our security men brought the items upstairs and eventually located me in the canteen, saying they were for me. In the carrier bag was a huge fluffy toy rabbit, and the parcel contained about fifty packets of sweets for a hospice appeal in which I was involved. It took a truck-load of guts to open that box, I can tell you. I was shaking like an alcoholic going through detox. Each minute was like an hour as I sat in that room, listening to the traffic roaring along the bypass, watching the headlights zoom by, wishing I could just zoom away myself.

Finally, the telephonist arrived, totally unaware of my worries, and I took over the show at 10 p.m. and used it, as I often did, as the place to lose my worries. My stomach was squashing about once again and as 2 a.m. neared I began to shake so much I could hardly write. I have known fear of a thousand kinds in my life, but this was so sour I could taste it, my stomach flooding my mouth with it every now and again as I felt physically sick. I ended the show believing that once again I'd managed to shield the programme from my own problems, and now it was time to get home. I had a baseball bat in my boot and carried a long knife in the cab of the car. Had I been able to get myself a hand gun I would have taken it. The only weapon I could have obtained was a shotgun from a colleague who goes shooting, but it wasn't something you could hide. So before I left the building I watched out of the canteen window, waiting for the police who had promised to keep me secure on the way home.

At 2.05 a.m. a tiny panda car arrived, drove once around the car park then disappeared up the road. That was my security. So at about twenty past I decided to get home, running from the building to my car, snapping open the boot. As I placed my case and bag inside I almost fainted on hearing footsteps behind me. I grabbed the baseball bat and swung around, and there behind me was the watchman from a nearby factory. He screamed and backed off as I went for him: 'For fuck's sake, Alan, divvn't hit 'is.'

I recognised him and apologised, briefly explaining that someone had threatened me. 'Rather them than me, but take it easy son!' Then he clumped across the car park, waving at our security desk on his way back to patrol the yard. I felt foolish, perhaps the entire thing was crazy, maybe I had never been at risk at all. I slammed the boot shut, slid into the driver's seat and took off.

Each evening I had been taking different routes home to my little semi in Cramlington. The only place that remained constant was Scotswood Bridge, as the new bypass had yet to be completed. I was very peeved that the police had promised to help, yet on this occasion had failed to deliver. Then on crossing the Scotswood Bridge I noticed that two cars had started following me. I felt so relieved, the police had been waiting to follow me home. I was genuinely elated and kept looking back in my rear-view mirror saying to myself 'good lads' and feeling totally confident for the first time in ten days.

Then as we drove along Scotswood Road and the streetlights were brighter, I was able to see the type of cars behind me. I expected a traffic car or an unmarked Rover; instead to my horror I saw an A registration Cortina and a souped-up Ford Escort. There were two people in each car and they certainly weren't dressed as policemen. Once I got through Newcastle I decided to put my foot down at every opportunity and travelled at a ridiculous speed up the A1 roaring on to the slip road towards Seaton Burns Holiday Inn and driving for Cramlington town centre. Both cars were in hot pursuit and I was buzzing with a mixture of desperate fear and intense adrenalin following the show. It clears your mind like nothing else, and with the cars less than 100 yards behind me I screeched into the courtyard of Cramlington police station. I raced in and tried to explain as coherently as I could: 'I'm going to be shot, I've been chased, quick get more men, you're outnumbered!' The policeman totally unimpressed by my stark terror said, 'Now slow down son, what is it?' I gave a brief explanation and he seemed not to believe a word.

'So you've been chased by two cars full of terrorists, eh?'

I nodded, as he walked out beside me and towards the door. To the surprise of both us, there parked on the main road was the Cortina and the Escort, their windows wound down, the men inside laughing.

'Now had away,' said the policeman.

The two cars began slowly driving off, the driver of the Escort giving a high-fisted salute from out of the side-window.

'There you are, now get yourself home,' said the policeman.

I got into my car and drove the other way, going through Seaton Delaval, Dudley, along to Blyth then across to Bedlington until I was absolutely sure I wasn't being followed.

Three days later I received a Christmas Card from the IRA. I didn't believe such things existed, but there it was with the Irish tricolour and the black imprint of a terrorist holding up a rifle. Inside the wording was in Gaelic and I didn't know what it said. I had it translated on air by someone from Newcastle University. It said: 'There Are Always Two Sides To Every Story. You Have Been Warned.' I believed that this was a lesson in how to get your message across. Fear is a very effective form of intimidation. I haven't changed my views and my criticism remains constant, but it did take me a few months to regather my bottle following this, before continuing my onslaught. That day onwards I knew that as I was always out among people, I would always be a soft target. I have spoken to experts in self-defence, the police and many others about self-protection, and at one stage I even took up kung fu, but perhaps Doris Day was right: *Que Sera Sera*. Whatever will be will be!

Every single call that anyone makes to a phone-in show causes ripples somewhere, sometimes good, sometimes bad. What always surprises me is that the audience always chooses what runs, for if they don't wish to discuss a subject it disappears without trace.

One call seemed to really hit the mark. It was from a man in his middle forties who had been with his family to Plessey Woods near Bedlington in Northumberland, and there, in the middle of a bright sunny afternoon, they had seen a couple making love in the car. Totally oblivious to the swarms of people driving in and out of the woods, it rocked and rolled until the dirty deed was done. If people want to make love in cars I have no difficulty with that, but it seems obvious that you shouldn't do it where you'd be seen, least of all by young children.

Floods of calls agreed with the caller, and each asked what could be done to stop this kind of thing from happening again. So in jest I said, 'Why not have a great bonk alert? If anybody sees a car parked, take its colour, make and registration, then ring me and tell me where it was and I'll announce it.' Before I knew where I was it was happening, dozens every single night. I received calls from American television asking if I was a killjoy. Most certainly not, for one of my happiest frisky memories was up against a battered Metro down a country lane. I only wanted people to report those that didn't give a damn whether they were seen or not. This alert caused ructions. I never gave the full registration, instead I'd miss the letters off so you'd get, 'A black BMW is parked at Causey Arch, registration H556'. Then three calls later a woman came on: 'That's my husband, the bastard. He told me he was playing snooker! I'll pot his balls when he gets in. It's that bitch of a woman from his work, she lives near there!'

It may well have been compulsive listening but it was, well, dangerous, and there was a degree of inevitability that should I ever stop for a snog the press would be leaping out of every bush. Sexually, I'm not in the slightest repressed, but I do believe that the act of making love is a private one. It's not that I'm a great lover, it's just that it has the chance to be a glorious experience and shouldn't be cheapened by onlookers. The bonk alert ran for months and must have led to divorce, arguments, fights and I'd be surprised if someone hasn't been firmly hoofed in the wedding tackle. Big Brother wasn't watching, instead it was Big Alan!

This activity of censorship voyeurism became an active sport. People would take their dogs for a walk to all the well-known lovers' lanes, making a note of all of the makes and registration numbers, then race home to ring me. On at least one occasion it may have led to pregnancy. A man called Bryan from Perkinsville, Jarrow, wrote in. I still have his letter:

> Dear Alan
> I was parked in a really dark back street where no one ever walks. After the garage shuts, no one drives or walks anywhere near. Well, I had only an hour before starting nightshift at midnight, so I took my girlfriend down there, because we get no privacy at either of our houses because we still live with our parents. So there we are in the pitch-black, the radio was on low, and you were talking to various people. Now we're both Catholics so we use the withdrawal method of

> contraception. Well, I was just getting close when I heard my car being described by a woman who was watching us out of her window. Well, I just came, I couldn't help myself. As I was coming the girlfriend was screaming and tugging at her clothes, while I dived out of the car, my trousers around my ankles. Then on the radio I heard the woman say 'He's waddling about like a penguin, his trousers around his knees. Eeeh, I can see his thing!' Surely this has gone too far. Give us a break, we weren't actually in public. We both think it's funny now, but at the time it ruined a very special moment.

He was right. Then came calls from others who had suffered coitus interruptus. One said a woman had actually knocked on his car window screaming, 'If you don't stop that, I'll tell Alan!'

So really not wanting to stop the fun the region was having, I tried to take a step sideways. Yet each time I tried to move to something else, we'd get another batch of calls. Right from the beginning of my involvement with *Night Owls* it was obvious that the people had to be trusted to decide the way. On my very first show I had said, 'It's my first night tonight and let's talk about aeroplanes and travel.' It ended up being the only subject not one single person touched upon. Instead a caller said that taxi-drivers often accepted sex from drunken girls late on a Friday and Saturday night if they didn't have enough money. At this one of the girls who worked at a taxi office rang in, confirming that this was true. Up to two-thirds of all of her cabs could be tied up having sex at any one time. She named all of the places where they parked up, and once again we were doing for Relate, the Marriage Guidance Service, what King Herod did for Mothercare. Wives of taxi-drivers would lie in wait and take photographs of these cars and pass them on to the relevant wives and all hell would be let loose. What had been a throwaway remark had snowballed into remarkable radio but with devastating consequences.

On one occasion while I was live on air a caller from a mobile phone said that he was actually in the process of having sex at that very moment in Metro's car park. I asked security to check and there in a steamy blue mini were a couple who declared that the bonk alert had improved their sex lives. Because now making out in the car was riskier than ever, therefore more exciting.

Finally it petered out, if you'll pardon the pun, and the show headed back into general calls, until another subject would grip them, and then we'd be away again. There are a million stories, far too many to even think about listing.

The *Night Owls* Crazy Nights were well received, involving singers, musicians, jokes, anecdotes, poems – a sort of late night talent show. The good are usually excellent, the bad ones excruciating. One man who was in fact as loud as anyone I had ever heard genuinely believed he was terrific, and every Crazy Night he'd appear singing his heart out. I was happy to let him, despite some of the audience saying how bad he was. I was in the game of building people up, not knocking them down, so continued to encourage him. His name was Alfred, so I named him 'The Great Alfredo'. He only knew about four songs and once he said, 'I'm going to sing a song in Italian, but I don't know the words so I'll sing it in mock Italian.' I questioned what 'mock Italian' was, and he said, 'Words that sound as if they're right but don't mean anything!' It could only happen on *Night Owls*. I think he is brilliant, a genuine star, and he still honours me with a song.

Another man who people accept cannot sing, yet had a number one hit, is footballer Paul Gascoigne who has sung on Crazy Night too. I'd first met Paul at Metro's studios after months of having a go at him for his weight problems. He took it as a joke and we had a laugh about it. The next time we teamed up was following a call from a lady in Newcastle's West End, when he dived in to help. The lady's grandson was dying and the entire family were bringing Christmas forward, because they didn't think the gutsy young lad would still be with us then. I promised to come to the party and Denny Ferguson, who was in panto with me at the time, agreed to come too. After the show, Paul's girlfriend called to say that he'd like to come too, so we met up and joined in the family 'do'. Sadly, the bairn wasn't totally with it, but bless his heart he had a ball. The family were all dressed up, one as the littl'un's hero Batman. Paul took a batch of goodies, so did we and tried to make it extra special. To be honest, the family did that – had I not seen it I wouldn't have believed how much love you could get into a single house. The youngster did see Christmas too, proving just how brave he actually was.

Apart from charity football matches I wouldn't see much of Paul. So I was well pleased when he called up out of the blue from a party determined to have a bit of a crack. I asked him how things were going, then told him he was on a Crazy Night so had to sing or tell a joke. He decided to give us a very wobbly version of his record 'Geordie Boys' which was as funny as it was entertaining. Paul has the knack of singing without using proper notes.

Following Paul's call we got another from the self-same party, and a man, prompted by someone, told a dubious joke: 'Why didn't Jesus move to Saudi Arabia with his money?' Answer: 'He was frightened that he'd be hammered with tax.' Tasteless, not funny, but the kind of dopey joke that goes around at parties, particularly the ones where you sink a good few gallons of the loopy juice. Yet within two minutes of that call two national tabloid newspapers were on the phone, asking if the voice in the background prompting the joke was Paul Gascoigne? How would I know? Yet so desperate were they to find some mud to stick to him they harried and harassed the telephonist, Metro's security man and even called my home at 3.45 a.m. chasing a story that didn't exist. I was involved in panto at the time, and all the following day, freelance journalists were plaguing me in a way you would scarcely believe. Is it any wonder the likes of Paul get sickened by the constant hassle from these people? Each time, these so called investigative journalists twist words in an attempt to invent the kind of story they've already made their minds up about. The following day one of the papers had it on the front page in banner headlines: 'GAZZA IN RELIGIOUS JOKE FURY'. This was just prior to his move from Tottenham Hotspur to Lazio in Italy, a devoutly religious country, where this sort of publicity, had it been true, could've wrecked his move. The story was pure invention and I was involved in a legal case against the paper. Rather than tell the truth, that Paul in a daft mood had sung a song on air, they'd rather transform it into something far more damaging. Apparently the Italian newspapers had all picked up on it and it could have destroyed a multi-million dream move with wages that would make him secure for the rest of his life.

The following night Paul walked on stage at a full house of the panto at Newcastle's Playhouse, donating a performance to underprivileged kids and pensioners from Dunston. Not *one* single newspaper, local or national covered that. This says more about the press than anything else. We are fortunate in the North to have a few genuine reporters, yet others want the big name, and try to build it by carving a slice off the genuine people.

While Paul was on stage he kicked five or six footballs out to the crowd. I said to him, 'Watch the lights Paul.' No sooner said than a ball rebounded off the overhead gantry hitting me hard between the legs. Gazza must be a genius because it was such a small target.

The Robson clan has been heavily involved in the fighting forces over the generations, from way back when they were Border reivers. I never fancied the army myself, although it was suggested to me when it seemed likely that my exam results would be dubious. However, the nearest I got was one morning when I was called upon to do an outside broadcast on a bitterly cold Saturday morning. The venue was to be Gateshead's Team Valley Trading Estate and there I would be meeting up with the Parachute Regiment. I had already jumped from a balloon, parascended, hang glided, abseiled, etc., but that didn't prove that I had what it took for the forces, but I was fully qualified to deliver boxes of Milk Tray.

The Paras were there to gather any young people who were interested in joining and about 120 turned up, all well prepared for the frost of that mid-March morning, with vests under T-shirts under sweatshirts under jackets under kagouls. As for me, I had on a T-shirt and shorts as instructed by my outside broadcast producer, Big Jim Brown, who himself wore a vest under his T-shirt under his sweatshirt under his skiing jacket. I thought I'd really been set up until the Paras arrived, each one in a vest and shorts and cursing at the coldness of the bright sunny day.

I interviewed the commanding officers, chatted with the lads, was taught how to strip down an assault rifle and was then told that I had been challenged to see if I was made of 'the right stuff'. I had been doing a charity show in Middlesbrough the night before, not getting home until almost 4 a.m. and had had less than five hours' sleep. This really was all that I needed. The first challenge was a three-mile run, along with the other would-be Paras. I managed to keep up with everybody, beating most of the wannabes. Then came the crunch. Before we had time to regain our breath they began unloading a massive green truck and there were two large metal stretchers. Each one was made out of steel and had a huge weight welded to it. On my own I couldn't even lift an edge off the ground. Then I was told that we were going to run two miles carrying it! I really didn't want a hernia that badly, but the ego takes over and you go along rather than shame yourself. I tried to rationalise that they would never give me a task to perform that I couldn't do.

I watched the first of the young lads trying to do this. Only four managed and they were all far bigger than I was. I was to go last. It really is awful watching people giving their all and failing, because they really did want to join up. (They would later still be given the chance.) Then came my turn to take my corner of this back-breaker. The sergeant explained that I had to hug the weight tight to my neck otherwise it would bounce around and break my shoulder. This meant that apart from the huge weight pressing on my shoulder, I had to press down creating even more. The other disadvantage was that the three guys on my stretcher were all about six foot two and I was barely five foot ten, so I knew this wasn't going to be fun.

Before I had a chance to think of a plausible excuse we were off, the stretcher hammering down on my shoulder each time I tried to steady it, clenching it in my sweating palms, tight on to my skin. We changed position twice, but each change kept the weight on my right shoulder as we pounded our way to the edge of the estate, rounded a flag and made our way home. The jeep following us shouted that we were in second place, as each run had been timed, which instantly put a spring in the step of the Paras and I panted and wheezed trying to keep up. I was fairly fit, but not close to these fellows, then with 400 yards to go we were only a second and a half from first place. To my horror, they practically started to sprint. By this time I was hanging on for dear life, the metal stretcher hammering down on my shoulder. We crossed the line in first place by over a second and as we did they hurled down the weight on to the grass and I fell, my shoulder aching under the pounding it had taken. The other lads shook my hand, which was agony, and the sergeant said, 'We might just be able to make a paratrooper out of you, after all, Alan!'

'Please,' I replied. 'Don't frighten me. I've gone through enough!' On getting back to my car the lads had let down all four of my tyres, so my exertions were far from over as I had to pump them back up again. Later that night during the rock show my shoulder was so numb that I could hardly feel it. I popped into the accident and emergency unit at Newcastle's General Hospital on the way home, where they told me that I'd broken my collar bone. I had always thought that doing the 'out and about' show would be full of fun, yet every week a new and horrifying challenge would be given to me.

Our moods change like the direction of the wind, one moment soaring to great heights of happiness, other times plummeting with the chill of loneliness, isolation and depression. It pains me to admit that I have been, and still am, as vulnerable as anyone else, yet as the Isley Brothers sang, most of my unhappiness is hidden 'Behind a Painted Smile'. I can't even count the amount of times on stage, on radio or on television that the sadness in my personal life has had to be covered up. Yet when working every day of the week and every night too, the stresses and strains sometimes begin to appear. The shows on radio and television involve real people, quite often wanting you to solve their problems. This in turn usually means that after the show they are feeling better and I am feeling worse, my mind carrying the weight that they've just unloaded.

One that I remember vividly came at a time when my life at home was in turmoil and I was desperately unhappy with the way things weren't working out. Yet on the show I was free, free to put everything behind me and fly with the Night Owls. If it is true that some people have used the show as an emotional prop, then I am proud to say that I have too on many occasions. So the night was whizzing along, one man had just had a dental bridge installed and it was picking up the show. 'I'm not putting words in your mouth, am I' I asked. 'Yes' came his reply, 'and my wife Sara can't sleep for it, because she hears your voice coming from my mouth in the dark!'

I was quiet for a while and then said, 'Sara come to me, let our bodies merge in lust, passion and desire.'

I heard her giggle so continued: 'I must have you and I must have you now!'

She was obviously reciprocating, and I heard the male caller say 'Get off, you idiot' and then he started giggling too. Things could have got very racy if I hadn't ended that call there and then. It was one of those wonderfully easy nights, when people didn't want to argue, instead they were just swapping daft stories and laughing along with each other. Yet these intense calls always happen when you least expect them, and reach into your chest and heave at your heart. The caller was a man in his sixties calling from Newcastle's West End and I identified him as not dissimilar from my own father. Everything seemed to fit, he had worked all of his life in the building trade and there was no doubt that he was quite rough and ready. 'Alan, my wife's just died and I can't cope, son!'

Then he began to cry. Not just sob, he broke his heart.

I tried to calm him, asking if there was anyone we could call to go there to be with him.

'No, I can't go on Alan, there's no point. I loved her with all my heart and now she's gone!'

Words seemed so inadequate.

'We never had nothing you know, just each other, and she's gone and I'm all alone! We had almost fifty years together, now I'm lost. I just can't handle it.'

I suggested contacting his family for him.

'No, I just want to talk to you. No one can really do me any good now. This is going to be my last night on this earth and I just wanted to talk to a friend!'

My Adam's apple was already almost reaching basket-ball proportions and I could feel tears welling in the corners of my eyes. I closed my microphone fader and swore at myself. My job was to be strong. He needed someone to cling to. I couldn't turn to mush too. This man, who was in such pain, was living out my fear, to be left alone, and I was in agony with him. I let him talk, telling me how he met his wonderful wife, how he'd married her, the things they had rowed about, laughed about and struggled over.

While he talked I was desperately trying to find something, anything, that I could grasp on to, to pull him to me, and then back towards life and not away from it. Having covered literally hundreds of suicidal calls this was by far the toughest, for everything he spoke of I had lived through, either in my life or through the lives of my parents. They too have been totally and completely in love for over 50 years, while I thrashed about in the world, more often than not sinking in broken relationships while they just swam on. I am so very proud of them, but being the brusque, outwardly thick-skinned northerner that they've made me, I just never got round to telling them as much as I should. He underlined my own personal thoughts by exposing his: 'You know, there was so much I should have told her. You just never think that one day she'd be gone and then it's too late!'

'Surely, she'd want you to go on,' I whispered. 'She'd expect you to, now, wouldn't she?'

'It's no good, I've tried.' Then he broke down again.

By this time I'd run the full gamut, and I was fast running out of road.

'My family will be so hurt that I'm not saying all this to them, you know. My friends too, but without her life is just so empty, there's really no purpose. I might as well just go after her, no one will care!'

The fact was that in households all over the North people really did care and our switchboard was bombarded with people who had been bereaved, all offering their help and their experience, often far more valuable than what I could offer. I told him this. 'No, Alan. I don't want to talk to them. I just had to speak to you. You've always been a good friend to us both!'

I'd never met nor spoken to either of them, yet they had done me this honour. I felt my bottom lip begin to tremble, but I couldn't let it go. I had to hold everything inside me. There still was a slim chance that I could find a way through this casket of surrender he had placed himself in.

I played the final card. I told him that his wife was watching him, knowing that she'd be with him again on the other side of the curtain, the great divide, whatever he chose to believe.

'Well, I'll be with her very soon,' he replied, in words of steel that made me certain he wasn't bluffing. This wasn't a person who was ill, out of control or mad. He was totally in control. He just couldn't cope. A hospital or a secure unit wouldn't change his resolve and much as I'd tried neither had I.

'You know Alan, we used to do the pools,' he said, his voice choking with emotion, 'because we never had much. When she was filling in the coupon she used to say "One day we'll beat these bastards!" '

Those words were the answer. Like a bolt of lightning, the way ahead exploded into my mind.

'Well, do you not think that she's with you every step you take and if she could she would say to you, get a hold of yourself, now it's *your* turn to beat those bastards?'

My words were tougher than before, shielding the upset I felt, my hands trembling on the desk in front of me.

He didn't speak for what seemed like minutes.

'Yes, Alan,' he cried. 'I think she would!'

I wanted to cheer because I knew that all of his defences had fallen.

'She bloody well would. What a fool I've been.' I could feel the life pouring back into him. It was at this point that I made my big mistake. Knowing that he was safe I had relaxed. All of my own personal burdens piled under his and I let it all go. Instead of focusing my mind, I let my guard down and he finished me off with a kindness that destroyed me.

'Alan, God bless you. I've been a fool.'

I assured him that all he'd been was human, and most of us are guilty of that. I was on the verge of ending the call when the final blow arrived, delivered almost as a thank you, yet none the less devastating.

'She loved you, you know, Alan. During her last months she was in great pain, and would always say "If it wasn't for Alan, I would have died long ago." Thank you for those extra months. We'll never forget you!'

The call was over and I couldn't speak. All of that love, given freely, a sincere love without any hidden motive. It hit me hard and I was a wreck. I mumbled something incomprehensible and played some adverts whilst I fell apart. I was screaming at myself, punching the walls while my chest heaved with sobs. The adverts were all too swiftly over, so I played more and slapped my own face trying to regain a grip and then reopened the microphone to talk to someone else. They were aware of the sensitivity of the previous caller and wished him the best of luck. I hung together as best I could until the end of the show, then I collapsed like a heap in the corner. It took me almost an hour before I felt capable of driving home. I sat like a zombie in the programme's office, tears falling in streams down my face. The security man offered me a coffee. I never even replied. I had totally flipped. I wanted to quit. The weight was too great to bear. Why should it be me that had to suffer like this? I now knew why I enjoyed doing the Saturday music show. Records can't hurt you like people can.

On many occasions people have said that my association with my listeners was 'meant to be'. Having such a loyal listenership occasionally draws flattery, so I was grateful for their kindnesses, yet never thought much more of it. Yet there is something that I really cannot explain. To understand this story it is important to realise that any music that I select for the programme is often chosen the week before. Once it is picked it goes into my case and is there until its time comes up. As producer and presenter of the show I can select any music I deem appropriate, and it ranges from jazz to heavy metal, reggae to chart hits. The studio has a collection of CDs but they are only the current top forty plus some classic pop compilations. The tracks I choose to play tend to be rather more obscure, and once I am in the studio for the phone-in it is impossible to find time to go up to the record library and dig out additional music. I have to play what I have selected the week earlier.

It was a Tuesday evening, just after midnight, when a lady called in. She was very upset indeed and had recently lost her husband of over forty years. I tried very hard to calm her down, trying to establish her own beliefs about death, so I could guide my conversation to support and endorse them, whatever they were.

'I don't believe in God any more. No God would take him from me like that!' She was angry and hurting bad.

Trying to stem such an aggressively unhappy tide would only isolate her from me, so I let her sound off.

'It isn't fair. I really loved him. Why did God take him from me? He was all I had in the world, yet now I've got nothing!'

So she went on for almost twenty minutes, shrieking in torment, cursing at God, and then turning on her own greatly loved husband. I tried every approach, including the standard Christian attitude that the loved one isn't dead, has only slipped into another room, to wait for you, until your time is due. This was like poking a snake with a stick. She hissed at me angrily: 'That's what he said. He promised if there was something on the other side that he'd let me know. If I knew that I would see him again, then I wouldn't feel like this. He's been dead now for almost six weeks. Every single day I wait for him to come to me. He doesn't. He's dead. Dead is dead, there is no more!'

She sobbed and cried as I battled with tears to try to remain her stalwart. She was inconsolable and I was losing her, in the same way that she felt she had lost him. I had tried sympathy, I had tried shaking her up, but whatever equation I attempted it always equalled tears of frustration and emptiness. I knew about emptiness and would have done anything to save her from that. I suggested getting her friends around, or her family, I even suggested that I go to her home following the programme. All fell on stony ground. Then she began making noises to end her call, and I was thoroughly disappointed. She had looked to me for help and I had been found wanting.

'Alan, thank you for letting me go on at you. I'm sorry,' she said. I was the one who was sorrier, but she continued: 'But he promised that he'd give me a sign. I loved him so much. He always said that no matter what, he'd move heaven and earth to let me know that he was waiting for me and he hasn't.'

'I know,' came my resigned reply. 'Isn't there *anything* I can do to help?'

'Alan, there is,' she said, fighting back her sobs. 'He always had a favourite song that he used to play for me all the time. It was very special to us. I know you'll probably not have it, but if you could get hold of a copy it would bring him closer to me!'

'Whatever it is, I promise it will be done.' I was still desperately trying to lift her.

'The record is Mario Lanza singing "Only A Rose".'

My blood turned to iced water. For there on the turntable was Mario Lanza, the needle waiting on the song 'Only A Rose'.

On telling her this, it was like she'd won the pools.

'That's his sign, God bless him, he's done it!' she screamed joyfully. 'He is waiting for me. I'll be with him again!'

She thanked me for everything that I'd done, which had in effect been little, and said an ecstatic goodbye.

I played that song with all of the hairs on the back of my neck standing to attention. I hadn't played anything by Mario Lanza in almost four years; could any coincidence have been that precise? It was one of thousands of amazing episodes that has made me firmly believe in kismet, fate and destiny.

I have often mused about becoming this 'Flashing Blade' character for real, believing that the hokum world created on screen by the likes of John Wayne and Errol Flynn was so much more preferable to the way the world really is. A world where men protect and defend women and children, not attacking, molesting and murdering them; where the young look up to those who set a good example, waiting for their time to defend the helpless and keep the faith. Yet life has proved to me that what may sound exciting often is nothing more than adrenalin-induced panic. On three occasions I have found myself on the wrong side of a knife.

One evening I arrived at Metro FM to find a young man waiting to steal a quick word. It appeared that everything was going wrong with his life and he wanted to end it all. I had spoken to this lad on air and he was a decent bloke, but life hadn't been kind. We talked for a while and then he told me that he would slash his wrists that evening. I tried to instil a bit of confidence into him without success, and finally he got up to go. I told him that I wouldn't let him go until he agreed not to do anything stupid. But he had completely switched off and finally I ended up wrestling a knife from his hand. Ultimately the police were involved and we got some help for him. He was back on the telephone to me within a fortnight to say how much better he felt.

The second, and by far the worst, happened again quite early into my *Night Owl* tenancy. This time, in the middle of a busy Saturday afternoon, he asked if I'd come out into the car park because his mother wanted to meet me. I duly obliged, having met hundreds of people this way, and followed close behind him. Once at the car I saw that it was empty, and asked him what he was playing at. He broke down in tears saying that his mother had died that morning. He was sitting in the passenger seat of the battered Renault and crying into his hands and I went down beside him, resting my hand on his shoulders. He was telling me about how she had always wanted him to be famous, how he did a little singing at the karaoke nights that are now so common. He swore that he'd be famous one day, no matter what it took. I spent about twenty minutes with him, talking quietly and trying to rebuild his confidence. Then totally out of the blue he picked up a knife and said, 'If I kill you, I'll be famous!'

Before I could even begin to talk him out of doing anything stupid, he thrust the knife at my stomach. I grabbed the blade with my right hand and he pulled it away. I felt my fingers being cut and felt the blood begin to trickle out of my hand. Rather than defend myself, for a reason that to this day I can't understand, I said, 'Look what you've done now, you dickhead!' I had seen this happen to Clint Eastwood's phone-in host in *Play Misty For Me* but hadn't realised it was compulsory. On seeing the blood he dropped the knife and started crying again. My hand was aching, and I felt like crying too. Instead, I raced back to the radio station, got the police called and they arrested him. It made the front page of the papers the next day, but I didn't press charges. He had enough problems.

Fortunately, the cuts were not too deep. I patched them up with three plasters and a bandage on the deepest gouge on my thumb. I suffered a few months' worth of sleepless nights after this happened. There was I trying to help him with kindness, yet still he could've killed me. I really couldn't fully understand the complexity of it all. His pain over his mother's death had temporarily deranged him, yet my thanks for coming to his aid was a slashed hand.

The third occasion wasn't long ago. Three lads, one carrying a Stanley knife, walked towards me at a service station near one of the bridges over the River Tyne. One said he was going to 'do me', because I had slagged off his brother who had been one of a gang who had been imprisoned for assaulting an elderly lady. Purely by chance, I just happened to have a large knife that I'd been given in the car, and on seeing that, rather like the classic scene in *Crocodile Dundee*, they changed their minds. It is a sadness that in certain areas this country seems rather closer to being the Wild West than the great North.

The show has been the sad showcase for many things and once they go out live there is so very little you can do about them.

On one occasion, there was a debate about a young murderess who had been released from prison after killing two young children. She had been given a new identity and set up home in a small village. As the years had passed she'd married and had a family of her own; however, a divorce was pending and there were discussions over custody. This generated many calls, mostly against this woman having two young children in her care, when she had so savagely taken the lives of two other youngsters. The tide was completely against her when a woman, who lived near the murderess, came on to defend her, alleging all kinds of improprieties against the woman's husband. This was slander so I had to use my six-second digital delay to dump what she'd said. But because she was the only voice in support, I didn't want to end the call, preferring to continue with it, to give the show its necessary balance. At that very second the woman gave out the murderess's new name and I had no delay to wipe it. We were very fortunate not to become embroiled in a court case over that one.

Then there was the time the police heard a young man from Sunderland talking on the show about a murder that had been committed there. The police were certain that he was in fact the murderer. Tapes were requested of the show and he was subsequently arrested.

One night in September 1989 a man called William phoned in from Bedlington, claiming that his wife used to attack him every time she came in drunk. He'd been stabbed with a kitchen knife, beaten unconscious with a frozen turkey and scarred by her fingernails. At first I thought he was joking, until half-way through the call we heard the door go, and in walked his wife. He tried explaining that he was just chatting to me about something else, but she had heard him on the radio in her taxi home. She tore at him, and a real battle started. He was trying to defend himself, shouting, yelling, begging for help. We notified the police, leaving the entire thing running for almost seven minutes, when the police burst in. She was charged with assault and they are no longer together.

When you deal with such complex problems night after night, you begin to use your own emotions rather like the gears of a car. Sometimes you can be in top gear, attacking back at someone having a go at you, other times you can be in cruise, just laughing along with some light-hearted tale. Then there are the times you have to be in 'sympathy' mode, a low gear, going at the speed of the person on the line who has suffered some kind of trauma. There are a thousand levels and techniques, but in general terms this is accurate. One evening a woman came on air, and said, 'Alan, I want to talk about death!'

I told her to go ahead and she continued: 'I lost my husband three weeks ago!'

Instantly, I was in 'sympathy' mode: 'I'm very sorry to hear it.'

'I found him dead in bed. Eeh, it was awful!' She was talking to me as if to an old friend over the garden fence, she was so at ease. 'It was six in the morning and I heard his alarm, so I reached over and shoved him saying, "Come on, you lazy sod. Out you get. It's Sunday, double time, and we need the money!" '

As she continued, I felt myself starting to get the giggles. I couldn't give any reason for it, and fought desperately to contain my chortles. There is a thin line between tragedy and farce and I kept skidding from one side to the other. Yet it seemed that everything she said from that point on made me even worse.

'Eeh Alan, when I touched him I felt that he was stiff!'

That started the girl on the switchboard crying with laughter. This in turn stopped a technician dead in his tracks. Everyone in the building was glued to this call.

She just carried on: 'And you know, Alan, he's not normally stiff in the morning!'

My stomach was sore trying to stop the laughs. I was shaking like a jelly on the waltzer.

'Well, I said to him, "If I have to open my eyes, I'll never get back to sleep. So get up will you!" '

No comedy sketch could have been so funny, until finally she brought us back to earth with a bump.

'So then I looked around and saw him. He was sitting bolt upright, his eyes staring out in front of him, his mouth was open wide and he was green!'

I was so shocked I was speechless, until she said: 'I knew he was dead! You're not married to someone for forty-three years without knowing when they're dead!'

In my second year on *Night Owls* a woman said on air that her neighbour had stolen her pet Jack Russell, because it had run amok in his garden. The neighbour had denied it, yet he called the show saying that he was up on his mate's farm. When I asked him why, he said: 'Because up here we've had domestic dogs worrying his sheep and he's entitled to shoot them if he finds them on his land!' Then there was a huge explosion and he laughed, 'Oh dear, there was a Jack Russell worrying his sheep. But it'll not worry anyone ever again!' At that he hung up. The Jack Russell was never seen again.

One chilling evening a frantic mother called the programme because her tiny six-year-old hadn't returned home. I instantly put out an appeal, asking everyone in the Sunderland area to pop out and check their gardens, backyards, streets, lanes and avenues in a desperate search to re-unite the family. The following morning the tiny battered body of the little girl was found. I was driving when the news broke on the radio and I felt sick in the pit of my stomach.

Every evening the *Night Owls* programme changes peoples lives, and often shares their tragedies. One girl regularly rings the programme following a bizarre suicide attempt that went sorely wrong. She leapt from a block of flats, landed on concrete yet still survived. She regularly calls the programme, despite having trouble speaking. She's a spirited girl, now in a wheelchair, who is fighting to live a happier life.

One of the most amazing stories to run and run on the phone-in featured a girl from Alnwick called Tikana who had also been put into a wheelchair after being run down by car thieves. We often talked of how lonely she was, not believing that she would ever find someone able-bodied who would fall in love with her, in her wheels of steel. She told of how she would drive to shopping centres and wait until a good-looking man would walk by and then ask him for help. She didn't actually need help, but it broke the ice and she'd try and subtly chat him up. During the Gulf war she was one of the first recruits in my trawl to find people to write to squaddies over there. She had been on the verge of doing silly things in the past, and I felt that this would be a boost for her as well as helping our blokes overseas. Almost 40 per cent of the British troops in the Gulf were northerners and I was flooded with letters from them everyday. We sent truckloads of stuff and thousands of letters to show we were thinking about them. Then close to the end of the conflict, this young lady rang to say that the young soldier she'd been writing to was coming home and had asked her to meet him at Newcastle's Central Station. Tikana said that she couldn't possibly meet him because she had never once mentioned that she was in a wheelchair. My advice was firm: 'Go and meet him. If he is to know you properly, he must know everything!' It took almost fifteen minutes of persuasion to get her to agree, but agree she did. Three weeks later I spoke to her again and she was elated. She had met him and he had fallen in love with her. This nervous and sensitive soul was brimming with happiness. It poured over me and the entire North-East as we talked. Within the year they were engaged, married and the story was complete when she became pregnant too.

The fairy tale had come true and I would love to say that they lived happily ever after, but tragically Tikana's sister phoned in a year or so later to say that she had died. But at least she'd found that happiness she'd long been seeking, and known the true love she'd wanted so desperately.

I was chatting to a man called Wayne from Sheffield who was on his car phone explaining that he was sick of women drivers. He lambasted them completely saying that they spent more time looking at what was on sale in High Street shop windows than paying attention to the road. He said, 'Alan, I'm driving past a scrapyard right now, and when I look at all of the mangled wrecks in there I know that most of them are the results of bad women drivers!' At that second there was the sound of a huge crunch. He'd driven right into the back of a police van! On air we heard the police talk to him, breathalyse him and ultimately walk him away – his phone off the hook all that time!

Many people have said that nothing ever happens in the North until *Night Owls* begins. Certainly on the two separate occasions that riots broke out in the North fate gave me a ringside seat. The evening had just begun and during the first hour I heard that a disturbance had begun on the Meadowell Estate in North Shields. By the time I started the phone-in all hell had been let loose. On contacting the police, they said that they couldn't get on to the estate at that time because it was too dangerous. Then the people who lived there began calling. One said: 'Alan, I'm in my seventies and there's a group of young boys setting my house on fire!' and another: 'I can see now that these idiots are burning down our community hall. I can see it burning. Other boys are stoning a fire engine that they've trapped down a narrow street!'

Every call came from a decent, law-abiding citizen trapped in a nightmare from which there was no escape. I had alerted our news team who got down there and reported back from the estate, talking to many who had just come out to watch the perverted circus from their gardens. Cars were being burned out and tipped over as more calls came in. One woman sobbed: 'Right outside my door they're burning my car. I've saved up for almost eight years and it's burning. Why are they doing this?'

Some suggested that it was connected to the deaths of car thieves who had crashed their stolen vehicle. Hundreds of car thieves had killed themselves and innocent people before, yet it hadn't led to this. The truth began to filter in. Yobs from various parts of the North had hired mini-buses, organised vans and transport to get to the Meadowell Estate, long before the deaths of the thieves. This was organised and choreographed, all at the expense of the majority of good people in the area. The nation would see the disgusting pictures and once again the image and reputation of the North had been dragged into the gutter by scum.

All through that night the calls became even more desperate: 'Alan, you must help me. I'm pregnant and I'm trapped in a house. My baby is coming! I can't get out and there are fires everywhere!' So behind the scenes I managed to organise some people to get in there and get her out.

The police were using the *Night Owls* show as the only way to find out what was going on. I had thousands of eyewitnesses who were reporting every single thing that was going on. I was advising that they kept their curtains closed, in case bricks shattered the glass, but also asked them to watch out of their upstairs windows, to tell us what was going on. There were over fifty calls in three hours from the estate until eventually order was restored.

The following night, the wife of a police officer rang: 'Alan, if it hadn't been for your show, I wouldn't have been able to get through last night. I was with half-a-dozen other police wives and we didn't know what was going on. Yet you brought the entire thing into perspective and kept us calm. Thank you!'

TV agony aunt Denise Robertson heard the amazing show and

told me: 'It was quite simply the most incredible piece of radio I think I've ever heard!' Then she arranged for a camera crew to come up to the North to film an item using some of the recording on her *Good Morning* TV show.

I have always thought that much of Britain chooses to believe the stereotypes rather than accept the truth of what the North is really like. Proof came when there was a smaller violent outburst in my old homeland, the West End of Newcastle. The thickheads had decided to wreck as much of the area as they could, blaming everything and everybody else, when the truth was they were themselves to blame, the morons. The national press announced: 'Second night of violence in Newcastle'. Not so. North Shields is fifteen to twenty miles away from Newcastle, yet the media wanted to continue the city's character assassination.

Once again, the air was filled with callers pointing out what was happening and who the local ringleaders were. There were more incredible calls and the most amazing was from Joan: 'Alan, I can see my own son down there. He's throwing a petrol bomb at a shop. All his mates are with him and it is as if they've all gone mad. They're crazy. I've already called the police to tell them it is my son. I'm so ashamed, I love the West End, it can be such a special place. We might not have a lot, but we've got our pride, and these little bastards are trying to take even that away! Well, he's never getting back in this house again, damn him, no more. He's been in little bits of trouble and I've tried to get him back on to the straight and narrow, but no more. Not after this!' Like every other decent person in the North, I was heartily ashamed too!

20 A Series of My Own

IT WAS ALWAYS my ambition to get my own television series. I wanted desperately to have that thrill of seeing my name in *TV Times* and the *Radio Times*. It was finally going to happen, but not in any role I really wanted to be cast. Nina Myskow was involved in putting together a series for Tyne Tees Television called *Getting Personal*, a sort of visual 'problem page', and I was invited along to be an agony uncle on a show totally dominated by women. *Getting Personal* was an attempt to show that Nina Myskow wasn't just a 'hit-woman critic', who was all attack, that there was another side to her character. Deep down she is a softy. During the show's run they tried out several people, including other radio hosts and magazine problem pagers, but I did the entire run and was often used by Nina as her foil, being relied upon to give a slightly more outrageous answer.

This was demonstrated by a woman who had bought a washing machine and didn't know how to use it, and had written in to the show. While one of the problem-page types said, 'Oh, this is a common problem. I *do* understand how difficult it is. Many of us can identify with this lady,' I said; 'What a dozy dollop. Why doesn't she read the manual or ring the shop, instead of waiting a whole week for us to sympathise with her!'

It wasn't long before Nina was chomping at the bit to have digs at me, and we did have a lot of knockabout fun, firing volleys at one another. I was on the show because my job was to think quickly and always to have an answer, no matter what subject was raised. Nina was soon aware that if she went for me I would bite back.

There was one occasion when I noticed that she was about to slag me off, because her witty comment was actually on the autocue. To be honest if someone has a dig, I'll come up with an answer, but to allow me a few minutes to think of a really solid reply is really suicidal. I could see the words on the autocue: 'Well, Alan do you work out, or are you happy being a slob?' I was dischuffed about this, because I'd actually spent more money on clothes than I was getting for the series, trying to impress enough to get offered more work. Three minutes later, after a commercial break, Nina delivered her lines. I smiled. 'I don't believe that exercise does get rid of fat!'

She rounded on me at once. 'What do you mean?' She'd walked straight into the trap.

I answered: 'If exercise gets rid of fat, how come with all the talking you do, you've still got four double chins?'

'Cut,' she shrieked, ordering the crew to record another version.

She rephrased her question and the joke was lost forever on the cutting-room floor. I must say, though, that against all odds I did really like Nina. She is straight as a die. You may not always agree with her opinions, but at least she means what she says unlike so many entertainment types who have ambition but no real substance.

It was Nina who gave me my first real break in a roundabout way. She had just published a book and had been offered a slot on *Wogan* that was worth about 20,000 copies sold, but it was on the same night that *Personal Call* was recorded. She tried everything to get out of it, bringing in another host, changing the recording date, but all to no avail. Tyne Tees were not prepared to foot the extra costs. So I said 'Just get yourself away, I'll do it.' The producer dismissed it out of hand, but as the time came closer, he knew that Nina would go. So I had my very first slot as host and I loved it. I did so well that everyone commented on it, and soon the people in power were discussing the possibility of a series of my own. On the last recording day a producer pulled me to one side and told me that a show was in the pipeline. I was elated and believed that at last I was on the ladder I had fought to get on.

Having in the past failed badly as a singer, it was still my ambition to cut a record, and eventually I realised my dream. As well as having interviews with me used by various bands on their albums, and being a bit-part singer on the Geordie Aid single, I was invited to take part in a tribute to the late and great Scott Dobson on an album called 'RADIO JARRA SLAX'. Along with the great 'Larn Yersel Geordie' duo, Mike Neville and George House, I had a ball, creating a very strange but amusing album. On one track I was the caller to a phone-in show instead of its host. You've got to be able to laugh at yourself, any man who can't should take a long look at himself standing naked in front of a full-length mirror.

Indirectly this would lead to me writing an album of comedy sketches and songs that would later be released as 'Two Sides Of A Flashing Blade'. At the time I believed that it would rocket me towards being another Mike Harding or Billy Connolly; instead it showed just how naive I was. The album was put together on a shoestring and it showed. Some of the gags still stand up, but it could have been done so much better. It did realise a number of ambitions, for I did get a chance to sing with one of my all-time favourite bands, The Blues Burglars, and releasing a single backed by Bob Smeaton's Loud Guitars.

At that time Newcastle United were going through a very bad spell. The club was floundering with no direction, so I decided to write a song about it called 'Sack The Board'. It caused ructions. At that time a businessman called Sir John Hall was trying to take over the club and this song backed him to do it. He was from another family of pitmen and I could relate to his aspirations. He'd made a brilliant job of building Europe's biggest shopping complex, the Metrocentre. Surely if anyone could turn Newcastle into a successful business it would be him? The record was universally banned, even by my own radion station, but victory was eventually secured. Sir John Hall did take over the club. He brought in Kevin Keegan and guided Newcastle back to the very top. Once in position he invited me to host all of the pre-match entertainment at St James's Park.

Although I'm a self-confessed 'failed comic', I still collect jokes and have published a book called *Simply The Best: Geordie Jokes and Stories*. Once again the best tales always coming from the people!

21 Playing the Name Game

ONE OF MY all-time pet hates is the 'star syndrome', when celebrities of any kind lay on their fame with a trowel. I have always believed that everyone deserves respect, no matter who or what they are. Therefore, to me a good plumber is worth as much as a good singer, nothing more.

Over the years I have had the chance to collect thousands of interviews with notable stars and quite often this would lead to more adventures. My most demanding interview without a doubt came one evening when I heard I would be interviewing Eartha Kitt. I hadn't thought too much about it, arriving at the radio station around 6 p.m. to prepare the studio for her arrival an hour later.

Whilst I was waiting, I clicked on the local television news and there she was, being interviewed. The newsman was asking very sensible, if rather dull, questions and she was walking all over him. Finally, in a split second, she turned the full weight of her fury upon him, called him a few choice names and then stormed out of the studio. The interviewer was destroyed and dumbstruck, and could only try and pad until the cameras ended his humiliation. She was in a blazing temper and she was on her way to see me.

To say I was intimidated by this was rather like saying that water is wet, and I pawed through her biography to make sure that I had as much information crammed into my head as possible. As I paced about Metro's canteen, occasionally glancing out of the windows for car headlights, I saw her arrive, her face like thunder, in a long, sleek, black limousine. When she stepped out a long white fur coat trailed behind her on the ground. I'm against furs, but in the industry they are not unknown, and you can never be sure if they're real dead things or very expensive fakes. She looked magnificent, but none too happy.

I went out to meet her in the reception area and guide her up to the first floor.

'And who am I going to talk to?' she purred, in a way that only she can.

'Me,' I replied, as I watched her face drop to her knees, then climb warily back up to her shoulders.

She said to her manager, in a voice just loud enough for me to hear: 'This boy is going to waste my time too!'

Gathering as many of my wits about me as I could, I sat her down at a table, switched on the microphones and then sat next to her. Whilst I was getting the recording levels set, I heard her saying things about the length of my hair, it was long at the time, and barking her displeasure in general.

I began: 'Miss Eartha Kitt, it's a great pleasure to welcome you to . . .' I didn't even get a chance to end my first sentence before she took over: 'What do you think of woman as an ism?'

She might as well have spoken Urdu. I didn't have a clue what she was talking about, but knew enough about interviewing to lob that one back over the net. 'That's an interesting concept. What's your view?'

From that point she lambasted me with her views on how women had to suffer men, how men had so little value and how the world would be a far better place without them. It was more a speech than the answer to a question and continued for almost ten minutes. Finally, I decided to try and get her to warm to me with a little humour: 'Surely, if the world was purely made up of women you'd become extinct?'

She grimaced at me. 'We would always be able to find the seed.'

'But you'd need a man for that!' I countered.

'Sadly,' she pouted, 'that is true, but only one man.'

I chirped, 'If the job's going, I'd like to apply.'

To my total shock, she pulled her fur coat off her shoulders and said, 'Well, come on then!' Her face still looked as angry as nettle rash.

I felt I had no option. I grabbed her and started undoing my shirt.

She screamed her anger, forcing me back into my seat. Then just as I began to wonder what would happen next, she roared with laughter, all the severity of her expression melted away and she was another person. From then on I asked all manner of unorthodox questions and sailed through an in-depth, but fun, interview. Half-way through she asked for a drink, and to visit the smallest room in the radio station, so we took a break and I walked her along. Once again, just loud enough for me to hear, she told her manager: 'He's the best one this year.' Many interviews are battles like this, some you win, some you lose, but this one gave me most satisfaction. After the interview she invited me to accompany her to her performance that evening. She really is tremendous, but once you have earned her respect you have no problems at all.

When Metro FM began the big stadium shows, it was decided to bring the big names to St James's Park, since there are no venues bigger than 2,000 seats in the area. The first show featured Santana, Bob Dylan and local heroes Lindisfarne. I grabbed an interview with Lindisfarne and Santana without any problem, then I walked up to Bob Dylan and asked for a few words. Suddenly I was pushed away by two minders, big American men with no hint of compromise in their eyes. Dylan seemed frightened that someone he didn't know was backstage. But it was my gig too, so he could do nothing about it. I later heard that he had demanded that a patio be built behind the stage with goldfish in a pond. It was done. I found him very strange indeed.

I interviewed Mick Jagger and Bill Wyman at the Rolling Stones show at St James's Park, and found them far more 'normal'. Metro helped bring a huge catalogue of stars to the North, including Guns 'n Roses, Simply Red, Bryan Adams, David Bowie, Queen, Tina Turner, Extreme, Dire Straits, Status Quo, Bruce Springsteen and many more. Metro even played a part in bringing Michael Jackson to Anfield, Liverpool, the closest to the North-East they could persuade him to go.

I had cut my teeth as one of the support DJs with Led Zeppelin at Knebworth, but my first actual show as host was at Gateshead International Stadium. It's a superb venue, they look after your every need, but this was their very first concert. The four bands were The Lords Of The New Church, The Beat, U2 and The Police with Sting, as headliners. What a strange crowd it attracted, rude boys, punks, pop fans, skinheads and practically every other 'cult' imaginable. It really was an audience recipe for disaster. I was probably the only person there with long hair, much to the disapproval of many. So I decided to make the most of it, and before long I had this bunch of crazies doing the world's longest conga, singing along and enjoying the show.

My co-host was another local lad, Mark Page, and he had brought along a batch of duff records to throw out. I warned him against it, but to no avail. The records ranged from The Tweets to the Nolan Sisters. I knew that that crowd wouldn't value them, that the records would be discarded or thrown back. They were, and we were nearly all cut to ribbons. A single seven-inch record out of its sleeve can kill you if it catches you in the wrong place. Finally, I dived into the audience and gathered them back in, dishing out a few T-shirts. They wanted the T-shirts, that wasn't a problem. Having taken a microphone into the centre of the huge crowd, I decided to get them singing and at one stage persuaded one huge, musclebound bloke to do an impromptu strip-tease. He obviously worked out and lapped up the applause. By the time I brought the first band on the atmosphere was happening and the show was a success.

22 The Lord Loves a Trier

All the way through my life I have been aware that I have hurt my parents, being a particular disappointment to them in the area of my personal relationships. My personal life has always been my Achilles' heel and the area where my judgement has been found badly lacking. It's strange that whenever I've been asked to help people discuss the most intimate problems on radio, in the press or on television, I do seem to be able to help. Yet the only problems I couldn't solve were my own. Perhaps I was too near the wood to see the trees.

When I met a young lady called Kristina, after a while, rather than rush into marriage, she decided to move in with me. Despite having this need for companionship, it felt awkward to have someone close to me again. It is not gallant to discuss those private times. Suffice to say that the good times were indeed good, the bad were very bad! The first couple of years were particularly filled with a sense of hope and purpose, yet all the way through there seemed to be something fragile just beneath the surface. It was a pairing of opposites, for she came from a big Catholic family and wanted children, while I am almost allergic to them. Once that initial period passed we were guilty of falling into a 'comfortable' relationship. For almost seven years I hadn't taken a holiday. I felt that I had to consolidate my position before allowing myself the freedom to recharge my batteries. I knew that I was beginning to suffer from stress and visited a doctor about it on several occasions. Yet really the only thing I was told was that you either have to live with it or take heavyweight drugs. So I read up on stress management and found it was easy to cope, provided you don't let yourself get out of control.

My relationship with Kristina continued uneasily, she as ever devoted to her family, whereas by choice I distanced myself from them. I didn't intend to be hurtful, but rather to keep myself to myself. I hardly saw my own family, so it seemed inconsistent that I should spend time with someone else's. I did and do like her brother very much, yet we lived in different worlds. They tried so very hard to involve me, despite the fact that I didn't really want to be involved. The more they tugged, the more I refused to budge, leading to a variety of long-running arguments. It felt to me very similar to all those people who have tried, unsuccessfully, to teach me to swim. In the pool, I know that I am safe, but I still need to keep my hand on the edge, or a foot on the floor. I never had the confidence nor the will to let go and join in completely. Whenever I was invited to visit any relative, I always made sure that I had an excuse to leave early, nearly always to work. This in turn would lead to the inevitable conflict at home later.

I did love Kristina, and I had failed far too often in the past so I wanted it to work. I wanted my parents to see me happily settled once and for all. What I am sure they failed to realise was that each time was an effort towards that very end. I just wasn't very good at it. All my life has been a desperate race towards security. I've worked hard with that being the only prize I wanted to await me at the finish line. Yet as we neared our fourth year together, things were sliding very badly. Apart from the annual fortnight's holiday we really weren't close, using friends to fill our only night of the week together. Sharing laughs and smiles with others made our own growing emptiness feel not quite so vast. We had reached that sad time that many couples reach, when the physical hunger disappears, the petty arguments that once would be instantly forgotten become major battles and the talk of leaving becomes a weekly centrepiece. My weakness is a desperate need for reassurance, my hidden insecurities need a 'fix' of positivism. I needed to know before I left for work that everything would be all right, yet the rows seemed to blow up just before a big show, just before I left to go to work. I couldn't count the number of times that I'd watched her packing her bags, filling a case in readiness to go back to her mother. This never happened during the week, when I could escape to work, but always on a Friday, my only night off, when we were beginning to find that when left alone together it was becoming less like Rhett Butler and Scarlett O'Hara and rather more like Kathleen Turner and Michael Douglas in *The War of the Roses*. It soon became a very uneasy routine; she would scream and pack and I would reason, then beg her to stay.

I just wanted things to be good and happy, yet what made me happy was not to her taste. I love old movies, she hated them. She liked being with her family, I preferred not. Then there was the constant burr under our mutual saddle – children. She was becoming increasingly impatient, for despite being ten years my junior she seemed to be highly aware that her body clock was ticking. I really did try to see myself as a father of a tiny baby, and yet deep down I have always hated the very thought. I put off and put off; there was always a work project that I would selfishly choose to think more important. Our dreams were just so very different. She wanted, maybe even needed, to be surrounded by a family, her family and her children, while I was in a career with no security. Having seen a presenter decide to get a huge mortgage, have a baby, then lose his job, I knew the risks only too well. He was unemployed for almost two years and his relationship was destroyed. Maybe this was just another excuse, along with the thousand others I tried to justify myself by using. I just didn't want a baby. Finally, I took the entire mess to a new low.

For a period of almost seven months of that fourth year it was like being with a stranger. When we weren't fighting, we were trying to be civil just to get through the day. We were no longer loving, just getting by. Every week or so the talk of ending came up and her clothes would be torn from the wardrobes and hurled on to the bed yet again. Right throughout I was frightened, not just of yet another relationship ending, but to fail my parents again. Yet I wasn't happy and I so desperately wanted to be.

Finally, after a particularly bitter row, believing that it was all over, I had the opportunity to see another woman who I had met whilst actually with Kristina. To my eternal shame this proceeded and without love ever being mentioned we started seeing each other. This created countless more petty arguments because I was never home. Kristina was used to me working all hours of the day and night, but this was now being used as a smoke-screen. I felt flattered that someone was prepared to give me the affection I wasn't getting at home, and maybe there was a degree of excitement in an illicit relationship too. It was almost as if I was positioning myself for the ending of the pairing, so that I would not be left alone.

Then I realised that this other girl was feeling that there was far more to the relationship than I was willing to give. At that time she was very important to me. She filled a huge void in my life, though she had no real idea what misery lay behind my smiling face. Eventually I realised that rather than making things better this situation was just throwing more petrol on the fire, and my conscience hammered me towards a depression. So I pulled back, and tried to restart the engine of my relationship with Kristina.

A few months passed without any marked improvement. I was trying harder, but I was still losing myself in my work at every opportunity, rather than constantly seeking out times to escape with her. On the verge of a big show we had yet another major set to. The cases came out again and I was sorely tempted to just let her go. In retrospect it may well have been better to make a clean break. Instead my courage failed me. I didn't want to hurt her, or her parents, nor mine, yet I was trapped in this circle of unpleasantness. My depression tore me apart. To all who knew me everything was fine, life was going along swimmingly, yet all the while I felt as if I were carrying the weight of the world on my shoulders. It was slowly crushing me. Despite the fact that I was a single guy, I felt committed to this disintegrating relationship and I was terrified that I would be left alone, once more.

That weekend, by chance, the 'other woman' contacted me, and it started all over again. The strange thing was it wasn't anything to do with sex. It was to hear a kind word, someone who would be nice instead of always turning everything into a fight. Yet being sensible about it, it was probably this situation that would make the relationship with Kristina untenable. This other woman wanted me to fall in love with her but I never did. I never said that word, because I never felt that emotion. Many would have lied to gain sexual gratification, but that was never what it was about.

I wanted to tell everybody how I felt, yet instead I just buried it inside me, allowing it to fester like a disease. I was positive that it was all over between Kristina and me; she was on the verge of actually going; all that was stopping us parting was the upheaval and the actual sorting out of our affairs. The heart of our pairing had long stopped beating. To be honest, I finally said 'stuff it'. I was on the verge of a one night stand with an Ashington girl who had chased me from show to show. It never happened, and it finally shook some sense into me. I knew that I felt nothing for these other women, yet I so desperately wanted to be loved. Instead I was trapped in this swamp of insecurities, and no matter how many tearful nights or evenings I spent locked in the editing suite at Metro shaking with fear I could see no way ahead.

It was then that I finally decided to treat the entire mess as if it were a *Night Owls* problem, not mine. The answers were very simple. Either I had to cut myself free of Kristina and live the single life in full or commit myself fully and try to live up to that responsibility.

Looking back, I chose the wrong route but for all the right reasons. Guilt had piled itself atop of all of the miseries and I so wanted to be forgiven. Yet I couldn't forgive myself, so how could I expect anyone else to? I had never been in so much turmoil. All I was really positive about was that I didn't want to be alone. In these nightmare times of uncertainty, I felt as if I was trapped in the middle of a long tunnel and the light that was merely a distant glimmer at each end was attracting me towards a future that wasn't what I wanted, but I had to choose one or the other. I was falling apart, unused to this degree of deception. I knew that whatever road I chose to take I would have to confess to Kristina about everything that had happened. In my life I have had two major depressions and this was the first. I tried to rationalise that maybe life sends these to us to demonstrate the error of our ways, to repay us for the misery that we have given others. If so, I almost wish that I had been much worse, for I paid twenty-fold for my indiscretions.

All this while Kristina and I were going through the motions of a normal relationship, our friends seeing the happy façade and accepting it on face value alone. I really didn't want to go hunting for love again. I'd failed so miserably in the past. I'd always believed that true happiness needed a healthy mental attitude, a clear conscience, a heart full of love and the conviction that someone loves us in spite of ourselves. I had acted dishonourably, going against everything I believed in, and couldn't shake off that burden. Having transgressed my own self-imposed moral code made me feel sick over what I had done, yet I felt powerless to make it all better. I should have sorted it out long before, but in amongst the depression, what was right seemed blurred and distorted. Late-night drives to the coast by the sea at Alnmouth just to think, to take some air and clear my head didn't really help but at least kept my mind away from the nightmare. At times I hated Kristina for the way she constantly left me hanging, wondering if we were together or apart. I felt totally without value to anyone, I couldn't eat or drink, I would burst out crying for absolutely no reason and didn't know why. Once in an attempt to cheer myself up I watched the movie *Scrooged* and cried for almost two hours afterwards without being able to stop. My concentration was shot, and my memory, normally very sharp whilst on air, had started to let me down. I really wasn't interested in the normal day-to-day activities and I wasn't sleeping at all well. My doctor told me that much of my behaviour was typical of a depression heading towards a complete breakdown. I thought I'd done all the right things, even to seeing a doctor for guidance, but still I was really screwed up!

So, in a desperate attempt to jump-start my life again, I decided to attempt to retrieve whatever degree of honour I had left. This would involve the unpleasant and gut-wrenching task of telling Kristina everything! I was fairly certain that the shaky relationship would crumble into dust, but I couldn't live with it any more. On three separate occasions I positioned myself to tell her, but instead found myself sidetracked into another row or losing courage at the last moment. It was as if I was becalmed in a stormy sea, unable to move forwards or backwards, yet the fuse was lit on a time-bomb that would inevitably blow up in both our faces. We were still shouting far too much or spending entire days in a huff. My mood swings were getting worse and the only refuge I had was my work. All the while I was exorcising my problems by talking to other people about theirs. The entire North was a party to my therapy as well as theirs yet they never realised. I was also just beginning rehearsals for a pantomime too; there was no such thing as too much work; it got me out of the house and away from the sadness that lived there. Finally, whilst walking through a park, I told Kristina what I had done. Once I started, it just poured out. No matter which way you deliver that kind of news, it has a devastating effect. Kristina had no illusions about how bad things were, but even so it hurt her badly. She gave me what I deserved, a bruised cheek and all the phrases that were most deserved, blasphemous but deserved.

I had hoped that part of that mountain of guilt that I heaved after me like some septic snail would have gone, yet instead I was even more riddled with guilt. Despite our seemingly insurmountable problems, I decided that I had no option but to try somehow to make it up to her. I really had no idea what I could do, for had I been in her position I could not possibly have forgiven. Chauvinist hypocrisy at its very worst! We talked for weeks, we argued and we physically fought whilst every sordid detail oozed out like a festering slime that I had carried for so long inside me. I felt sick and so did she, but we seemed to be making some headway. I was surprised that she was still with me, particularly as we had been so close to finishing.

Two days later hell arrived on my doorstep. The 'other woman' had discovered where I lived and was proving that there was no fury like a woman scorned. Throwing things, stamping and leaving the most hurtful of letters casting us both back into the pit again. It didn't stop there, for almost a year she would appear at my live shows to try and unnerve me. Sometimes egged on by a friend to scream and shout, other times writing notes distorting what had gone on between us. It was as if she had told all of her friends and didn't want to lose face; instead she lost her dignity. Whilst in panto I would often swing on stage in my role as 'The Flashing Blade' to see her right in the front row glowering at me. It didn't unsettle me, for I was at work, my haven from everything. Throughout this entire period my radio shows had also been incredibly supportive and I clung like a drowning man to the only things untouched by the whole mess.

Around this time, another girl appeared claiming that I had made her pregnant. The truth was I had never even met her. But she involved me in her fantasy and I had to deal with it. There was one amazing show when these two women actually sat in the same front row, never knowing that they were both out to get me. I still did my best on stage, but perhaps I did deliver my lines marginally faster that evening.

Finally, I decided to do what I considered to be 'the right thing'. In retrospect it was precisely the wrong thing, yet I felt duty-bound to make amends in whatever way I could. We were appalled about the way we had both behaved; we had both made huge errors and were both to blame; so we decided that we had suffered enough and that we should try and bring everything back to the way it was. I asked her to marry me, to give us a brand new start and recapture the good times we had once known. The omens weren't good, for despite my genuine will to put things right we were already falling back into our old ways, she involving her family and friends in the arrangements for the big day, whilst I would sneak back to my little office and write. But things did begin to turn out for the better and I was beginning to feel that maybe we did stand a chance after all. Yet even on our wedding day, as we entered Morpeth registry office, there stood 'the other woman' with her friend. A day designed to be happy was already tainted.

I went on air immediately after to host the rock show and declared my love to everyone. This would ultimately lead to comments like 'I bet your next marriage licence will be made out "to whom it may concern" ' and 'You must be addicted to wedding cake'. One of my closest friends had no confidence in it whatsoever, saying, 'I'll give it a year!' Although we both really tried to pull together, things really were never the same again, and I was always the weak link. I never really ever forgave myself and fourteen months later we found ourselves back where we had been all over again.

Many of the symptoms of the depression I had suffered started again, so we were looking at ways to put things together once more. Kristina had the opportunity to take a holiday on her own to stay with her Italian family, visiting Venice in the process, and later that year I took two of her friends on holiday to America with us, just to help keep things sweet. But by the end of that holiday I felt very much that it was me and them, and once home we were snapping at each other again. Around that time, as if to prove that I really did want things to work, I agreed to try and start a family. So began a period of sex for sex's sake with thermometers and head stands that had little to do with love and nothing to do with lust. It was after about six weeks of this that I realised that a child really wasn't the cure for our shaky relationship.

We were on the verge of splitting up once again, so I began to stock up with as much work as I could, to help me weather whatever lay ahead. I was about to fulfil another ambition, to put on my own panto, a story called *Sherlock Holmes And The Case Of The Christmas Curse*, at Newcastle Playhouse. It was a tale I had written based around some of my friends in the business, particularly designed to bring the very best out of my mate Denny Ferguson, who had almost died earlier that year. This would be the tonic to bring him back to his very best. Trying to involve Kristina, I asked if she would be prepared to make the costumes for the show and she agreed. But we regularly fell out over the production, and it was taking up far too much of my time, particularly as I was still doing all my radio shows too. By the time we needed all of the costumes finished, and even though we had tried to buy as many period costumes as we could from second-hand stores to save time and effort, her preparations were far from complete and we had to bring in a costumier called Allan Graham to save the day. I was under immense strain being responsible for everything and that pressure finally showed when a gold Charleston dress was ripped and Kristina refused point-blank to mend it, despite it being needed for two shows the following day. Shame-faced, I had to drive to Ashington and beg our choreographer Mary Hunter to come to my rescue. Things actually never recovered from that last straw that snapped the camel's back. I involved her with nothing else from that point.

By the spring we were fighting like never before and I was beginning to lose it all over again. This time I was absolutely certain that I was heading for a breakdown. As the arguments became more heated, I started to suffer from stabbing stomach pains and convulsions. Things were getting worse and worse, yet still to the outside world it was a brave face. Then finally the day came, as always on the verge of a special gig, my very first book signing session in Blyth, Kristina asked if I could first give her a lift to her mother's. Minutes away from her mother's house she proclaimed, 'I'm leaving you and I won't be coming back!' She had chosen her moment to perfection. She knew that I wouldn't let down all those people; I had no option but to let her go. She did eventually come back, to start yet another round of threatening to leave, packing her cases and posturing. Then my depression came back with a vengeance, and it wouldn't leave me for months. I was well used to suffering from stress, the jobs I do are filled with it. It's where

I live and I am aware of it but never let it affect my work. I hide it away inside myself. I cannot live in an atmosphere of unhappiness and misery, inside myself I knew that whatever we had was slipping away from both of us. I spoke to a *Night Owl* colleague from Relate, the marriage guidance people, in the strictest confidence; I talked to another Owl who is a psychiatrist and also my doctor as I tried to cover every avenue to sort it all out. We tried various separations as Kristina did the sad rounds of her family and friends, clinging on to the belief that suddenly things would right themselves, and the problems would just go away. They didn't and although everyone tried to help, the chasm between us was far wider than had ever been perceived.

I wish her well and hope that she gets out of life whatever she wants. Maybe right from the start her dreams had never been mine and vice versa. Divorce eventually followed.

It's always better to look where you're going than to see where you've been, for those who fear the future will waste the present. Yet following the breakdown of my third marriage I was as low as a man could possibly go. The very last thing I wanted was to start again, to have to go through the game of meeting people, courtship and the like. I was hurting and once again plunged headlong into work. And all the while there were the angry recriminations, the screamed phone calls as the relationship finally writhed to its final demise. I sat at home, weathering the various verbal storms from friends and family alike. My parents were once again totally dismayed. I chose to tell them that I was to blame, for deep down I believed that to be true. There were two sides to the story, but it was easier for me to accept the responsibility because I had eventually struck the final blow. I had won my freedom but at a terrible cost.

On the day that the second and biggest van load of things left, I sat in my small living-room in Cramlington. I couldn't bear to pack them up, however large or small, for they were special to me. Kristina had sent several lists of items she wanted me to send to her, and it was eventually decided that I should send everything. I didn't have a knife and fork, nor a plate. I couldn't remember how many times in my life that all of the things I had built up over the years had been handed over, leaving me nothing. Whilst friends marched around the house collecting everything from plant pots to curtains, I just sat next to my fireplace and couldn't stop the tears pouring down my face. Once more I was trying to be fair at my expense, and it would hurt my heart much more than my wallet. I had worked so hard, for seven days a week, for over twenty years and yet there I was with nothing. Deep down, if I could have exorcised all of the pain I had given others, friends and family alike, I would gladly have surrendered everything, but this was not to be. Instead the horror of it all began to sink in. Perhaps I wasn't meant to be with anyone forever; all I was certain of was that I never wanted to feel pain like this ever again. I thought of the high life many of my work colleagues had, many with the 'love 'em and leave 'em' philosophy. Many of them had slept with more women in a month than I had in my life, yet none seemed to have a fraction of the problems that I did. I had believed that if you love someone, you marry them, and live happily ever after. My parents were the proof and as always I was the pudding.

It took almost three hours to put everything in that van, the washer and tumble-drier the last to go in, surrounded by plants in their exotic pots. I thanked my friends for helping, then they were off to deliver the van load.

The following days were filled with those moments when I would go to iron a shirt, but find I had no iron. So with what little I had left in my bank account I'd buy an iron, then discover that the ironing board had gone too. I quickly bought some cheap plates and cutlery, as I decided to start eating at home instead of relying on one takeaway each day at the radio station.

I had spent months of unhappiness and torment, yet even now I was alone, it was still with me. I carried it like a curse and it began flooding every part of my life, except work. Work was always my escape. In the same way that I could lose myself in an old movie, I could allow my duties on radio or TV totally to envelope me, and I could be safe and relaxed for a while. I hated being alone. I have always been guilty of thinking far too much, and each time I would scratch my way back through all of my mistakes wondering if only I had handled things differently. It was all such a painful waste of time, yet I felt that it had to be done. My friends began making choices and rightly or wrongly I felt that I had to cut myself off from everybody. I believed, quite wrongly as it happened, that everyone had taken sides and I chose isolation rather than having to constantly explain myself. Then I interviewed a lady from one of the women's magazines on the phone-in show about making choices. What she said made so much sense. 'Each person has a right to do whatever they want with their lives. They don't owe anyone an explanation! . . . Every person must try and find true happiness and contentment, and you can't do that if you're trying to always keep someone else happy!' And finally the clincher, 'It's hard to do what needs to be done, but if you don't do it, it won't get done!' It was almost as if fate had decreed that I was given precisely the message I needed as my spirit was beginning to ebb. I had done the only thing I felt I could do to give myself a chance of happiness in the future. I had enough qualms and regrets to fill an ocean, but I had to look onwards, and off I headed without any real focus or direction.

Life has a way of coming up with something when we're in our darkest hour. I was lost in the blackness and had no idea where my help would come from. I had no romantic associations, my friends had been frozen out and the only people I had any dealings with were my work colleagues or the Night Owls. Whilst at work my life was busy and satisfying; outside that circle it was an empty desert. Janis Joplin once said, 'On stage I make love to 20,000, yet I always go home alone!' I was the life and soul of the late night phone-in, problems were solved, friendships made, laughs shared. Then at 2 a.m. prompt it all stopped. My social life, my family life, my friends all vanished into the ether and once again I was alone.

Whilst suffering my second great depression, I tried desperately not to let how I felt show on air, but one Wednesday night the programme had been totally taken up with divorce stories. By 2 a.m. I was totally demoralised and I couldn't have felt worse. All of the ins and outs, the sideswipes and unpleasantness, the cut and thrust of the frightened loneliness was upon me. After weeks of unhappiness my direction in life had been eroded to such a degree that I no longer seemed to have any control. My search for peace had left me alone (again) and I was far from happy. In my heart I knew that I was right to have made the decisions that I had, yet they had hurt just about every single human being that I cared for. The surest way to be lonely is to tell the truth, and although none had wanted to hear it, I had told the truth. I was hurting as badly as I ever had, the pressure I was feeling all wanted a release. So there was I roaring down the road at some ridiculous speed, almost tempting my own self destruction. Each night I was carrying the weight of others, yet this night my own weight was too heavy to bear. I raced onto the slip road near Newcastle's Holiday Inn and ground to a halt in a parking area. There I broke down, I wallowed in self-pity. The millions listening that week believed that life was so sweet for me, yet I was drowning in my own misery. By four in the morning I was still there, the sky was beginning to brighten, it was the very edge of a new day. The most lonely place in the world is the human heart when love is absent. There was no one left in my life. I was alone.

My home was an empty shell littered with memories that in each case had led to heartbreak. I just didn't want to go back there, but I had nowhere else to go. That house was still reverberating with arguments, rows and all of the horrors of a failing relationship. I was on my own and that is always the last place I wanted to be. Yet fate seems always to do something that gives you courage, rouses your ebbing spirit and pulls you to your feet again. At that moment I was lost, then almost on cue a huge brown owl swooped over the windscreen of the car. It gave me such a shock that I twisted my neck so severely that I could barely turn my head to the left. Yet again and again the owl swept down and all the while its eyes, caught in my headlights, seemed to look straight at me. It was a real Night Owl, showing solidarity with the man who had stolen his name. He perched on a fence within yards of the road, chest thumping, eyes electric green and showing no fear of me. I pressed the button to lower the passenger side window. 'You understand, don't you friend?' I mumbled. The owl didn't move, but stared at me. I continued, 'But what can I do? I'm alone just like you.'

I stepped out of the car and the bird, almost a foot in height, stayed still. Its neck followed my path as I leaned against the same fence upon which it stood, though I was at least ten feet away. There we both looked at the horizon as the sun began creeping up on us. I talked quietly to that bird and it paid me the ultimate compliment of listening, as I always did when Night Owls talked to me. Some say that birds are the spirits of those of us who have gone before, others say that owls in particular are wise. Whatever the truth I was grateful to that bird. Out of nowhere he was there for me when I couldn't cope with being alone. All my life friends had gathered around me, wanting things from me, yet it took a bird to give without taking!

The lengthy conversation, the spilling of all my woes had helped me. Finally I slowly walked towards the bird and thanked it. It sounds stupid but that is what happened. Maybe all the time it was thinking, 'Who is this wally?' But it stood watching and I just smiled at it – a most unlikely Samaritan. Then, almost as if my audience with it was over, it launched itself off the fence, missing my face by centimetres. It circled the car and, looking back at me, it flew away over the fields towards Blagdon.

The truth was I didn't have any friends; maybe that old owl didn't either, but I chose to believe he understood. I had a guest appearance less than five hours later. It was a waste of time going to bed so I made some toast and had a bath, watching some rubbish on television before putting on my glad rags to face the public. At 9 a.m. prompt I was waiting to get into the butcher's shop where I bought a skinned rabbit. Later that night on my way home after that evening's phone in, I placed the carcass on the fence where the owl had been. The next morning it was gone.

23 Reach Out and Touch

ONE THING THAT has always bugged me about the entertainment industry is that it has a great number of people who love the 'star' trip, believing they are somehow different from ordinary people. The real stars rarely exhibit such traits, but these semi-celebrities seem far too wrapped up in their own self-importance. Out of the masses of mail and calls I receive people often describe themselves as 'fans', and each time I chastise them. I don't want 'fans', I want friends. Fans are fickle, moving from one favourite to another. I want it to last longer than just during fair weather. To this end I have always made myself approachable, whether this is for those schoolkids who used to gather around my front door by the hundred at lunchtimes for signed photographs or for the pensioner who stops me in the street with a gripe about her coal supply. However, by far and away the most usual place for people to reach me, has been at the studios of Metro FM and it is there that a variety of things have happened.

One evening around 7.30 p.m. one of Metro's security men told me that a woman had arrived to see me, and that she'd fallen and was bleeding. She was wearing expensive clothes, yet her nose was bleeding and her stockings were torn at the knees and her skin was grazed. She looked late forties, early fifties and spoke in a very posh accent. I tried to calm her down, showing her to the downstairs ladies' toilet, so that she could wash and tidy herself. This she didn't do. In fact she didn't even wash the blood off her face. Thinking she was in shock following some assault, I phoned the police. She talked very calmly to me about her family, then about how much she loved the programme, saying that we shared very similar opinions about things. Suddenly the conversation became as if I was talking to two people, each one battling to take over the other. She said: 'Alan, I want to thank you for helping me because DON'T YOU FUCK WITH ME YOU BASTARD, I'LL FUCKING KILL YOU your programme helps me at night, just listening to a friendly voice makes YOU HATE ME, IF YOU DIDN'T YOU'D HAVE FUCKED ME BY NOW, SO NOW I'M GOING TO KILL YOU, DON'T THINK I WON'T, I'VE KILLED BEFORE AND can you not see I'm unwell. I've tripped and fallen, but I'm all right.'

I was terrified, yet tried to look as if there was nothing wrong. This continued for about another ten minutes until the police arrived. I briefed them as to what I believed her to be, mentally ill or schizophrenic, and they guided her to the car. Even then in one voice she was thanking me, in the other she was swearing at me. She returned on two other occasions, each time needing restraint and ultimate sectioning into the hands of the professionals.

On thousands of occasions callers would ask for things, and inevitably whatever they wanted would be found. Quite often they couldn't arrange for a place where goods could be exchanged, so they would bring them down to Metro's main reception. There people would leave the goods ranging from physical aids, motorbikes, CB radios, sacks of toys for a local children's ward, cakes and on one occasion a hand-made wishing well, and over the following week those seeking the goods would arrange to pick them up. On one occasion I felt a total mug following a call from a woman who had been robbed on the verge of her child's birthday. She said that she and her husband had nothing and that all she wanted was enough money to buy a small present for her child. As ever, I asked if her family could help; she said no. I asked if neighbours could help; she said no. I suggested asking the bank for a small overdraft until she was back on her feet again; she said no. She seemed sincere, so, as I had done on hundreds of occasions before, I asked her, off air, to call in and I'd help her out. At times like this I am very aware that people are often very reluctant to take a helping hand, so rather than make a big deal of it, I stuck some cash in an envelope, along with a note saying, 'Buy the bairn something decent. Happy birthday. Alan Robson.'

By chance, I was in Metro's canteen, directly above main reception, when a brand-new car arrived in the car park. It wasn't long after August so I noted the new registration. A couple flounced out of the vehicle dressed up to the nines as though they were on their way to a big night out. They took my envelope, and I just knew that no child would see a penny of that money. More likely I'd be paying for their night out. I rationalised that just because some people lie, this shouldn't lead to those who genuinely need help from missing out.

In one single year we average about 3,600 requests for help of one kind or another, and 95 per cent of those were met. Yet on one occasion we were almost conned by an exceedingly clever person in Red Row, Northumberland. A distraught woman had called the programme just before Christmas, saying that she'd been burgled and all of the presents had been taken. As a single parent, there was no way that she could replace them, or the television, video and hi-fi that had also gone. The thieves had cleaned her out to such an extent that they'd even stolen all her food. It was six days before Christmas and I had commitments all over the place, yet I felt that I had to do something. She explained how both she and her child had been abused by the child's father and all in all it was a very sad story. The wave of sympathy, enhanced by the time of the year, was incredible. Within minutes people began promising goods. Within 24 hours we had pledges of a microwave oven, three food hampers, turkeys, dozens of presents for the child, a local hypermarket had offered a free stack system, another shop a walkman, a second-hand store offered a video recorder, an electrical shop in Blyth came in with a colour television and countless presents wrapped in Christmas paper arrived at Metro and at Tyne Tees Television where I had a chat show. A rough estimate of the overall value was close to £3,000, not counting the dozens of people offering money to her. So stealing every spare minute I zoomed all over the North collecting these items, aided by a young man from Cramlington who had offered his services. Once they were all in one central place, I headed up to Red Row to deliver them. The entire listenership was thrilled to be able to help the lady and her daughter who had been so badly treated. Now we do check as best we can in most cases, and on my way to her home I called into the small police hut at Red Row. I explained what I was going to do and they looked in puzzlement at one another. They had heard the show and weren't aware of any burglary in Red Row around that time. I told them that they were mistaken, so they even checked their log. No one had reported any burglary on that estate for almost four months. However, they knew the woman concerned and it seemed that eight months earlier she had reported a burglary, which had proved upon investigation to be 'an insurance job'. The glass broken to get in was all outside, not inside where it should have been. Some of the articles she claimed to be stolen were in fact hidden around the house. So I pulled the plug at the very last moment. After three days of driving over 1,000 miles between us to collect stuff, I was left with returning everything to its rightful owner. Humble pie always sticks in my throat, but I refused to lie to these people whose kindness had been genuine. Some members of the public asked me to keep the gifts, handing them on to local hospitals or worthy causes. This was easily done. I told the woman precisely what I thought of her, yet even that didn't alleviate my anger.

There will always be those I describe as the 'owt for nowters' (anything for nothing) and they do more to dissuade people from helping those in need than anything else. Yet thankfully the vast majority of appeals for help are genuine and I'm filled with immense satisfaction when all does work out well. Such was the case of Charlie, an exiled northerner in London who could barely walk, but his local Social Services couldn't offer any assistance at all. What he needed was an electric wheelchair, but at around £2,000 each, he certainly couldn't afford to buy one. The Social Services had tried to get him one on the National Health Service but without success, and he found himself trapped in his house, with no way to get out at all. After an appeal was put out on the programme, the Render family wrote saying that they had such a thing that was no longer used. Within a day of the appeal, they had solved a problem that changed old Charlie's life. There was no easy way to collect the chair, so I sent a van to collect it and had it delivered to my home, where we tidied it up, checked it over, then shipped it to London. We sent some flowers to the Renders for their kindness, and paid the fees to get it moved. We've always tried very hard to 'make a difference' in whatever way we can, and this was a price well worth paying. On hearing how much it cost a colleague said, 'Alan, you'll never be rich!' That to me is only too obvious; there's so much red ink on my bank statements it looks as if my account is haemorrhaging!

Over the years we've collected well in excess of 300 pianos, organs and keyboards for old people's homes and provided wheelchairs, visual aids, furniture, cars, companions, cash, helpers, friends, countless electrical gadgets for hospitals, hospices and community halls. I am proud to have played a tiny part in so many amazing stories. There are about ten to twelve every single night. Yet still the shows are filled with serious stories, hilarious home truths and callers who become the star of the show, simply by being themselves. An intoxicating combination that once sampled can't be missed, by me, nor anyone else.

Some of the visitors that arrive to see me are definitely unwelcome. On several occasions women have declared their love for me, often based purely on my voice. On seeing my face that cures most of them, but for the others it is often harder to get the message across. One girl used to send me disgusting photographs of herself, but with the head cut off. Some women have walked straight up to me and said, 'Do you want to have sex with me?' It sounds like the answer to a man's dream, yet for me it is closer to a nightmare. Although I would love to think of myself as a sex symbol, I know my limitations. I always wanted to be a sex maniac, but I failed the medical. I have never fully understood why women bothered with me at all, for my work has always been so all-consuming that it has excluded much from my life that a woman would expect in a relationship. Often it would seem all right at first, then eventually she would find herself competing with it. Once that happened the end would loom into view. Would I ever find someone who could be as comfortable as I am living my job as my life?

My job is to talk to people and whether they're famous or not, they all deserve the same amount of respect. In fact, ordinary people are often far more fascinating.

Having said that, my biggest regret is not having met my great hero, Fred Astaire. Out of all the stars I've crossed paths with, he was THE ONE! A penniless immigrant, he worked hard to become the world's most stylish and sophisticated man – not bad for someone else born on the wrong side of the tracks. He was due to come to England in the summer of 1987 and I had already made preparations to snatch the interview I had been seeking. Then on 22 June 1987 he died. I was so near yet so far! I am sure many had told him how wonderfully talented he was; I merely wanted to say how proud I was that a little kid with nothing had made his mark. The back streets are a long, long way from the very top, yet he'd got there and I wanted him to know that I understood. I believe he would've known what I meant. Most of us can only work hard and hope, yet he was the beacon that shone out, proving that it can be done. Rather like a card someone sent me once: it was blank on the front except for a tiny star at the top of the page, and written in small letters on the bottom was the legend 'Go For It!'

All sorts of things happened with the visiting celebrities. On one occasion Alice Cooper called me asking if I could help him with his snake. He was due to play at Newcastle's City Hall and his python was poorly, so I fixed him up with a 'guest snake' for the evening.

There was once a great flurry of excitement when an opportunity came for me to meet and interview Prince Charles. I was asked to send a list of all the questions that I would be putting to him to his secretary before permission would be given. This I refused to do. I talk to people every single day, asking them the most personal and probing questions, all without any advanced warning, so I couldn't go against their trust in me by giving preferential treatment to anyone. I wrote a polite note to his secretary and three days later the offer of an interview was withdrawn. In a way I regret that, because I do think that a genuine heart-to-heart with a broadcaster who would ask the *real* questions that the public would like to know would give everyone a much better idea what the Royals are really all about. These pre-prepared, sanitised interviews with 'harmless' reporters do nothing, say nothing and mean nothing.

My desire to be fair has upset callers in the past. Even callers who ring regularly must expect no special treatment. Everyone is on an equal footing. It is for this reason that I choose to talk to celebrities on the telephone rather than get them to come to the studio. Celebrities are no more important than anyone else and must be seen to be the same.

Before he became a household name Bryan Adams told me: 'I'll probably never make it, but I'll keep going. I'll be happy if I can keep writing and singing good songs, then maybe one day I could end up with a car like yours!' Within five years he was back in the North headlining at Gateshead International Stadium. I hosted the show and he was in a chauffeur-driven limousine as one of the world's biggest rock stars. Few people know that he offered Joe Cocker the song 'Everything I Do, I Do It For You' from the film *Robin Hood Prince of Thieves*, only singing it himself after Joe turned it down. Just prior to his show Prince Charles and Princess Diana had announced their split, so I played the record Bryan had made called 'Diana', all about how the singer had never understood what she was doing with a man like Charles and how he had wanted to run off with her. The following morning it was on the front page of *The Sunday Sun*.

Prior to David Bowie's gig at Roker Park I met the man and with him was a local dignitary who seemed to be boring his ear off. So I found out this man's name and walked up to him saying, 'Excuse me, but the press want a quote from you about today's concert!' The local councillor fluffed up like a peacock and strutted out the door I'd directed him to. The safety door swung closed behind him and he couldn't get back into the stadium. 'Thank you very much,' said a much relieved David Bowie who was more than happy to give an interview now he was freed.

It really is strange that although on stage most of the women in rock exude an animal sexuality, on meeting them face to face I must admit that I see more rampant friskiness on the local high street. Joan Jett, Lita Ford, Girlschool, Gypsy Queen and even the German Doro Pesch were so 'normal' it was untrue. Some were pushier than others but all were refreshingly ordinary. The nicest lady of them was Doro, a tiny waif with long blonde hair, unassuming and straightforward. I was flown down to London by her record company to meet her and when she walked along the hotel corridor, a waiter was delivering a tray to a room on the same floor. Half-way along the corridor she dropped some papers and bent down in her tight black leather suit. The waiter couldn't do anything else but stare at her bottom and walked into the closed door, covering himself with gravy and vegetables.

When that little red light goes on and you're at the microphone it's a different world, a place where you must live on your nerves every single second. Once when talking to *Playboy* writer Cynthia Heimal I got rather more than I bargained for. She had just written quite an explicit book and I was to have a bit of fun at her expense. Interviewing celebrities isn't difficult; if they've done a lot of interviews you just press the right buttons and off they go. However, Cynthia was in a pixie mood, and instantly launched into talking about the more full frontal chapters, about oral sex, and how more women should enjoy it. I tried to discuss it in a sensible way, because you can talk about anything, as long as you're not immature about it. She really got down to it, if you'll pardon the expression, signing off with, 'So come on, girls, give your man oral sex and he'll love you for it!' I swiftly moved on to a lady caller who instantly said, 'Eeh Alan, I'm shocked, oral sex, a man's doodah in your mouth! Eeeh! . . . What I want to talk about is . . . Eeh, it was on the tip of my tongue a minute ago . . .' A fellow presenter was sitting beside me and he burst out laughing at her choice of words! 'What's he laughing at?' she screeched. That took some explaining.

Over the years I've caught up with Iron Maiden on many occasions. I interviewed Bruce Dickinson in the ladies' toilets in the City Hall, and I've played football against them at charity games and in the studio. After an interview I was hanging out with the band just before they recorded the videos for 'Number Of The Beast' and 'Run To The Hills', which were filmed in Newcastle. On stage were huge monsters and 'Eddie', their mascot, looking menacing and men dressed in horny red devil suits prodded forks about. Then the band got up to do the biz for the cameras. Bruce was screaming 'Six, six, six, the number of the beast', looking as menacing as he could, when one of the devils missed his footing and fell on to the stage, rolling and bouncing towards the front, his backside stopping literally inches from one of the floor cameras. The entire band roared with laughter as he tried to climb back up without success and the take was curtailed.

One of my early interviews was with Judas Priest at Newcastle's Gosforth Park Hotel. Not being a drinker, I made a total fool of myself all because I got there early. The public relations man, a canny lad called Robbie, met me in the bar saying, 'The lads won't be long, Alan. Have a double whisky while you're waiting!' Before

I could answer, it was there. I hadn't drunk whisky since the days I was too keen on booze, but was polite enough to drink it. Time marched on and after visiting the loo I returned to find another double shot of whisky in the glass. I was already feeling its effect when singer Rob Halford came down and invited me to join them for lunch, then we could talk later. Most civilised I thought. During the meal a tough American security guard kept filling my wine glass to the rim, and bottle after bottle circled the table. By the time the sweet course arrived, my taste buds were dead. I could've eaten the table napkins or the beer mats; my sense of co-ordination was also seriously in doubt. Then came the brandy. By this time I could hardly talk, and nor could they. When an entire table is this drunk, you're all best friends. Everybody's laughing, even though nobody's cracked a joke. So finally it was time to do my interview and I had fun chats with Glenn Tipton, K. K. Downing, Ian Hill and Rob Halford – over an hour and a half of interviews. On getting back to the studio it was apparent just how drunk we all were: out of 87 minutes of tape I was able to use eight minutes on the show. The rest was either slurred, disgusting or both! To my eternal shame most of the worst remarks had come from me!

Out of the blue Inxs gave me a call, offering to pop in for a chat, and it was there that we recorded an entire show with them as co-hosts. It's funny how word gets round in the rock business, because whilst chatting to them I mentioned how good I felt fellow Australian Jimmy Barnes was. Within the week Jimmy phoned me to ask if he could come on the show. He did, sang live and was an absolute knockout! It is interesting to note that the Aussie bands are completely down to earth whilst many European and American bands like to heap on the pretensions. The Australian circuit is very tough, not dissimilar to the club circuit that I had worked, and you don't forget that kind of baptism of fire.

If I had to list some of my real heroes, the name of blues legend B. B. King would be high in the order. I've interviewed him on many occasions. Coming from an impoverished background, he's played guitar and sung for money since he was a street-corner entertainer at the age of four. When I first met him he was in his late fifties. In his dressing-room at Newcastle's City Hall I noticed him pacing back and forth. I asked, 'Surely, after over fifty years of working live, sometimes 250 shows a year, you can't possibly be nervous?' He replied, 'I ain't nervous, I'm concerned.' It made so much sense, he cared so much that the show was good. It's a phrase I've never forgotten and it is a feeling I have shared ever since in my own humble way.

I interviewed Motley Crue's Vince Niel while he was awaiting sentencing for the 'death by dangerous driving case' he was involved with. He said, 'I know I'm going to jail. I deserve to. I was a fool and I can't give life back where it belongs!' All the while I was learning from the lives of others.

From The Stones to Paul McCartney, Elton John to Tina Turner, I have been most fortunate in the thousands of names I've met. Yet it is those little guys that get to the top after years of knock backs that I really remember. I hammered into the ears of the north a band called Terraplane. Year in, year out, I kept pushing this really talented outfit, with good lads, but it only managed a snatched top 30 chart placing. Finally, after a name change and an image transplant they became Thunder and never looked back. Jon Bon Jovi, that young lad with stars in his eyes who told me his first album 'probably wouldn't light any fire', got where he deserved. Another band who deserve to be there is the current project the Little Angels. When I hosted Bryan Adams show with Extreme, Squeeze and the Angels, they were due on first and worried about it. I had the crowd for an hour before them and by the time they came out I'd revved it so high they couldn't fail. One of them yelled 'Thanks Alan, next time we'll be warm-up for you!' I was mortified to learn they were to split up in the summer of 1994.

On TV and radio I'm surrounded by the household names not just of the North but of Britain and the world, yet the catch 22 situation for me remains. To climb that same ladder I'd have to move South. This I refuse to do, choosing my beloved North every time. I do work away, as long as I can get a fast train or plane home. My base will always be in the North, and each night I'll be with my friends on Metro FM's *Night Owls*.

Over the years I have often been asked who influenced me. I always hated the old Neanderthal phone-in shows, refusing to listen to them, but one man who has had great impact on my career is my friend and gaffer Giles Squire at Metro FM. He has always left me to my own devices, to bend and shape the show, yet at key moments he is there to fine tune the package, always to best effect. In the early days when he was a fellow presenter he used to say, 'Don't prepare jokes. Fly by the seat of your pants. You can do it. You'll sound better and the show will be stronger!' At first I doubted him, but under his influence *Night Owls* has had the biggest audience for a phone-in show in Britain. Giles' ability to mould it into shape has been essential. He has never lied to me, never let me down and it is thanks to him that we are seeing off all comers. There are very few people in this crazy business who are as excited about what they are doing as I am, but Giles certainly fits that category. In many ways our lives have run parallel and no one was happier than I was to see him promoted through the ranks. Insight, intuition and a knowledge of what it is like to work at the rough end, that is why he's got where he is. His signings have been superb; his judgement bang on the button. He fights your corner and there is no one in Britain that I feel a greater sense of loyalty towards. My success has been his success! He's a good friend and a supportive boss.

24 See What Granny's Brought You

I HAD BEEN ALONE on and off from February, the formal separation from Kristina came in early June, and it was now October and I was still on rock bottom. The friends I was working with on my television series *College Cuisine* were stunned when they realised the kind of pressure I had been under. Yet as the series progressed the director, a smashing lady called Betty Bage, said that she thought that Rosie, my PA and already a trusted friend, was interested in me. The producer, Gillian Firth had noticed it too. Although I was well aware that Rosie was concerned about me, having witnessed many of my lowest moments, I was sure that she had no romantic inclinations. I had met Rosie at a shop opening where I had mentioned that we were interviewing for my company, Blade Enterprises. She said that she was a personal assistant, and half in jest, suggested that she could do the job. She had interviews with my manager and myself and was eventually given the job. She was also working as a *Night Owl* telephonist and I found her a warm and genuine lady. She was a mother of two and, although only in her middle to late thirties, a grandmother of a smashing little lass called Jayne Ashley. A week or so before the very last episode of *College Cuisine* the entire crew went for a meal in Chinatown, Newcastle; as it was Rosie's night on *Night Owls*, she had promised to come and pick me up from the restaurant and give me a lift to Metro FM where I'd parked my car, thus saving a taxi fare. Throughout the meal I had been given a thorough talking to by Betty, Gillian and the rest of the bunch, all of them saying 'Look, ask her out!' I really liked Rosie a lot, but conscious of my past record I felt that to ask her to take a chance on me would be rather like asking Eddie Murphy to join the Ku Klux Klan – and with a similar likelihood of success. All the telly folk knew that I had arranged a big Christmas party in November for everyone associated with Blade, so I promised them that over the next few days I would try and build up the courage to ask Rosie to accompany me to the 'do'. I promised Betty that if I was successful and if Rosie honoured me with a 'Yes' I would wear a feather in my hair on the set for the grand final of *College Cuisine*. The team all waited with baited breath, all wondering whether I had shown the courage to launch myself into the unknown again. The day finally came around and to everyone's surprise there I stood wearing a Red Indian's headdress.

The following few weeks I was very worried indeed, because Rosie had always appeared to me to be a bit of a hard-hitting woman, not frightened to give her views. She had suffered a lot in her private life, I really didn't want to risk hurting anyone else, least of all her. What actually made it more stomach churning was that we worked together, and it had always been drummed into me that you never make a mess in your own backyard. Rosie was a stunner, yet totally different from anyone I'd ever known, with eyes that could stop you in your tracks. Right from the start Rosie had said that she wasn't looking for a relationship at all, and neither was I. So what was that night going to be all about? I put it down to two friends choosing to team up, rather than be gooseberries among all of the other couples.

This 'forthcoming engagement' did put a little bit of pressure on our working relationship, as others seemed to be giving it more relevance than we were. All the while the personal pressures on me continued, and Rosie increasingly became my listening post. At this time she was being visited by echoes of her past too, so we were shoulders for each other to cry on. On the day before the Blade party I promised to give Rosie a lift to Metro for the *Night Owls*, since she lived nearby in Bedlington. Her car, a rather dodgy machine, had broken down, and it would save her a taxi fare. That night was very businesslike, then on the way home Rosie said the Blade party was her first proper date for a long time.

'A proper date!' That was the very first time it had been so described. Up until then it had had the same rating as a business lunch. I began to feel those 'naughty schoolboy' feelings, and grinned like the cat who had all the cream. She was beautiful, but had more balls than most men I knew. I felt thoroughly intimidated by her, a feeling not helped by the fact that her youngest daughter Sarah still lived with her and I had always fought off any thought of being a 'family man'. We sat in the car for what seemed like ages, then finally she invited me in for coffee – just coffee. We talked for a while and before we knew where we were the sun was rising, yet we hadn't noticed the time passing. She had to be at work for 9 a.m., and she barely had time for a shower and a change of clothes. Just before I left I thanked her for putting up with my series of grumbles, saying, 'Maybe the party will be special after all!' During that time I had toyed with the idea of kissing her, because you can tell a lot from a kiss, and I had felt so lonely for so long. Eventually we passed each other in a doorway and I went for it. First it was clumsy, then we started concentrating on what we were doing and the fireworks went off. I think she knew too, and swiftly bundled me out of the door before I got any other ideas. My privates had purely been ornaments for quite a while, in fact the only ornaments I had left, as my home was still very empty and bare. I got into my car and drove off. I felt good, the first time in months, yet I said under my breath 'Oh my God, what have I done now?'

It was going to be a long weary day for Rosie having had no sleep at all, and as soon as I got to bed, within twenty minutes the phone rang and my day had begun. What had I done? What was I going to get myself into now?

All of my preconceived ideas as to my 'perfect partner' had been shattered.

I had never wanted children. Rosie had two!

I dated girls much younger than I was. Rosie was almost my age.

I never dated people I worked with. Rosie ran my office.

I could see the cheap-shot headlines: 'The Night Owl and the Night Owl Girl' or worse 'ALAN ROBSON FALLS FOR GRANNY'. Yet when it all came down to it, whatever they wrote wouldn't matter, provided I could be with this woman. Having watched how she worked, seen her loyalty growing as we beavered through some turbulent water, my respect for her had grown enormously. I had very few real friends, because the surest way to loneliness is to always tell the truth. She really shone, almost radiated, and I was exposed to this day in and day out. No wonder I was drawn to her. No matter how confident I was in my day-to-day entertaining, it was quite a different matter when it came to women. Love at first sight might be wonderful, but I do think it wise to take another look. Having made a fool of myself with past flirtations, I wanted to make absolutely sure that this would be a proper relationship. I had made such a pig's ear of friendships and my love life, I wasn't even sure if I could trust myself, let alone expect someone else to. There seemed to be this invisible line around six years that caused my relationships to self-destruct. I'd never even managed to reach my seven-year itch.

My thoughts during the hours before leaving the house that fateful day were in turmoil. Had I been on air advising a fellow 'worrier', I'd have said, 'There will always be enough for today without taking on the burdens of tomorrow or yesterday!' Yet I have never been able to take my own advice, and thus always ended up that certain creek, usually without a paddle. I couldn't help worrying, but knew that worrying couldn't help me either. Following my show it was a quick change into my poshest outfit to go to the big end-of-year party and meet my 'date'.

I felt rather clumsy and cumbersome; it was all far too out in the open. Whether I liked it or not, I was still married and it did concern me that I wasn't completely free, that I could offer Rosie nothing concrete. I rationalised that, having been separated as long as I had, my feelings were bound to be jumbled up anyway, and after all I wasn't planning on sweeping her off her feet, merely getting to know her better. We'd spent a fair bit of time working together, but socialising was something else. In recent months my own self-esteem had fallen around my ankles like a wet swimsuit. Only bluff had kept me going, yet surely I was about to add to my problems not alleviate them?

The party was specifically designed for those who had been associated with Blade and Rosie had insisted that she should be there to 'meet and greet' all of our guests. I was on air until 7 p.m. so had no alternative but to meet her there. This concerned me because I wouldn't have the chance to break the ice in private before facing up to all of the people that I knew with a new partner. Driving to the hotel, my tummy gurgling like a manic dish washer, I even thought of taking the coward's route and turning around, blaming an 'urgent appointment'. The problem there was that Rosie was in charge of all of my appointments and that we'd planned a madcap cabaret that wouldn't happen without me. I was on automatic pilot to get to the Gosforth Park Hotel and before I fully knew where I was I was marching into the lift to go to the function suite where everyone was assembled. I must have been glowing like a Belisha beacon when I tentatively poked my head around the door, scanning the room for any sign of her. Would I feel the same way as I had when I'd kissed her, or had that been just a crazy moment with any real attraction dissipating seconds later?

There she was in an amazing leather outfit happily chatting away to a chocolate tycoon. People had actually spoken to me, but I'd been too wrapped up in finding Rosie. When she turned towards me, I reacted like a rabbit caught in the glare of car headlights and was waiting to be hit. Yet totally unconcerned, she waltzed towards me, kissed me on the cheek and acted as if nothing had happened. To me this kiss had been a major event, so my heart sank thinking that maybe it hadn't meant the same to her. I was carried along in her wake, intoxicated by her; whilst meeting all of our guests my mind was lost in her. Then it was time, following a very classy meal, to get on stage and perform a few silly songs to get everyone in the party spirit.

My friends from television knew that it was our very first dalliance and watched our every move, occasionally whispering words of encouragement to me during the night. Having discovered that it is virtually impossible to visit nightclubs without being hassled, I had finally found myself at a party that I could enjoy. It was costing me thousands of pounds so I had better make the most of it. Time had evaporated like spilled wine and before I knew where I was I was clutching Rosie tightly to me during a very smoochy 'Those Were The Days of Our Lives' by Queen, the DJ's last record of the evening. We were both totally sober but couldn't even go home together, for Rosie had her car and I had mine. My thoughts had moved from friendship into the realms of love and passion, and certainly lust was cropping up in there too. In an attempt to tempt her along that road, I chattered like an Arctic explorer's teeth to keep her beside me for longer, yet off she went. I watched as her car vanished along the road to Bedlington as I turned towards Cramlington to curse my hesitation. I was brimming with mixed emotions, I was happy but disappointed, pleased but dissatisfied and not really sure where we would go next. I had been a proper gentleman but my trousers insisted that I would have felt far better being an improper, ungentlemanly cad.

Now I had no choice. I had to begin my campaign to win this woman!

Only those who have had broken hearts will really understand how desperate you feel, how you yearn for someone to hold you, to make you feel special in any way, to make you feel alive again. I had made that mistake in the past, reaching out to someone who was there, but wasn't right, so this time I wouldn't allow myself to fail again. All the while my shows were doing very well, beating off all competition, yet behind the scenes I was in complete turmoil. Rosie and I were growing closer, spending hours talking about our lives, our fears, our hopes for the future. I was horrified to hear some of the things inflicted on her by those purporting to have loved her in the past, for she had been very badly treated indeed and had many emotional scars. I was carrying a great deal of weight too and to share it with anyone was most therapeutic. I had never told anyone these things before, yet out of my mouth they tumbled, like escaping squirrels, bounding to her. Maybe in the past my insecurity had made me feel that younger women were best suited, they are easier to impress, easier to please with material things, money, being in the public eye. Here was a woman of my own age who didn't give a jot as to whether I was a clerk or a carpenter, she just wanted things to 'feel right'. It sounded too simple yet that is exactly what I wanted too. I had always felt so very proud of my mam and dad, my mother ever supportive, my dad working every hour that God sent, and to be sure I was following that example, I never had a moment to myself yet I wanted to steal time to actively court this woman. She worked all week so we would steal Fridays whenever work allowed, to vanish into the countryside, or just barricade ourselves in her house or my house trying to avoid the phone or the fax.

Towards Christmas it had felt as if we were 'sneaking about' so

I finally decided that this was not correct. I was legally separated and had gone through a very sad and depressing year, now was the time to start pulling my life together properly. I still suffered those melancholy times where I would think about all the things I had done, wondering about all those 'What if . . . ' scenarios. The truth is that they are a waste of time, you've got to live for now, not for then. So with Christmas just around the corner I decided to invite Rosie and her daughter to stay for the festive season. I had no experience of children, but Sarah who was fifteen at the time seemed to like me. This would be a major test for us all. I must admit that I was incredibly jealous at first, because there is an amazing bond of love between them. No matter what was said, whether in anger or in upset, you just knew that their special feelings for one another would never change. My family life was quite different. I had gone through long periods in my early teens actively hating my dad, because he wouldn't let me get away with the things I wanted. I had lengthy periods of being dischuffed with my sister too, yet even if I'd fallen out with my mother I could never bring myself to do anything other than love her. Always a strange blend of grace and dottiness, my mother was a bottomless pit of affection throughout my formative years.

That week or so over Christmas and into the New Year was a great success, although it was very much a 'family' occasion. My rather more lewd and lascivious intentions went to the wall, neither of us wanting to make Sarah feel alienated. Instead my libido was alienated; in fact I locked it in the back garden until early January when they returned to their home in Bedlington. Rosie was amazing: she seemed to juggle a very demanding job, sometimes involving seven-day weeks, and her many family commitments, and still managed to race around after me in the evenings for a stolen hour whenever possible. It was a most unsatisfactory way to woo, but all we had.

Early in 1993 on a blustery Monday night Rosie called around after work to watch *Robson's People*, my chat show, which had been recorded some months before. It had been a long hard day and we had flopped in front of the TV when the doorbell rang. Leaving Rosie in the living room, I clumped to the front door and opened it. It was my Kristina!

In a blind panic, I slammed the door firmly in her face,

correcting in seconds to open it again. My heart was doing a Buddy Rich drum solo as she asked to come in. I explained that I had company and didn't think it was a good idea. We talked for over an hour on the doorstep, both of us speaking from the heart, both hurting. What I had no idea about was how badly Rosie was feeling; she wanted to get out yet we were blocking the only door. She had found a bottle of sherry but it wasn't helping. She was trapped and had no choice but to wait, no matter how uncomfortable it was. She would catch the odd word, the occasional sentence, and string them together out of context.

We had needed to talk, to affirm what was happening and where we were both going in our lives. Yet by talking we had hurt each other again, and in turn I had hurt Rosie too; so all things considered it was a most unsatisfactory night. My relationship with Kristina had ended because I wanted to stop hurting her and stop being hurt myself, not for purely selfish reasons. Yet still the pain was being dragged out, causing heartache to whatever or whoever it touched. I had explained that Rosie was inside and Kristina had asked, 'Do you love her?' Even at that moment I was far from certain so replied, 'Time will tell!'

As she left, Kristina had wanted a hug, even asked for one, but I refused saying it would have given her false hope, that it wouldn't have been fair. I am the most tactile person I know, I hug everyone, yet I couldn't allow it on this occasion. I felt ashamed at the same time, knowing how desperately unhappy she was feeling.

It was a devastatingly sad evening all round. I was sick with sorrow, and marched back into my living room seeking a hug from Rosie. Instead, I found a she-devil – she was stotting mad! 'Let me out of here,' she screamed. 'I don't want any of this!' I kept chasing Rosie round and around the sofa as she yelled and cried as insecurities flooded from her. I wanted to hold her as much for myself as well as to reassure her, but it was so early into our courtship that it caused our first major upset. I wasn't the kind of man that would cause hurt unnecessarily, I had spent most of my life trying to make people happy, yet there I was, with the woman who I was slowly but surely falling in love with, trying to cork a volcano.

It is Rosie's way to want to protect me. Even had she been still just a friend, it is how she would act. She had seen me so desperate and unhappy that she wanted to save me from going through all that again. In retrospect, it was really funny the dozens of laps around the furniture, but at the time we were in so very much pain, both of us filled with uncertainty. Finally amidst the tears we ended up clinging on to each other as if we were on a cliff face, knowing that so easily we could fall.

The time we made for each other began to change the kind of person I am. I started to feel more confident. Despite work increasing to such a level that we could barely cope, I knew that I could rely on Rosie completely. We were getting on like a house on fire so we began to plan for the future, our future together. We talked things over with Sarah, Rosie's daughter, who could see that things were picking up speed. Everything looked set for a new beginning for everyone.

I decided that, not having had a single day off in sixteen months, I needed to get away from it all for a while. It would be another opportunity to get to know Sarah and Rosie, and to consolidate our relationship. So I booked a holiday in America and off we flew. Once again I had ensured that Sarah wouldn't be left out by letting the two ladies share a room, while I was in by myself. There certainly were teething problems, as Sarah showed signs of jealousy over this man who had the audacity to fall in love with her mum, but they were few and far between. By the end of the trip we were closer than ever before. I had watched in wonderment as Rosie had to adopt different roles during our time away, from an in-control mum to a wide-eyed tourist, a happy companion to a thrilling lover, a worried woman to a very special friend. Months before I had realised just how little of the world she had seen, when on visiting a stately home she had burst into tears on seeing the beauty of it all. She had such a tender heart yet it had endured hardship rather than true love. I would change all that. If I had my way I would give her the world on a plate, show her its wonders and try to demonstrate that no matter how incredible they were they paled into insignificance next to my love for her!

There was now no doubt whatsoever: I was finally sure that we were in love! I can honestly say that I had never laughed so much as during that time. I was at last able to cast off all my chains of worry and just be *me*. I was so unused to that, and I would be forever grateful to Rosie.

Whenever Rosie got excited she would get a scared pain, and

this would be a constant source of joy to me. She knew something wonderful was going to happen, but was terrified at the same time. I would constantly seek to find ways to bring out those 'scaredy pains', to attempt to share with her some of the special times that had been so lacking in her life. In turn they would make me feel as if I was achieving something. Words could never express how this woman overwhelms me.

Returning home, it seemed stupid that we should part, Rosie and Sarah returning to their home in Bedlington and me alone to Cramlington, but that is what Rosie insisted. We had talked about the possibility of her moving in, but Rosie had stamped hard on that idea. The Cramlington house had been home to two failed relationships and although she would agree to come and stay occasionally at weekends with Sarah, she would never move in. A view I understood and respected.

We decided that we had to have a new start. The house held too many unhappy memories and I was reaching an age where I was nearing my last chance for a mortgage. Once you reach your middle thirties you realise that another 25-year term will see you into your sixties, and how many of us will still be working when we're that age? So we started house-hunting and I put mine up for sale. The market was totally flat so we approached various companies with a view to a part-exchange and we eventually secured the very last house on a new estate just outside Morpeth. What little furniture I had left from Cramlington I just gave away; sofa, chairs, tables, beds were all found new homes. We had chosen a brand-new start and, regardless of how long it would take us, it wouldn't be built on remnants of the past. It would be totally 'ours'.

One afternoon Rosie and I had stolen an hour together, choosing to spend it wandering along the malls in Gateshead's Metrocentre. I had my arm around her as we enjoyed an all too rare break in our busy schedules. We were just returning to our car, when a couple in their middle fifties approached us, the lady saying, 'Alan, can I just say that I've always hoped to meet you. I really enjoy your programmes!'

I was very flattered and thanked her.

Seeing my arm around Rosie, she added, 'And this must be your wife?'

I replied: 'No, actually it's not!'

Her reply was marvellous: 'Well, can I just say that she's lovely anyway!' Then off she went, probably feeling as if she'd put her foot in her mouth, but we were both thrilled by her reaction. The press, on the other hand, began plaguing us for stories. My private life was my own and I had no intention of giving those kind of interviews, trying to shield Rosie as best I could. Reporters visited the house hoping to catch us together and on one charity occasion, when I was asked to start a sponsored walk raising money for the children of the North with 'The Yellow Brick Road', they even had photographers with telephoto lenses hiding in bushes hoping to catch us. On tumbling to their plan we merely kept our distance throughout the afternoon. It wasn't easy for Rosie to find herself in the glare of the public eye, choosing to keep out of the limelight whenever possible. Still we kept our relationship private, despite outrageous attempts by people to smoke us out.

Thankfully the house exchange was finalised and we moved in to what we could only describe as our dream house. We named it God's Little Acre. The drawback was that we would have to work even harder to guarantee keeping it. Yet at last we were together under the same roof. It was strange yet wonderful. Finally, all that hard work for well over twenty years had borne fruit. I had a new house, a new love and a new chance!

At last, I felt confident that Rosie was to be *the one* for me. The search was finally over. We had found each other. It is amazing that we both said the same things to one another, that we both wished that we had met all those years ago, so we could be the first as well as hopefully the last. To say that we had been through hell was an understatement, for hell had actually come to visit and stayed around far longer than we deserved, yet we had faced it and fought off all comers. I knew that Rosie had suffered the kind of stress I had lived with since my middle teens, and it takes some handling! So all of those old-fashioned feelings began to take me over. The decree nisi had long been awarded, we were waiting merely for the rubber stamp of the decree absolute, then I would be free. Now was the time that I really wanted to settle down, once and for all. Rosie had said early in the relationship that she didn't want to marry me, having no desire to be the *fourth* Mrs Robson, and perhaps I had no right to expect her to change her mind, but over the months I would do my damnedest to achieve that very end. Whenever I was away from her I felt so desolate, needing to be with her every second possible, even being at work seemed too far away. I had to make her mine!

How is it that someone can take you over so completely? I had never known anything like it before, yet to use Rosie's very own rule of thumb, it 'felt right'!

The only real ambition that Rosie had ever shared with me was to visit Paris. She had come close several times in the past, but had never actually had the money to make her dream come true. Every time that Paris featured on TV or cropped up in conversation, Rosie would go all mushy. It had been the one place above all others that she really wanted to see, particularly that amazing tower named after its designer Gustave Eiffel and built back in 1889. Once she said, 'But you've got to go with that special person!' Knowing the city as well as I did, a devious plan began hatching.

In September 1993 I booked us for a week in Paris, while Sarah stayed with friends. Off we went and for the very first time we were actually alone together. It was quite simply the most amazing week. Never have I felt so totally and completely at one with someone. We shared the same thoughts and the same dreams.

I had decided that I would take her to the top of the Eiffel Tower and propose, then from that day on whenever we would see pictures, films or TV programmes, that image would remind us of the day we pledged our love to one another. I know it's a bit sloppy, owing more to Cary Grant and Deborah Kerr in *An Affair to Remember* than to Tom Hanks and Meg Ryan in *Sleepless in Seattle*. On arriving at the hotel, minutes away from the Champs-Elysées, Rosie noticed a sign saying that breakfast in bed was optional at no extra cost and her eyes lit up. She is a coffeeholic, and the thought of limitless coffee and croissants every morning, without having to stir herself was too much to pass up. Next morning the waitress duly brought the tray. Sleeping nude, I grabbed a towel, wrapped it around me, and with my hair sticking up like Tin Tin I headed to open the door. As the waitress handed me the tray my towel slipped, and I could do nothing but thank her and back away. I tried to kick the door closed to hide my ever-shrinking dangly bits, but the towel was jammed tight underneath. I turned and almost sprinted bare-buttocked to deliver the tray to the still snoozing Rosie, then darted back to remove the towel and restore my dignity.

After a couple of days wandering around the city I was building up to ask her to marry me. The visit was incredible. I was seeing everything through her eyes, and it was affecting me more deeply than ever. Rosie was in tears of joy after seeing the murals and mosaics at the white-domed basilica of Sacré-Coeur, sobbing on seeing the beauties of the Louvre Museum and even the hurly-burly of Montmartre. In between we were laughing and giggling like two sixteen-year-olds; this was how life should be lived! We'd partied at the Moulin Rouge, chewed on crêpes at the Opera House and shopped till we dropped. We used this week to give us back all of the things stolen from us at home, and every moment was filled with activity. In one day we visited Euro Disney, had two meals out and went to the cinema. It was non-stop and we loved it. Then came *that* time and I told Rosie that we were off to visit the Eiffel Tower. Finally her dream was about to be a reality.

Now I was the one with the frightened tummy, thinking that if she refused me, I would have ruined the dream experience that Paris was to her. I had to take the chance. It was my only hope of giving her my love and trying to show her just what she meant to me. How I wished that this was my very first love – my life would have been so different. Workwise I would change very little, for I have been so very lucky in that area, but elsewhere I would have laughed so much more.

We arrived at the foot of that mighty structure and got into the long queues as hundreds of tourists prepared to journey to the top for that awe-inspiring view. I had planned to make it even more memorable with that question to pop. I was so wound up, worry nagging away at me like a toothache, and once again there was a glint of cowardice, as my mind suggested leaving well enough alone. But I *had* to go through with it and grabbed Rosie tight, putting all of my welling emotion into a kiss to her neck. Nothing could possibly go wrong now.

Just then Rosie said: 'You'd better say hello to them!'

I was puzzled. 'Say hello to who?'

She pointed to the adjacent queue. There were two coach loads of schoolkids from Newcastle and Sunderland on a trip to Paris, and every single one had recognised me. I waved and tried to sign as many autographs as I could, so I wouldn't have to once at the top. I had much more important things to do there. Yet the twenty kids turned to forty, then to sixty, then to eighty. When we got to the top they were still following me. After hundreds of photos had been taken, I finally said, 'Thanks everybody, but I'd like to take a look around now! Come on, Rosie!'

One eagle-eared young lad said, 'Rosie. Are you Rosie off the *Nights Owls* switchboard, the one who sets those really hard competitions?' Rosie nodded, and from that moment everyone who had my autograph came running back to get Rosie's and to take her photo. The teachers cracked jokes, saying how terrible it was for us. They didn't know the half of it. It was a tragedy. I was greatly honoured by them bothering, yet totally devastated that the special moment had been stolen from us. It was as if the sky felt sorry for us too, as when we descended back to earth it started to rain. So I dragged Rosie into the park directly beneath the structure, and there beside a statue of Aphrodite I asked her to marry me!

Thank the Lord she said 'Yes!'

25 Feels Like Forever

WHAT LIES BEHIND us and what lies before us are tiny matters compared to what lies within us. It seems that I am doomed to spend forever searching for 'security' in the same way that flashing blades of old spent their lives seeking their own holy grail.

To outsiders, what I do may appear to be 'just radio and TV programmes'; yet those programmes have changed so many lives and I too have had so many hilarious nights making them that I am as addicted as those that listen. Even when I am away from the show, around 10 p.m. my palms begin to sweat and my mind begins to focus, ready to take on the hundreds of different subjects and problems that I'm bombarded with. With so many high-profile activities, I'm working up to eighteen hours a day to keep them all going. During the run of a television series I don't have a single day or night off for over three months. The job has taught me to always do what I'm hired to do, then give even more. If you do, they will come back and hire you again.

My biggest regrets are hurting those people in my life who didn't deserve it, yet in every case I paid for it with interest. Now I am trying to build a new life with my new family, something I never believed I would have. Rosie and Sarah love me in a way I would have said was impossible two years ago. I love them so very much and now I have even greater incentive to work harder, achieve more and go further than ever before. It is as if I have had to suffer the failures, the pain, the tears and depressions to get where I am now, to find my Rose! How often we sit and hold each other, wishing that we had met each other first, so that those years we've been with others, we could have enjoyed together. Yet each smile I've had in the past, each battle, every single up and down has brought me to where I am, and I thank God for it! Now at last on the domestic front I am content, a word I've always wanted to say and finally can. I have been like everyone else, searching for that one special person that I'd always been told was out there somewhere waiting for me. After so many mistakes I never believed that everything could suddenly fit into place in the way that it has. Like most men, sometimes I'm sweet other times sour, but I know that no matter what happens in my life, I will always be in love with Rosie.

I found myself falling headlong in love and trying to please her. She didn't like my clothes, hated my socks and despised underwear of any kind. It was like being hit by a hammer and I had no choice but to go along with it. My entire wardrobe was started from scratch. Following my second TV series the public wrote their approval and it was all down to Rosie and Brian Smith from Leaf in Newcastle. Coming to terms with life without trollies (underwear) takes a little getting used to, but gone are those tell-tale underwear lines on tight clothes, gone are those unsightly cricket-ball size lumps in tight jeans caused by Y-fronts, and I could never bear the discomfort of a piece of elastic up my bottom from those G-strings. I have been set free in so many ways, even in my trousers!

When I first met Sarah, through inexperience I treated her as if she was a child, instead of the young lady she is. Now we are great friends and she seems to understand me very well. I was recently giving her a lift when I asked her: 'How do you *really* feel about me having been married before?' Her reply was: 'That was then, you can't change what has happened in the past. That's what has made you what you are now, and we love you for what you are, not for what you've done!' Pretty damn sharp for a 16-year-old! There is a kind of friendly rivalry between us as we constantly seek Rosie's love and approval, and we regularly spend nights screaming with laughter. Now I find myself swamped in love from a grandma and a child. Two black sheep and a special lamb. All we seek is the chance to share as many special times together as we can. For the very first time my parents, sister and uncle all declared that they have never seen me so at ease, and they put it all down to Rosie's love. They love her almost as much as I do!

The insecurities loom as large as ever, but we will try and face up to everything together, and perhaps Rosie's 'tiny steps' will end up taking me further than my old style of charging into the unknown. Everything that I've done, whether great or small, successful or a flop, has always started by me deciding to give it a try. One of my bosses wrote a reference for me once: 'Alan has a habit of biting off more than he can chew, then chewing it!'

Those people who labelled me as common and ignorant, purely because of where I come from, now have another view. That battle was very hard won. I left home to set the world alight, and although all too often I had to return home for more matches, the fuse is now well lit. I believe that Rosie is the first person really to understand my all-consuming need to work, fuelled by having been unemployed and never wishing to return to be lost in its limbo again. Nothing can stand in my way when a job needs to be done, whether it's a day spent sorting out a widow's pension that won't earn me a penny, or if it's a major live show that will earn me a week's wages. The fact is that I am never happy unless I am striving for something. Rosie knows that and is always there for me. I hope and pray that this is my heart's final port of call. I have had too many lovers, yet not enough love. Sometimes my fingers tremble when I hold her, for what I hold is so important to me. She is my true companion!

I have never sought riches, for I only end up giving them away or losing them to worthy causes. I have also been savagely ripped off by those professing to be friends.

As always, I dive back into my twilight world where the Night Owls fill my life, a ready salvation for the lost, the lonely, or the game for a laugh.

Being asked at only 38 to write my autobiography was very flattering, yet it has caused me an enormous amount of soul searching. It is also spurring me on towards so many other objectives not yet reached. The hopes that well inside me let me see the invisible, feel the intangible and reach for what seems impossible. I may never get there, but I have no choice but to try. I have a thousand ideas for new TV shows I want to do, I must conquer the Network from the North, I've books to write and live shows to script. Having persuaded 52 per cent of the North to become Night Owls, I must now win over that lost 48 per cent. My work has hardly started!

I make no excuses for what I've done, for I have always believed I was doing what felt right at the time. I went with the flow and often found myself aground and having to begin my journey again. In life there must be no surrender. Instead I continue to try and make a difference in any way I can!

Alan was awarded an MBE in the Queen's New Year's Honours List for his services to broadcasting.

26 Alan by his Mam

BORN TWELVE YEARS after his sister, Alan was very much unplanned, but not unwanted. He was the biggest baby born at that time, 9 pounds 5 ounces, and was known as 'Big Boy'. At the age of ten, almost overnight, he seemed to gain his independence. His music was *always* far too loud! We don't see very much of him now because he seems to work all of the time; when he's not on TV, on radio or writing he's working for all the charities he can possibly help. I've still got a poem that he gave me when he was fourteen and it portrayed the world as he saw it at that time. I think it's poignant and perhaps set out his principles that early.

THE WAR OF LIFE

A pollution chokes a people grand
as trouble spreads throughout the land.
The striking of men that never seems right,
just 'up the union' and fight our fight!
The chemical plants spreading death and hate.
Can it ever end or is it too late?
The violent men who kill and maim
and terrorise people with bullet and flame.
The wars that plague us throughout our earth
ask us 'What can we offer a child at birth?'
Must our children live in a world like this
with so much hate, a lack of peace?
They say they are fighting to win, honour and defend
but are we all striving towards the end?

I am really very proud of him because he's my boy, even though it's not really a proper job for life. He's self-employed but I suppose it's good he can do something that he enjoys. I am a happy Mam, lucky to have a son and daughter like mine!

27 Alan by his Dad

As a young lad he did the normal boyish things. I taught him to box and we'd go fishing together but then he decided he wanted to be a singer. Well his voice was nothing out of the ordinary, and this is when he grew his hair really long. His Mam and I weren't too happy about that, but at least he was in good health. He settled into an office job and seemed pretty happy when he worked in the discos. It was a bit worrying when he packed in a good job to go full time on the radio, but I admit that he must have known he had it in him to make a go of it. I am very proud, though to be quite honest, I don't say it out loud. He has had his setbacks in life; sadly his marriages didn't work out, but he always seems to bounce back and I hope the future will bring him what he hopes for. We would be happy to see more of him but we know that it's not possible. We are content to know that he keeps us in his thoughts and contacts us when he can. We did have many a battle when tempers ran high. The worst of these was when he used to play his music so loud at home that he would deafen his mother, who is hard of hearing to start with!